New Casebooks

SHAKESPEARE, FEMINISM AND GENDER

New Casebooks

POETRY

NOVELS AND PROSE

DRAMA

GENERAL THEMES

New Casebooks Series
Series Standing Order
ISBN 0-333-71702-3 hardcover
ISBN 0-333-69345-0 paperback
(*outside North America only*)

You can receive future titles in this series as they are published by placing a standing order. Please contact your bookseller or, in case of difficulty, write to us at the address below with your name and address, the title of the series and the ISBN quoted above.

Customer Services Department, Macmillan Distribution Ltd
Houndmills, Basingstoke, Hampshire RG21 6XS, England

New Casebooks

SHAKESPEARE, FEMINISM AND GENDER

EDITED BY KATE CHEDGZOY

palgrave

First published 2001 by
PALGRAVE
Houndmills, Basingstoke, Hampshire RG21 6XS and
175 Fifth Avenue, New York, N. Y. 10010
Companies and representatives throughout the world

PALGRAVE is the new global academic imprint of
St. Martin's Press LLC Scholarly and Reference Division and
Palgrave Publishers Ltd (formerly Macmillan Press Ltd).

ISBN 0–333–71651–5 hardback
ISBN 0–333–71652–3 paperback

This book is printed on paper suitable for recycling and
made from fully managed and sustained forest sources.

A catalogue record for this book is available
from the British Library.

Library of Congress Cataloging-in-Publication Data
Shakespeare, feminism, and gender / edited by Kate Chedgzoy.
        p. cm. — (Contemporary critical essays)
    Includes bibliographical references and index.
    ISBN 0–333–71651–5 (cloth)—ISBN 0–333–71652–3 (pbk.)
    1. Shakespeare, William, 1564–1616—Characters—Women. 2.
Shakespeare, William, 1564–1616—Political and social views. 3. Feminism
and literature—England—History—16th century. 4. Feminism and
literature—England—History—17th century. 5. Women and literature–
–England—History—16th century. 6. Women and literature—England–
–History—17th century. 7. Gender identity in literature. 8. Sex role in
literature. 9. Women in literature. I. Chedgzoy, Kate. II. Series.

    PR2991 .S54 2000
    822.3'3—dc21

                                                            00–042066

10   9   8   7   6   5   4   3   2   1
10   09   08   07   06   05   04   03   02   01

Printed in China

Contents

Acknowledgements

Thanks to Rebecca Lemon and Suzanne Trill for encouragement and advice; to Diana Paton and Ramona Wray, whose rigorous and generous comments on drafts of the Introduction were very much appreciated; and above all to Martin Coyle: among editors, he stands up peerless.

The editor and publishers wish to thank the following for permission to use copyright material:

Frances Dolan, for material from *Dangerous Familiars: Representations of Domestic Crime in England, 1550–1700* (1994) pp. 89–91, 110–20, by permission of Cornell University Press;

Lizbeth Goodman, 'Women's Alternative Shakespeares and Women's Alternatives to Shakespeare in Contemporary British Theatre', from *Cross-Cultural Performances: Differences in Women's Re-Visions of Shakespeare*, ed. Marianne Novy (1993) pp. 206–26; copyright © 1993 by the Board of Trustees of the University of Illinois, by permission of the University of Illinois Press;

Barbara Hodgdon, 'He do Cressida in Different Voices', *English Literary Renaissance*, 20:2 (1990) pp. 254–86, by permission of *English Literary Renaissance*;

Jean E. Howard and Phyllis Rackin, for material in *Engendering a Nation: A Feminist Account of Shakespeare's English Histories* (1997) pp. 195–215, by permission of Routledge;

Ania Loomba, for 'The Colour of Patriarchy', from *Women, 'Race' and Writing in the Early Modern Period*, ed. Margo Hendricks and Patricia Parker (1994) pp. 17–34, by permission of Routledge;

Kathleen McLuskie, 'The Patriarchal Bard: Feminist Criticism and Shakespeare: *King Lear* and *Measure for Measure*', in *Political Shakespeare: New Essays in Cultural Materialism*, ed. Jonathan Dollimore and Alan Sinfield (1985) pp. 88–108, by permission of Manchester University Press;

Steven Mullaney, for material from 'Mourning and Misogyny: *Hamlet* and the Final Progress of Elizabeth I', *Shakespeare Quarterly*, 45:2 (1994) pp. 139–58, by permission of *Shakespeare Quarterly*;

Diane Purkiss, for material from *The Witch in History: Early Modern and Twentieth-Century Representations* (1996) pp. 199–202, 206–14, by permission of Routledge;

Alan Sinfield, for 'How to Read *The Merchant of Venice* without being Heterosexist', in *Alternative Shakespeare*, vol. 2, ed. Terence Hawkes (1996) pp. 122–39, by permission of Routledge;

Ann Thompson, for 'Feminist Theory and the Editing of Shakespeare: *The Taming of the Shrew* Revisited', in *The Margins of the Text*, ed. D. C. Greetham (1997) pp. 83–103, by permission of the University of Michigan Press;

Valerie Traub, for material from *Desire and Anxiety: Circulations of Sexuality in Shakespearean Drama* (1992) pp. 122–44, by permission of Routledge;

Every effort has been made to trace the copyright holders but if any have been inadvertently overlooked the publishers will be pleased to make the necessary arrangement at the first opportunity.

General Editors' Preface

The purpose of this series of New Casebooks is to reveal some of the ways in which contemporary criticism has changed our understanding of commonly studied texts and writers and, indeed, of the nature of criticism itself. Central to the series is a concern with modern critical theory and its effect on current approaches to the study of literature. Each New Casebook editor has been asked to select a sequence of essays which will introduce the reader to the new critical approaches to the text or texts being discussed in the volume and also illuminate the rich interchange between critical theory and critical practice that characterises so much current writing about literature.

In this focus on modern critical thinking New Casebooks aim not only to inform but also to stimulate, with volumes seeking to reflect both the controversy and the excitement of current criticism. Because much of this criticism is difficult and often employs an un-familiar critical language, editors have been asked to give the reader as much help as they feel is appropriate, but without simplifying the essays or the issues they raise. Again, editors have been asked to supply a list of further reading which will enable readers to follow up issues raised by the essays in the volume.

The project of New Casebooks, then, is to bring together in an illuminating way those critics who best illustrate the ways in which contemporary criticism has established new methods of analysing texts and who have reinvigorated the important debate about how we 'read' literature. The hope is, of course, that New Casebooks will not only open up this debate to a wider audience, but will also encourage students to extend their own ideas, and think afresh about their responses to the texts they are studying.

John Peck and Martin Coyle
University of Wales, Cardiff

Introduction

KATE CHEDGZOY

I

'Head bans *Romeo and Juliet*' ran the front-page headline in London's *Evening Standard* newspaper on 19 January 1994. The prohibition of a Shakespeare play that is one of the cornerstones of the National Curriculum in British schools would, indeed, be a newsworthy event. But, in fact, the story that followed merely reported that Jane Brown, headteacher of a primary school in Hackney (an ethnically and culturally diverse, economically disadvantaged London borough) had turned down a charitable foundation's offer of cut-price tickets for a performance of the ballet *Romeo and Juliet*.[1] The *Evening Standard*'s decision to accord such prominence to this minor incident is surprising enough, yet in subsequent weeks the story proliferated across all the London-based national daily and Sunday papers, and even received international attention, in Australia, New Zealand, and the USA. The intemperate rhetoric of prohibition and exclusion used by the *Evening Standard* was echoed through this coverage, strongly suggesting that the case was symptomatic of something larger than itself, for it hardly seems fair to equate the polite refusal of subsidised tickets for a single ballet performance with an all-out ban on Shakespeare's play. That one of the small daily decisions a headteacher made about what was best for her school turned into a major media preoccupation tells a complex and revealing story about the cultural politics of Shakespeare in 1990s Britain. It is a story which discloses

1

how thoroughly concerns about cultural hierarchy and value, epito-
mised by the name of Shakespeare, are entangled with anxieties
about gender and sexuality.

The *Evening Standard* and other papers alleged that Jane Brown
refused the tickets for *Romeo and Juliet* because she considered it 'a
blatantly heterosexual love story'.[2] In fact, the determining factors
in the decision were the cost of the tickets and transport, which
would have been beyond the means of most children in the school.
The press coverage failed to acknowledge that material factors af-
fecting wealth and mobility might genuinely have an impact on children's access to culture. At the same time, journalists ignored the
highly praised, participatory, community-based work on dance and
drama being done at Kingsmead School – work that strove to
involve all children in the pleasures of making theatre, rather than
giving a select few the opportunity to consume a high-cultural
version of it. At stake in this story, therefore, is an unacknowledged
struggle between competing understandings of culture. One, embodied in the ensuing controversy by *Romeo and Juliet*, represented
the highly valued aesthetic recreations consumed by a privileged
élite as a treasury of the British national heritage that should be
graciously extended, in special circumstances, to the uncultured
masses. As so often, Shakespeare was constituted in this crisis as
the site where élite, popular and national interests converged. The
second understanding of culture, articulated by Jane Brown's supporters, conceives it as a set of social and artistic practices, which
can be made and shared by a collectivity of people – a collectivity
that may be internally diverse in terms of class, ethnic or racial po-
sitionings – and which are valued according to the pleasure and satisfaction derived from this active participation.[3] The *Evening
Standard* and its allies thus position themselves as the defenders of
one version of what Raymond Williams called 'official English
culture',[4] standing firm against the incursions of 'political correctness' and an implicitly anti-English multiculturalism represented by
the Hackney school under Jane Brown's headship. In the Jane
Brown affair, Shakespeare became the sign under which these different understandings of culture were brought into conflict, even
though the controversial trip was not to a performance of his play
Romeo and Juliet, but to the ballet based on it. This fact was
swiftly occluded in the press coverage, with the result that ballet's
associations with élite foreign culture and effeminacy – troubling to
the populist English conservatism that led the attack on Brown –

were replaced by the unproblematically masculine Englishness of the national bard. This conflation of concerns about national identity, race, gender, sexuality and class on the site of Shakespeare's iconic persona was paralleled at the local level, where the situation became polarised around the personalities of white, middle-class, lesbian headteacher Jane Brown, and Gus John, one of her key antagonists in his role as Hackney's heterosexual, African-Caribbean Director of Education. As a result, some very painful and problematic connections between racism and homophobia were made by participants on all sides of the case.

The distinctive set of concerns laid open by the Jane Brown affair returned to the agenda of public debate about cultural identity and cultural participation on an international scale the following year, with the remarkable success of the movie *William Shakespeare's Romeo + Juliet*.[5] Widely praised by critics and enjoying massive commercial success, Baz Luhrmann's film was seized upon by teachers of Shakespeare because of the opportunities it offered to construct a bridge between contemporary popular culture and the Shakespearean classroom. Most high school and university students are very sophisticated readers of popular culture: juxtaposing Luhrmann's film with Shakespeare's play has proved a fruitful way of enabling them to bring their complex understandings of representational politics to bear on the less immediately accessible Renaissance text. Moreover, Luhrmann and his team were quite knowing about the extent to which the film was performing such important work of cultural mediation, as the 'Production Notes' posted to the official website bear out.[6] To take just one of many possible examples: *William Shakespeare's Romeo + Juliet* opens with a news broadcast, in which the words of the play's Prologue are uttered by a black, female newscaster. These famous phrases serve as news headlines and as annotations to an onscreen montage that makes the movie's Shakespearean reconfigurations of gender, sexuality, race, parent–child authority issues, religion and cultural conflict into a media event, a newsworthy take on the concerns of a 1990s society self-consciously anxious about its identity and its stability. For Alison Findlay, this breathtaking opening sequence does not 'moderniz[e] Shakespeare beyond recognition', but rather 'brilliantly captures the essentially public nature of family politics and alliances in Renaissance England'.[7] But of course it does also modernise Shakespeare, in a way which ensured that the movie made his play newly accessible and exciting for exactly the kind of youth audience whose interests were invoked for such different purposes in the Jane Brown affair. The same gesture thus both returns the play to its history, and underlines its continuing relevance. Similarly, feminist criticism of Shakespeare characteristically weaves between past and present, driven by a commitment both to intervene in contemporary cultural politics and to recover a fuller sense of the sexual politics of the literary heritage. In doing so, it has made its mark on the way that Shakespeare is reproduced and consumed in schools, theatres, cinemas and many other public sites, as well as expanding and enriching the range of interpretations of the texts and their original historical location.

Feminist criticism has recently contributed to the rejuvenation of the practice of local reading of literary texts, showing how carefully contextualised interpretations of particular cultural moments can open a window onto larger social concerns.[8] In their different ways, the Jane Brown affair and Baz Luhrmann's film both exemplify this, vividly demonstrating how anxieties about gender, sexuality, race, class and cultural hierarchy intersect on Shakespearean terrain, and thereby underlining why Shakespeare's plays and his continuing iconic status remain a matter of concern for the politically motivated critics whose work is included in this volume.

The essays here elaborate a range of answers to the crucial question about social relations posed by Alan Sinfield when he asks how 'readers not situated squarely in the mainstream of Western culture may relate to such a powerful cultural icon as Shakespeare'.[9] The complexity of what constitutes 'the mainstream', how its boundaries are defined and maintained, and how those who are outside it experience their simultaneous exclusion from it and proximity to it, is precisely what is at issue, of course, in the case of Jane Brown. As that incident demonstrates, the education system is a primary site where these practices of inclusion and exclusion are elaborated and Shakespeare's cultural privilege is sustained. The teaching of Shakespeare is profoundly entangled with questions of race, class, gender, sexuality, national identity and cultural hierarchy in post-colonial Britain as much as in those former colonies which got their Shakespeare via the institutions of imperialism.[10] In England and Wales, for example, just at the moment when the processes by which the literary canon is formed and maintained are being called into question, the imposition of national requirements and criteria for the teaching of English literature in state-maintained schools have ensured Shakespeare's continuing centrality in the curriculum as a specifically national writer. This privileging of Shakespeare need not in itself be a conservative phenomenon, of course: the popularity of *William Shakespeare's Romeo + Juliet* is just one of many possible testimonies to the radical potential that Shakespeare can embody within the education system – a potential which teaches in schools and colleges are constantly realising. But the punitive treatment that Jane Brown suffered when her resistance to the pieties of British cultural conservatism collided with Shakespeare also underlines just how compelling is the responsibility of feminist Shakespeare scholars to continue to make critical interventions in full awareness of those complex and difficult material realities that form the contexts of academic debate.

II

Anthologies of critical essays have their own cultural and intellectual politics: they participate in the formation of a critical canon, helping to define a field and shape priorities of interest and hierarchies of contributors within it.[11] A milestone in the history of feminism's encounter with Shakespeare is the 1980 anthology *The Woman's Part: Feminist Criticism of Shakespeare*.[12] Subsequently, one of the editors, Gayle Greene, reflecting on the production of that volume, remarked: 'While feminist criticism of Shakespeare is in some sense unlike other sorts of feminist criticism, in that it is more a matter of reassessing than of rediscovering a literary canon, still we found that we could, on the basis of our work with Shakespeare, describe elements of a feminist approach to literature that applied to the enterprise as a whole.'[13] Assuming that feminist scholars will mainly be interested in women's writing, Greene presents feminist criticism of Shakespeare as both representative and exceptional in relation to the larger project of feminist literary studies. Undoubtedly, the history of feminist encounters with Shakespeare has had a dynamic relation to that wider project. Though I have resisted selecting and ordering the essays in this volume to tell a single story about the development of feminist Shakespeare criticism in the last decade, nevertheless that period has arguably seen a series of distinctive re-orientations in the field. These changes have occurred in dialogue with shifting concerns and priorities in feminist literary and cultural studies, which are not themselves purely internal to literary criticism as a scholarly and pedagogical practice, but are shaped by the engagement of critics with political concerns in the world outside the academy, the world of which the academy is a part. Examples of such engagements in the present volume include Jean Howard and Phyllis Rackin's account of the construction of martial masculinity in the second tetralogy of English history plays, which is informed by feminist analyses of the 1991 Gulf War's impact on US cultural and sexual politics;[14] or the carefully nuanced readings of recent British cultural politics found in the essays by Alan Sinfield and Lizbeth Goodman.

The development of feminist criticism of Shakespeare through the 1970s and 1980s has already been charted retrospectively in a number of anthologies, survey articles and bibliographies.[15] The present volume accordingly focuses on the 1990s, offering a snapshot of a decade when feminist criticism of Shakespeare's plays both flourished and diversified. Like all snapshots, it offers a limited view, and a great deal has been left out of the picture. My priorities were to cover a range of widely studied texts, while showing how gender-inflected criticism has challenged the conventional hierarchies of scholarship and participated in a revision of the Shakespearean canon; to demonstrate a range of critical and theoretical approaches; and to give a sense of the breadth of intellectual and political concerns with which feminist criticism of Shakespeare has engaged. Many reluctant decisions to exclude important work had to be made, and the 'Further Reading' section gives clues as to some of the other ways this volume could have been organised, testifying to the extraordinary diversity of work in this field.[16]

As well as deciding what to include, I had to decide what to call the book. For both academic and commercial reasons, 'Shakespeare' clearly had to feature in the title, and the fact that his name was the one element of the title that escaped serious scrutiny tells its own story about just how difficult it can be to get a critical perspective on his overwhelming presence. The Casebook series, in treating Shakespeare so much more generously than any other author, is also complicit in the reproduction of this Shakespearean cultural hegemony, of course. So 'Shakespeare' it was to be, but 'Shakespeare and' – what? I liked the polemical commitment of 'Shakespeare and Feminism', which testifies to the enormous changes wrought in literary studies by the impact of several waves of politically committed scholars. But while it is clear that feminism has had a beneficial effect on Shakespeare studies, it is less obvious that international movements for the empowerment of women have anything to gain from Shakespeare's company, or that Shakespeare merits a high place on the agenda of global feminism at the beginning of the twenty-first century. In this light, the bold pairing of 'Shakespeare and Feminism' seems comically hubristic. Moreover, within the smaller field of Shakespeare studies, it does not seem a precise descriptor at a moment that has witnessed a shift away from a consideration of the pro-, anti- or proto-feminist qualities of Shakespeare's representations of women, to the concern with gender and sexuality as interrelated analytic categories that now animates much work in this area. The desire either to bury Shakespeare or praise him has given way to analysis of the ideological and cultural work done in his own time and since by his plays' representations of gender.

The dyad of Shakespeare and feminism did not seem to offer the right title for this volume, therefore. But because I find some justice in the claim that attention to gender as a central category of analysis can sometimes be a way of recuperating the energies of feminism for a mainstream that largely resists or shrugs off its challenge, I was also reluctant to let 'feminism' be superseded by the rubric of 'gender'.[17] Such a gesture would be politically and intellectually premature, running the risk of ceding some of the hard-won and tenuously held gains achieved by the efforts of feminists. Introducing their critical anthology *Shakespeare and Gender*, however, Deborah Barker and Ivo Kamps assume that such a supersession of 'feminism' by gender has indeed taken place, and that this development is a welcome one. They state that '"gender studies", which has recently come to replace "feminist studies", recognizes that issues of gender are not limited to a focus on women', and further claim that it 'exposes the heterosexual bias implicit in various feminist discussions of eroticism' (p. 11). Their presentation of 'feminist studies' is a partial one: from the start feminist work on Shakespeare has tackled the construction of masculinity and femininity, sexuality and gender.[18]

More worrying is that by positioning 'feminist studies' and 'gender studies' purely as choices to be made from a menu of academic approaches, Barker and Kamps overlook the fact that feminism's primary energy came from political engagement, a desire to transform gender relations in the world. As Eve Kosofsky Sedgwick says, '[t]o assume that the study of gender can be definitionally detached from the analysis and critique of gender inequality, oppression, and struggle (that is, from some form of feminism) ignores, among other things, the telling fact that gender analysis per se became possible only under the pressure of the most pointed and political feminist demand'.[19] Changing agendas for the academic study of gender and sexuality, and for feminist interventions in the politics of teaching and research, exist in a dynamic relation to developments within the discipline and in the wider culture. Pertinent instances include the impact on feminism of queer politics and theory, which demand that we suspend what we thought we knew about the relation of sex to gender and think again;[20] or the various gains and losses which have marked feminism's progress as public discourse and social practice through the last couple of decades. It would be too easy to describe this as a process in which the naïve and simple protests of feminism give way to the more sophisticated negotiations of gender critique, or to characterise recent work on gender and sexuality as the output of disobedient daughters, ungratefully rejecting the worthy but now embarrassingly old-fashioned efforts of their intellectual foremothers.[21] Recent work is informed by and emerges from the earlier studies, as the women who might – though not, I suspect, without protest – be cast as the 'mothers' of feminist criticism of Shakespeare continue to extend the challenges and provocations of their own work, while generously enabling new scholarship.[22]

The final choice of title thus reflects my sense that it is important to record and testify to these debates, and not to occlude them by tacitly taking up one position or another. Triangulating the three terms 'Shakespeare', 'feminism' and 'gender' in the title is intended to signal that none is less important than another, and to hold open the possibility of a range of relations among them, which may involve – in various combinations – mutual support, reinforcement, stimulation and opposition. These complex dynamics are reflected not only in the individual essays, but in the relations among them established by their juxtaposition in this volume. The book opens with Kathleen McLuskie's emphasis on the diversity of feminist criticism, and its grounding in political commitments.[23] The essays which follow reflect this diversity in terms of their choice of texts, thematic concerns and critical approaches. They also make manifest the multiple political differences that exist within feminism.

III

Kathleen McLuskie's opening essay is one of three reprinted here that range widely and seek to establish the fundamental relevance of feminism to several crucial areas in Shakespeare studies: textual editing, teaching, academic research and performance. Each of these essays is attentive to the material contexts in which the meanings of Shakespeare's plays are produced and circulated, and the institutional settings in which feminist interventions are called for. If McLuskie's 1985 essay, the earliest piece included in this volume, is placed first, this should not be read as an assertion of chronological priority, so much as a reminder of what continue to be some of the most important issues in the field. In 'Feminist Theory and the Editing of Shakespeare' (Chapter 2), Ann Thompson investigates feminism's relevance to the editing of Shakespeare, and emphasises that this endeavour should not be seen as an arcane scholarly task, but as one that is of crucial importance to all who are interested in bringing feminist perspectives to bear on his plays, whether in educational or theatrical contexts. She traces the reproduction of Shakespeare in the male editorial tradition, showing that nothing is neutral or innocent, not even 'the words', and argues that it is vital for feminists to intervene in this ongoing process of mediation. Lizbeth Goodman's essay (Chapter 3) extends this interest in the cultural mediation of Shakespeare in the crucial direction of contemporary performance practice, comparing the diverse strategies of the subsidised mainstream and the feminist fringe. Her investigation of the sexual politics of Shakespearean performance privileges the contemporary British context, while posing questions of considerable significance to the field as a whole. In contrast, Chapter 4 engages with Shakespeare's place in the recent cultural politics of the USA, specifically the resurgence of a martial masculinity associated with the wars in Vietnam and the Gulf. Jean Howard and Phyllis Rackin examine the role of military culture in the construction of both masculinity and femininity in the sequence of plays about English wars and English history sometimes known as the second tetralogy. In drawing attention to this manifestation of transatlantic differences in feminist approaches to Shakespeare, my intention is not to reinstate the confrontational transatlantic divide that some histories of politicised Shakespeare criticism have delineated.[24] Rather, I want to stress the engagement of all these critics with the particular cultural location and specific political circumstances in which they do their work, and their shared demonstration of the value of using Shakespeare to engage with these conjunctions.

Next comes a series of studies that focus on just one or two of Shakespeare's plays, moving through the dramatic canon in a roughly chronological order. Refusing to separate formal, generic concerns from questions of thematic or political content, Alan Sinfield's essay (Chapter 5) uses *The Merchant of Venice* to show how playtexts do complicated ideological work across uneven terrain, inviting exploration rather than enforcing closure. A similar stance informs Valerie Traub's theoretically sophisticated discussion of *As You Like It* and *Twelfth Night* (Chapter 6), which works closely with the texts to interpret the dynamics of romantic comedy in terms of the constructedness of gender and the volatility of erotic desire. Though sexuality is not constitutive of the book in the way that gender is, I have been aware throughout the process of compiling it of the overdetermined connections between sexuality and gender, a matter which is explored by several of the contributors. Though their essays focus most directly on sexuality, Sinfield and Traub are by no means the only contributors who put into practice the complexly enriching implications of Eve Kosofsky Sedgwick's warning that the congruities and differences of feminist and anti-homophobic inquiry are always likely to be manifold and unpredictable.[25]

In Chapter 7, Steven Mullaney turns to the genre of revenge tragedy, and borrows interpretive tools from psychoanalysis and anthropology in order to investigate the interweavings of mourning and misogyny in *Hamlet*. Defining performance – in Shakespeare's time and in the play's afterlife – as a site where social meaning is (re)arranged as theatrical meaning, Barbara Hodgdon's account (Chapter 8) of *Troilus and Cressida*'s twentieth-century stage history explores the political meanings of spectatorial pleasure. Frances Dolan's discussion of *Othello* (Chapter 9) brings together issues of genre, the politics of the household (in terms both of marriage and domestic service) and racial difference, using a woman's text to throw new light on Shakespeare's. The strengths of all the essays in this volume are exemplified by Diane Purkiss's reading of *Macbeth* (Chapter 10), which puts theoretically nuanced close textual readings in the service of a political critique that opens up the texts to further interpretive possibilities.

Concluding the volume, Ania Loomba's essay (Chapter 11) meditates on the extent to which Renaissance and post-colonial literary studies have recently converged on the grounds of a 'common interest in marginalized peoples', coupled with a desire to 'theorize and recover subaltern resistance'.[26] Distinct in political and disciplinary terms, these undertakings have coalesced under the sign of female agency. Loomba's elegant tracing of the lines of intersection and divergence that delineate the boundaries of these projects emphasises the difficulty of theorising social difference in a way that does not merely dissolve all forms of oppression or constructions of socially marked identities into analogies of each other. Her essay is a salutary reminder of the care with which feminist Shakespeare studies needs to think through the complex relations of gender to other forms of disempowerment. In 1991, Valerie Wayne regretfully acknowledged, in the introduction to her influential collection *The Matter of Difference*, that the white contributors to that volume had largely failed to avoid what Dympna Callaghan, responding to Wayne, calls 'one of the pitfalls of feminist criticism, namely its habitual tendency to take gender as the diacritical difference of culture, and in so doing to erase other systems of difference'.[27] Wayne's rueful admission of the shortcomings of feminist criticism has been much discussed – three contributions to Margo Hendricks and Patricia Parker's agenda-setting collection of essays, *Women, 'Race', and Writing in the Early Modern Period* begin by alluding to it.[28] But as the very existence of the Hendricks and Parker volume shows, *The Matter of Difference* appeared at the beginning of a decade which has seen a striking extension amongst feminists of work on race, and on questions of ethnic and cultural specificity. Indeed, Peter Erickson now contends that feminist scholarship has played a crucial role in forwarding such investigations within the wider field of Renaissance literary studies.[29] As with the original impetus for the emergence of feminist scholarship, this development, too, may owe something to identity politics, with scholars' awareness of their own location in relation to discourses and structures of racial difference driving forward critical debate. The burgeoning of work that variously endeavours to critique whiteness or to trouble the dominant understanding of racial difference as a matter of antithetical binaries has increased the richness and sophistication of debate in this area.[30] Addressing similar political and historical concerns, critical analysis of post-colonial revisions and interpretations of Shakespeare, much of it informed by feminist perspectives, has extended debate by highlighting the material and cultural legacies of colonialism that continue to shape the circumstances in which his works are reproduced.[31] But a thorough integration of questions of gender and sexuality with issues of race and colonialism has not yet been achieved, and there is a pressing need for more work on the imbrications of gender, sexuality and race in the shaping of national identities and cultures.[32]

IV

In common with the rest of the New Casebook series, the scope of this volume is restricted to academic criticism. However, some of the most interesting and stimulating critical thinking about Shakespeare by women in recent years has gone on in theatrical productions, novels, poems and films, as Lizbeth Goodman's essay here demonstrates. There is, indeed, a long-standing tradition of female and feminist responses to Shakespeare, traceable at least as far back as the Ladies' Clubs formed to appreciate his works in the eighteenth century. Marianne Novy argues that 'by writing character studies and inventing biographies', nineteenth-century writers and actresses 'formed a female interpretive community, where Shakespeare's characters could be used to authorize defenses of women as a group'.[33] At the same time, many nineteenth-century actresses developed a sense of the outstanding opportunities some Shakespearean roles offered, and of the significant connections that might be made between these roles and the social condition of women, in ways that prefigure modern performance criticism of the kind exemplified here by Goodman and Hodgdon. Goodman, for example, traces a shift in recent British theatrical practice from this kind of individualist approach, preoccupied with the exceptional role and exceptional performance, to collective feminist activity. This development can fruitfully be understood alongside the critique, recently formulated in academic writing on Shakespeare, of the early dominance of literary-critical approaches rooted in liberal individualism, which have given place to increasing attention to structures, institutions and collective or collaborative practices of cultural production. In the introduction to their anthology of women's literary-critical engagements with Shakespeare before 1900, Ann Thompson and Sasha Roberts narrate the earlier histories of critical writing on Shakespeare and gender. They note that much of this work has been neglected because it was not in the dominant genres of the academic essay, edition, or monograph. For Thompson and Roberts, such women's work is also political – even if the authors would not choose to identify as feminist in the way

that modern scholars do – in so far as it addresses 'women's education, women's role in public life, and power relations between the
sexes in society and in marriage'.[34] Some of the most important
Shakespeare scholars of the twentieth century have been women
(among many others who could be named, Muriel Bradbrook,
Molly Mahood and Caroline Spurgeon come to mind). Until recently, few such scholars would have identified themselves explicitly
as feminists, but that certainly does not meant that their work is irrelevant to current feminist scholarship. They, too, form part of the
history of women's engagements with Shakespeare. Critical exami-
nations of the role of women in his reproduction through study and
social groups and Shakespeare societies, as well the interventions of
women directors, performers and adapters, offer a rewarding direction for future research. There is a continuing need to historicise
the material conditions of Shakespearean reproduction, extending
the reach of feminist scholarship beyond the thematics and poetics
of Shakespearean gender formations.[35]

One area of long-standing consonance between popular and academic approaches to Shakespeare is an attention to the fictions of
character generated by his plays. Among audiences and readers,
identification with particular characters has long been a favoured
way of expressing response to and affirmation of Shakespeare's
plays. Similarly, one of the dominant modes of feminist
Shakespeare criticism in the 1970s and 1980s was a realist, psychological approach informed by American feminist revisions of
psychoanalysis. Kathleen McLuskie's essay, reprinted here, critiques these mimetic approaches, which she sees as being rooted in
the critics' own desires and identifications. Feminist Shakespeare
criticism could now usefully investigate why the language of
identification has become such a powerful way of expressing en-
thusiasm and pleasure, arguably having a particular appeal to
readers and audience members whose responses to Shakespearean
drama are inflected by identity politics and a conscious affiliation
to oppressed minority identities. In an astute review essay covering
some of the most influential lesbian/gay/queer readings of
Renaissance texts, Jean E. Howard interestingly points to the tenta-
tive signs of a revivification, in a highly sophisticated form, of a
character-centred criticism which is not founded in a simplistic
identification of a stable reading self with a fixed, fictional character.[36] Ann Thompson seems right to note that 'current literary
theory, in discrediting the idea of a coherent, transcendent self, has

made character-based readings of texts seem unfashionably naïve, but has not really given us an adequate alternative'.[37] As she points out, identification with a dramatic character need not be founded in sameness; just as casting against race, gender and body-type has been stimulating and productive in many recent productions (examples might include Théâtre de Complicité's Kathryn Hunter playing King Lear at the Leicester Haymarket in 1997, or the 1993 Tara Arts/Manchester Contact Theatre production of *Troilus and Cressida*, in which the male British-Indian actor Yogesh Bhatt was a marvelous Cressida), so readers and audiences may identify with characters across difference. In this context, the recent emphasis on historicizing Shakespeare's plays as products of early modern culture is a salutary reminder that we *always* have to project ourselves across a chasm of historical difference. Paula Bennett's autobiographical essay 'Gender as Performance: Ambiguity and the Lesbian Reader'[38] demonstrates the creative potential of such identifications against the grain. Perhaps what is called for is a mobile, metamorphic response to match the metamorphic qualities found in Shakespeare's own works by Margaret Cavendish, in what we may see as the first contribution to the tradition of gender-oriented writing on Shakespeare by women:

> one would think that he had been Metamorphosed from a Man to a Woman, for who could Describe *Cleopatra* Better than he hath done, and many other Females of his own Creating, as *Nan Page*, Mrs. *Page*, Mrs. *Ford*, the Doctors Maid, *Bettrice*, Mrs. *Quickly*, *Doll Tearsheet*, and others, too many to Relate?[39]

The effect of all this is, of course, to change the way we perceive Shakespeare by changing the cultural and historical context in which he is located. Such a change has also been effected by the massive effort to recover and study Renaissance women's writing that has recently transformed our view of the literary landscape of that period. Many eminent feminist Shakespeareans have also chosen to work on Renaissance women's writing, yet so far there have been few attempts to establish a dialogue between Shakespeare's plays and the relatively less canonical writings of his female contemporaries. This relative silence can teach us useful lessons about gender, genre and periodisation, as well as prompting reflection on the reasons for the absence of women from the canon. One pertinent factor is that women, like many of Shakespeare's male contemporaries, often chose to write in forms that have not achieved the kind of longevity and prestige enjoyed by his plays and poems. The exception is Elizabeth Cary's *Tragedy of Mariam*, which corresponds more closely than almost any other women's text of the period to the genres privileged by modern scholarship, and as a result has often been discussed alongside Shakespeare plays (Frances Dolan's article in the present volume is a good example). Articles such as Lorna Hutson's 'Why the Lady's Eyes are Nothing like the Sun' and Mary Beth Rose's 'Where are the Mothers in Shakespeare?' demonstrate the value of work that does make these connections, however, and the essays in a special issue of *Shakespeare Quarterly* that brings together work on Shakespeare and on early modern women's writing indicate its pedagogical usefulness.[40] The feminist strategy of locating Shakespeare among his less famous female contemporaries can either be a way of re-placing him within a contemporary circulation of popular culture, in which he did not have the unique position we anachronistically accord him, or a way of exposing and critiquing the processes of cultural hierarchy which sustain his iconic status, and which mean that he in turn is used to shore up particular versions of and positions in culture. When I asked some of the contributors to the present volume what future directions feminist/gender-related criticism of Shakespeare might fruitfully take, several of them agreed that further work on the place of gender in the relations of early modern literary production is a crucial task. Studying men's and women's writing together will facilitate a richer response to their texts and a clearer understanding of the factors that shaped opportunities for Shakespeare and his male and female contemporaries. As Frances Dolan says, what is needed is 'a reconfiguration of the landscape, so that Shakespeare is no longer so much a lonely landmark'.[41]

Despite the exceptional status acknowledged by Dolan, Shakespeare studies form part of the wider field of literary criticism and will continue to share in and contribute to developments within the discipline as a whole. Shakespeare's institutional and cultural prestige means that his works are often the site where people seek to achieve credibility and success for innovation. As Valerie Traub notes in her essay (Chapter 6), Shakespeare studies in the last decades of the twentieth century were characterised by a marked procedural and political self-consciousness, and this is clearly a positive attribute of the field. At once exposing and contesting the spurious claims to neutral authority of some other kinds of scholarship, it is a product both of the rise of certain theoretical approaches, and the impact of political forms of criticism, notably feminism itself. Ann Thompson concludes her 1988 overview of feminist criticism of Shakespeare, '"The warrant of womanhood"', by insisting that feminist critics should 'continue to intervene in every way in the reading and interpretation of Shakespeare'.[42] This refusal to circumscribe the scope of the feminist project is echoed by Lizbeth Goodman, who ends her essay (Chapter 3) by arguing against an economy of scarcity in which competing voices have to struggle for dominance, and calling for the flourishing of multiple approaches to Shakespeare. The essays in this volume exemplify the value of such eclecticism, while the inclusions and exclusions performed by the act of editing it indicate how much more work still remains to be done.

V

I began by suggesting how an instance of the local reading of contemporary culture can enrich our feminist understanding of Shakespearean mediations, and I want to end in the same way, with some brief remarks on *10 Things I Hate About You*, a cinematic version of *The Taming of the Shrew*. Released in 1999, this is less a *fin-de-siècle* movie than one that turns its face to the new millennium, at the same time as it collocates Shakespeare, education, gender, sexuality, race and class in a way that returns us to the cultural anxieties symptomatically expressed by the case of Jane Brown. The film largely endorses the heroine's feminism: it is quite clear that there can be no question of her being 'tamed' in anything remotely resembling the way that Katherine is in Shakespeare's play, and in fact *10 Things I Hate About You* seems to draw as much on the reciprocal sparring of Beatrice and Benedick in *Much Ado About Nothing* as on Petruchio's struggles with the 'shrew'. Yet it remains anxious about sexuality: the film is careful to specify that being a feminist does not make the heroine 'a k.d. lang fan' (that is, a lesbian), and there are no obviously gay characters – a surprising omission in a movie which is sufficiently conscious of identity politics to offer a blithely inclusive representation of the ethnic and cultural diversity of a Seattle high school. Class is present in a rather occluded, not to say obfuscated, way, as a signifier of counter-cultural personal style that marks Patrick/Petruchio out as an intriguing outsider among the racially mixed but uniformly affluent teens of Padua High School. The film ends with a scene in class, when the students – in an exercise that will be familiar to present and recent school students – are invited by their rather embarrassingly funky teacher to rewrite in their own terms Shakespeare's sonnet 141, 'In faith, I do not love thee with mine eyes'. Kat eagerly seizes the opportunity to put her own voice in the place of Shakespeare's, to appropriate the site of the Shakespearean text as one that enables female speech. In a bold revision of Katherine's notorious speech of submission to Petruchio in *The Taming of the Shrew* (V.ii.141–84), she addresses her poem directly to Patrick. In its articulation of sexual and social ambivalence, her desires for him, and her fear of losing autonomy, it seems to speak very powerfully to the uncertainties of a generation that is in several contradictory senses post-feminist.[43]

10 Things I Hate About You shies away from some of the challenges posed by *The Taming of the Shrew* on the cusp of a new century; but it is still a funny and thoughtful exploration of many of the issues that have preoccupied feminist criticism of Shakespeare. Teachers and students of Shakespeare will no doubt quickly incorporate it into debates about the sexual politics of his plays. I am not suggesting that with this film Shakespeare's cultural prestige, Hollywood's desire to exploit the teen market and the imperatives of feminism have achieved a reconciliation as delighted and delightful as Kat and Patrick's at the end of the movie. But as they kiss and the camera soars away from them while the soundtrack insists 'I want you to want me / I need you to need me', it seems clear that the question of how far Shakespeare and feminism need and want each other is one that must continue to be asked, answered and asked again well into the new century.

NOTES

1. My account of these events is indebted to Debbie Epstein, 'What's in a Ban? The Popular Media, *Romeo and Juliet* and Compulsory Heterosexuality', in Deborah Lynn Steinberg, Debbie Epstein, and Richard Johnson (eds), *Border Patrols: Policing the Boundaries of Heterosexuality* (London: Cassell, 1997), pp. 183–202. Thanks to Debbie for her help with the present essay.

2. *Daily Mail*, 20 January 1994.

3. For an analysis of competing understandings of the term 'culture', see Raymond Williams, *Keywords: A Vocabulary of Culture and Society* (London: Croom Helm, 1976), pp. 76–82.

4. Raymond Williams, *Politics and Letters: Interviews with New Left Review* (London: New Left Review Books, 1979), p. 316.

5. Directed by Baz Luhrmann for Bazmark/Twentieth Century Fox (1996).

6. *William Shakespeare's Romeo + Juliet*, at http://www.romeoandjuliet.com. TM © 1996 Twentieth Century Fox Film Corporation.

7. Alison Findlay, *A Feminist Perspective on Renaissance Drama* (Oxford: Blackwell, 1999), p. 135.

8. For some fine examples, see the essays in Susan Frye and Karen Robertson (eds), *Maids and Mistresses, Cousins and Queens: Women's Alliances in Early Modern England* (Oxford: Oxford University Press, 1999), and Valerie Traub, M. Lindsay Kaplan and Dympna Callaghan (eds), *Feminist Readings of Early Modern Culture: Emerging Subjects* (Cambridge: Cambridge University Press, 1996).

9. 'How to Read *The Merchant of Venice* without being Heterosexist' (see p. 115 below).

10. See, for example, Svati Joshi (ed.), *Rethinking English: Essays in Literature, Language, History* (Delhi: Oxford India Paperbacks, 1994), and David Johnson, *Shakespeare and South Africa* (Oxford: Clarendon Press, 1996).

11. See Jane Gallop, *Around 1981: Academic Feminist Literary Theory* (London: Routledge, 1992).

12. Gayle Greene, Carolyn Ruth Swift and Carol Thomas Neely (eds), *The Woman's Part: Feminist Criticism of Shakespeare* (Urbana: University of Illinois Press, 1980).

13. Gayle Greene, 'Feminist and Marxist Criticism: an Argument for Alliances', *Women's Studies*, 9 (1981), 29–46 (29–30).

14. Compare Miriam Cooke and Angela Wollacott (eds), *Gendering War Talk* (Princeton, NJ: Princeton University Press, 1993).

15. Deborah E. Barker and Ivo Kamps (eds), *Shakespeare and Gender: A History* (London: Verso, 1995) is a wide-ranging collection of critical essays. For an antagonistic overview, see Richard Levin, 'Feminist Thematics and Shakespearean Tragedy', *PMLA*, 103 (1988), 125–38 (a letter of response in *PMLA*, 104 (1989), 77–8, signed by 24 feminist scholars, offers a succinct statement of a feminist practice of Shakespearean criticism). For more sympathetic accounts, see Ann Thompson, '"The warrant of womanhood": Feminist Criticism of Shakespeare', in Graham Holderness (ed.), *The Shakespeare Myth* (Manchester: Manchester University Press, 1988), pp. 74–88, and Peter Erickson, 'Rewriting the Renaissance, Rewriting Ourselves', *Shakespeare Quarterly*, 38 (1987), 327–37. Philip Kolin, *Shakespeare*

and Feminist Criticism: An Annotated Bibliography and Commentary (New York: Garland, 1992) is an invaluable resource.

16. Notably, I decided to concentrate exclusively on drama. The Sonnets and the narrative poems raise quite distinct issues, and many of the general claims made in these essays about the use of Shakespeare's works as a kind of cultural currency are less pertinent to the poems than they are to the plays. Including a single essay would not have done justice to the variety and interest of feminist criticism of Shakespeare's poetry; including several would have upset the balance of the anthology.

17. For a nuanced retrospective on these debates which also takes stock of the current political and theoretical situation, see Leora Auslander, 'Do Women's + Feminist + Men's + Lesbian and Gay + Queer Studies = Gender Studies?', *differences*, 9, *Women's Studies on the Edge* (Fall, 1997), 1–30.

18. This is true of many of the essays in the groundbreaking anthology of criticism *The Woman's Part*, edited by Greene, Swift and Neely. Among many other possible examples, see also Catherine Belsey, *The Subject of Tragedy: Identity and Difference in Renaissance Drama* (London: Methuen, 1985), Lisa Jardine, *Still Harping on Daughters: Women and Drama in the Age of Shakespeare* (Brighton: Harvester, 1983; 2nd edn 1989), Coppélia Kahn, *Man's Estate: Masculine Identity in Shakespeare* (Berkeley, CA: University of California Press, 1981), and Juliet Dusinberre, *Shakespeare and the Nature of Woman* (London: Macmillan, 1975; 2nd edn 1996).

19. Eve Kosofsky Sedgwick, 'Gender Criticism,' in Stephen Greenblatt and Giles Gunn (eds), *Redrawing the Boundaries: The Transformation of English and American Literary Studies* (New York: Modern Language Association of America, 1992), pp. 271–302 (p. 272).

20. The work of Judith Butler and Eve Kosofsky Sedgwick has been foundational here, as in other fields of literary and cultural studies. See especially Butler, *Gender Trouble: Feminism and the Subversion of Identity* (London: Routledge, 1989), and *Bodies that Matter: On the Discursive Limits of 'Sex'* (London: Routledge, 1993); Sedgwick, *Between Men: English Literature and Male Homosocial Desire* (New York: Columbia University Press, 1985), and *Epistemology of the Closet* (New York: Harvester Wheatsheaf, 1990). A rich gathering of meta-theoretical meditations on the encounter between feminism and queer theory can be found in *More Gender Trouble: Feminism Meets Queer Theory*, a special issue of *differences*, 6:2–3 (Summer–Fall 1994).

21. The politics of maternal and familial metaphors as a way of inflecting relations between 'generations' of feminists, and between feminist and other scholars, has been widely discussed, reflecting the scope for am-

bivalence and conflict in such relationships. See Lynda Boose, 'The Family in Shakespeare Studies; or, Studies in the Family of Shakespeareans; or, The Politics of Politics', *Renaissance Quarterly*, 40 (1987), 707–42, and Devoney Looser and E. Ann Kaplan (eds), *Generations: Academic Feminists in Dialogue* (Minneapolis, MN: University of Minnesota Press, 1997). Thanks to Ania Loomba for prompting me to think about these issues.

22. I would like to take the opportunity here to acknowledge the always enabling influence on my own academic life of Ann Thompson and Kathleen McLuskie.

23. 'The Patriarchal Bard' (see pp. 24–9 below).

24. See, for example, Walter Cohen, 'Political Criticism of Shakespeare', in Jean E. Howard and Marion O'Connor (eds), *Shakespeare Reproduced: The Text in History and Ideology* (London: Routledge, 1987), pp. 18–46, and Barry Taylor, 'Academic Exchange: Text, Politics, and the Construction of English and American Identities in Contemporary Renaissance Criticism', in Viviana Comensoli and Paul Stevens (eds), *Discontinuities: New Essays on Renaissance Literature and Criticism* (Toronto: University of Toronto Press, 1998), pp. 181–200.

25. Sedgwick, *Epistemology of the Closet*, pp. 27–35. For further examples of work on the politics of sexuality in Renaissance culture, see Harriette Andreadis, 'The Erotics of Female Friendship in Early Modern England', in Frye and Robertson (eds), *Maids and Mistresses, Cousins and Queens*, pp. 241–58; Mario DiGangi, *The Homoerotics of Early Modern Drama* (Cambridge: Cambridge University Press, 1997); Jonathan Goldberg (ed.), *Queering the Renaissance* (Durham, NC: Duke University Press, 1994); Elaine Hobby, 'Katherine Phillips: Seventeenth-Century Lesbian Poet', in Elaine Hobby and Chris White (eds), *What Lesbians Do in Books* (London: Women's Press, 1991); Bruce Smith, *Homosexual Desire in Shakespeare's England: A Cultural Poetics* (Chicago, IL: Chicago University Press, 1991); Valerie Traub, *The Renaissance of Lesbianism* (Cambridge: Cambridge University Press, 2000).

26. 'The Colour of Patriarchy' (see p. 236 below).

27. Dympna Callaghan, 'Re-reading Elizabeth Cary's *The Tragedie of Mariam, Faire Queene of Jewry*', in M. Hendricks and P. Parker (eds), *Women, 'Race', and Writing in the Early Modern Period* (London: Routledge, 1994), pp. 163–77 (p. 163).

28. In addition to the essay by Dympna Callaghan cited in the previous note, see the editors' Introduction to that volume, pp. 1–16, as well as Hendricks, 'Civility, Barbarism, and Aphra Behn's *The Widow Ranter*', pp. 225–39. The passage they are invoking is in Valerie

Wayne (ed.), *The Matter of Difference: Materialist Feminist Criticism of Shakespeare* (Hemel Hempstead: Harvester, 1991), p. 11.

29. Peter Erickson, 'The Moment of Race in Renaissance Studies', *Shakespeare Studies*, 26 (1998), 27–36 (34). This essay is part of a forum, 'Race and the Study of Shakespeare', which usefully takes stock of these issues. For further examples see Kim F. Hall, *Things of Darkness: Economies of Race and Gender in Early Modern England* (Ithaca, NY: Cornell University Press, 1995); Ania Loomba and Martin Orkin (eds), *Postcolonial Shakespeares* (London: Routledge, 1998); Joyce Green Macdonald (ed.), *Race, Ethnicity and Power in the Renaissance* (London: Associated University Presses, 1997).

30. These issues are addressed in the works cited in the previous note, but see also Barbara Bowen, 'Aemilia Lanyer and the Invention of White Womanhood', in Frye and Robertson (eds), *Maids and Mistresses, Cousins and Queens*, pp. 274–303; James Shapiro, *Shakespeare and the Jews* (New York: Columbia University Press, 1996); Andrew Murphy, *But the Irish Sea Betwixt Us: Ireland, Colonialism, and Renaissance Literature* (Lexington, KY: University Press of Kentucky, 1998).

31. See Thomas Cartelli, *Repositioning Shakespeare: National Formations, Postcolonial Appropriations* (London: Routledge, 1999), my *Shakespeare's Queer Children: Sexual Politics and Contemporary Culture* (Manchester: Manchester University Press, 1995); and several of the articles in Marianne Novy (ed.), *Transforming Shakespeare: Contemporary Women's Re-Visions in Literature and Performance* (New York: St Martin's Press, 1999).

32. For a sketch of some possible agendas for such work, see my '"Two, and More than Two": Nations, Genders', in Simon Mealor and Philip Schwyzer (eds), *Archipelagic Identities: Writing Nation and Region in the Early Modern British Isles* (forthcoming).

33. Marianne Novy, *Engaging with Shakespeare: Responses of George Eliot and other Women Novelists* (Athens, GA: University of Georgia Press, 1994), p. 18.

34. Ann Thompson and Sasha Roberts, *Women Reading Shakespeare, 1660–1900* (Manchester: Manchester University Press, 1997), pp. 7, 5.

35. Thanks to Kathleen McLuskie for this point (personal communication, June 1999).

36. Jean E. Howard, 'The Early Modern and the Homoerotic Turn in Political Criticism', *Shakespeare Studies*, 26 (1998), 105–20. See also Lorna Hutson's *The Usurer's Daughter*, which addresses the enduring productivity of the notion of character by explaining in meticulously historicized terms 'why Shakespeare's women have "characters"', proposing that 'the compelling emotional intelligibility, or probability

of his drama', and its 'innovative "characterization" of women' can be traced to the dramatic transformations he wrought on cultural materials prized and enjoyed by men of the sixteenth-century educated élite. See *The Usurer's Daughter: Male Friendship and Fictions of Women in Sixteenth-Century England* (London: Routledge, 1994), pp. 12–13.

37. Ann Thompson, 'Women/"Women" and the Stage', in Helen Wilcox (ed.), *Women and Literature in Britain, 1500–1700* (Cambridge: Cambridge University Press, 1996), pp. 100–16 (p. 108).

38. In Julia Penelope and Susan J. Wolfe (eds), *Sexual Practice, Textual Theory: Lesbian Cultural Criticism* (Oxford: Basil Blackwell, 1993).

39. In *CCXI Sociable Letters* (London, 1664); quoted in Thompson and Roberts (eds), *Women Reading Shakespeare, 1660–1900*, p. 13.

40. Lorna Hutson, 'Why the Lady's Eyes are Nothing like the Sun', in Clare Brant and Diane Purkiss (eds), *Women, Texts, and Histories, 1575–1760* (London: Routledge, 1992), pp. 13–38; Mary Beth Rose, 'Where are the Mothers in Shakespeare? Options for Gender Representation in the English Renaissance', *Shakespeare Quarterly*, 42:3 (Fall, 1991), 291–314; *Teaching Judith Shakespeare, Shakespeare Quarterly*, 47:4 (Winter 1996), guest editors Elizabeth H. Hageman and Sara Jayne Steen. See also the Forum 'Studying Early Modern Women' in *Shakespeare Studies*, 25 (1997).

41. Personal communication, May 1999. Thanks to all those contributors who responded so constructively and generously to my queries.

42. Thompson, '"The warrant of womanhood"', p. 84.

43. 'I hate the way you talk to me / And the way you cut your hair. / I hate the way you drive my car. / I hate it when you stare. // I hate your big dumb combat boots / And the way you read my mind. / I hate you so much it makes me sick – It even makes me rhyme. // I hate the way you're always right. / I hate it when you lie. / I hate it when you make me laugh – Even worse when you make me cry. // I hate it that you're not around / And the fact that you didn't call. / But mostly I hate the way / I don't hate you – Not even close, not even a little bit, not any at all.' *10 Things I Hate About You* by Karen McCullah Lutz and Kirsten Smith. From the film's official website at http://www.movies.go.com/-10things/skunk.html © Touchstone Pictures.

   The fact that both the Shakespeare films mentioned in this Introduction are complemented by official websites underlines a crucial aspect of Shakespeare's changing cultural location in the late twentieth and early twenty-first century. There is a pressing need for a feminist critique of the implications for the mediation of Shakespeare posed by the expanding possibilities for the reproduction and circulation of textual materials in various electronic media (e.g., hypertext, newsgroups, CD-ROM and DVD). Such technological developments can change procedures in a way that has implications for politically engaged criticism. The economic and social factors that make new media and communication technologies inaccessible to people in many parts of the world can exacerbate existing structures of exclusion and inequality: this is a matter that affects impoverished communities in Europe and the USA as well as the vast majority of populations in the poorer regions of the globe. Given the near-global interest in Shakespeare, there is an imperative on radical critics to support material and ideological efforts to hold the circles of debate open to Shakespeareans whose access to cyberspace is limited by economic constraints on their real-world existence. Conversely, in more affluent communities, phenomena such as the internet can open new spaces where non-academics and independent scholars, excluded from the institutionalised circuits of academic exchange, can make a significant contribution to the sharing of ideas about, and pleasure in, Shakespeare. The very different priorities and interests that non-academics often choose to bring to debate function as a salutary provocation to academic feminist Shakespeare criticism.

Discussions of the gender politics of electronic textuality can be found in Kathryn Sutherland, 'Challenging Assumptions: Women Writers and New Technology', in Warren Chernaik, Caroline Davis and Marilyn Deegan (eds), *The Politics of the Electronic Text* (Oxford: Office for Humanities Communication Publications, with The Centre for English Studies, University of London, 1993), pp. 53–67; Julia Flanders, 'The Body Encoded: Questions of Gender and the Electronic Text', in Kathryn Sutherland (ed.), *Electronic Text: Investigations in Theory and Method* (Oxford: Clarendon Press, 1997), pp. 127–44; and at the website of the Brown University Women Writers Project, http://www.wwp.brown.edu/.

1

The Patriarchal Bard: Feminist Criticism and Shakespeare: *King Lear* and *Measure for Measure*

KATHLEEN McLUSKIE

I

Every feminist critic has encountered the archly disingenuous question 'What exactly is feminist criticism?' The only effective response is 'I'll send you a booklist', for feminist criticism can only be defined by the multiplicity of critical practices engaged in by feminists. Owing its origins to a popular political movement, it reproduces the varied theoretical positions of that movement. Sociologists and theorists of culture have, for example, investigated the processes by which representations of women in advertising and film reproduce and reinforce dominant definitions of sexuality and sexual relations so as to perpetuate their ideological power.[1] Within English departments critical activity has been divided among those who revived and privileged the work of women writers and those who have focused critical attention on reinterpreting literary texts from the traditional canon. In the case of Shakespeare, feminist critics have contested the apparent misogyny of the plays and the resistance of their feminist students by directing attention to the 'world' of the plays, using conventional tools of interpretation to assess Shakespeare's attitude to the events within it.[2]

In a number of essays[3] the feminist concern with traditional evaluations of sexual identity has been used to explore the importance of ideals of violence in the psychological formation of Shakespeare's male characters.[4] Janet Adelman has analysed the importance of structures of psychological dependence in accounting for Coriolanus's phallic aggression[5] and Coppélia Kahn has described the feud in *Romeo and Juliet* as 'the deadly *rite de passage* that promotes masculinity at the price of life'.[6] These essays have built on and developed a feminist psychoanalysis[7] which places motherhood at the centre of psychological development, as Coppélia Kahn makes explicit in her book *Masculine Identity in Shakespeare*: 'the critical threat to identity is not, as Freud maintains, castration, but engulfment by the mother ... men first know women as the matrix of all satisfaction from which they must struggle to differentiate themselves ... [Shakespeare] explores the unconscious attitudes behind cultural definitions of manliness and womanliness and behind the mores and institutions shaped by them'.[8]

Modern feminist psychoanalysis could be applied to Shakespearean characters for the texts were seen as unproblematically mimetic: 'Shakespeare and Freud deal with the same subject: the expressed and hidden feelings in the human heart. They are both psychologists'.[9] Shakespeare was thus constructed as an authoritative figure whose views about men and women could be co-opted to the liberal feminism of the critic. Within this critical practice, academic debate centred on conflicts over the authors' views rather than on the systems of representation or the literary traditions which informed the texts. Linda Bamber, for example, reminded her readers of the evident misogyny of Shakespeare's treatment of his tragic heroines and placed her own work 'in reaction against the tendency for feminist critics to interpret Shakespeare as if his work directly supports and develops feminist ideas'.[10] While noting the fundamental inconsistencies between Shakespeare's treatment of women in comedy and tragedy, she explicitly resists the temptation 'to revel in them offered by post-structuralism'. She finds instead a cohering principle in Shakespeare's recognition of women as 'other', which 'amounts to sexism only if the writer fails to attribute to opposite sex characters the privileges of the other'.[11] In tragedy his women are strong because they are coherent – 'certainly none of the women in the tragedies worries or changes her mind about who she is' – and the attacks which are made on them are the product of male resentment at this strength – 'misogyny and sex nausea are born of failure and self doubt'.[12] The comic feminine, on the other hand, is opposed not to men but to a reified 'society': 'In comedy the feminine either rebels against the restraining social order or (more commonly) presides in alliance with the forces which challenge its hegemony: romantic love, physical nature, the love of pleasure in all its forms'.[13]

These assertions rest on a reductive application of feminist anthropological discussions of nature and culture but their primary effect is to construct an author whose views can be applied in moral terms to rally and exhort the women readers of today: 'the comic heroines show us how to regard ourselves as other ... the heroines laugh to see themselves absorbed into the ordinary human comedy; the heroes rage and weep at the difficulty of actually being as extraordinary as they feel themselves to be'.[14] These moral characteristics ascribed to men and women take no account of their particular circumstances within the texts, nor indeed of their material circumstances and the differential power relations which they support. Feminism thus involves defining certain characteristics as feminine and admiring them as a better way to survive in the world. In order to assert the moral connection between the mimetic world of Shakespeare's plays and the real world of the audience, the characters have to be seen as representative men and women and the categories male and female are essential, unchanging, definable in modern, commonsense terms.

The essentialism of this form of feminism is further developed in Marilyn French's *Shakespeare's Division of Experience*. Like Bamber, she constructs a god-like author who 'breathed life into his female characters and gave body to the principles they are supposed to represent'.[15] Although shored up by references to feminist philosophy and anthropology, this feminine principle amounts to little more than the power to nurture and give birth and is opposed to a masculine principle embodied in the ability to kill. These principles are not, however, located in specific men or women. When men are approved of they are seen as embracing feminine principles whereas women are denied access to the male and are denigrated when they aspire to male qualities. French suggests that Shakespeare divides experience into male (evil) and female (good) principles and his comedies and tragedies are interpreted as 'either a synthesis of the principles or an examination of the kinds of worlds

that result when one or other principle is abused, neglected, devalued or exiled'.[16]

The essentialism which lies behind Marilyn French's and Linda
Bamber's account of the men and women in Shakespeare is part of
a trend in liberal feminism which sees the feminist struggle as concerned with reordering the values ascribed to men and women
without fundamentally changing the material circumstances in
which their relationships function. It presents feminism as a set of
social attitudes rather than as a project for fundamental social
change. As such it can equally easily be applied to an analysis of
Shakespeare's plays which situates them in the ideological currents
of his own time. In *Shakespeare and the Nature of Women*, for
example, Juliet Dusinberre admires 'Shakespeare's concern ... to
dissolve artificial distinctions between the sexes'[17] and can claim
that concern as feminist in both twentieth-century and seventeenth-
century terms. She examines Shakespeare's women characters – and
those of some of his contemporaries – in the light of Renaissance
debates over women conducted in Puritan handbooks and advice
literature. Building on the Hallers' essay 'The Puritan Art of
Love',[18] she notes the shift from misogyny associated with Catholic
asceticism to Puritan assertions of the importance of women in the
godly household as partners in holy and companionate marriage.
The main portion of the book is an elaboration of themes –
Chastity, Equality, Gods and Devils – in both polemic and dramatic
literature. The strength of her argument lies in its description of the
literary shift from the discourses of love poetry and satire to those
of drama. However, her assertions about the feminism of
Shakespeare and his contemporaries depend once again upon a
mimetic model of the relationship between ideas and drama.
Contemporary controversy about women is seen as a static body of
ideas which can be used or rejected by dramatists whose primary
concern is not with parallel fictions but simply to 'explore the real
nature of women'. By focusing on the presentation of women in
Puritan advice literature, Dusinberre privileges one side of a contemporary debate, relegating expressions of misogyny to the
fictional world of 'literary simplification' and arbitrarily asserting
more progressive notions as the dramatists' true point of view.[19]

A more complex discussion of the case would acknowledge that
the issues of sex, sexuality, sexual relations and sexual division
were areas of conflict of which the contradictions of writing about
women were only one manifestation alongside the complexity of

legislation and other forms of social control of sex and the family. The debates in modern historiography on these questions indicate the difficulty of assigning monolithic economic or ideological models to the early modern family, while the work of regional historians has shown the importance of specific material conditions on both the ideology and practice of sexual relations.[20] Far from being an unproblematic concept, 'the nature of women' was under severe pressure from both ideological discourses and the real concomitants of inflation and demographic change.

The problem with the mimetic, essentialist model of feminist criticism is that it would require a more multi-faceted mirror than Shakespearean drama to reflect the full complexity of the nature of women in Shakespeare's time or our own. Moreover this model obscures the particular relationship between Shakespearean drama and its readers which feminist criticism implies. The demands of the academy insist that feminist critics reject 'a literary version of placard carrying',[21] but they cannot but reveal the extent to which their critical practice expresses new demands and a new focus of attention on the plays. Coppélia Kahn concedes that 'Today we are questioning the cultural definitions of sexual identity we have inherited. I believe Shakespeare questioned them too ...',[22] and, rather more frankly, Linda Bamber explains: 'As a heterosexual feminist ... I have found in Shakespeare what I want to imagine as a possibility in my own life'.[23] However, the alternative to this simple co-option of Shakespeare is not to assert some spurious notion of objectivity. Such a procedure usually implies a denigration of feminism[24] in favour of more conventional positions and draws the criticism back into the institutionalised competition over 'readings'.

A different procedure would involve theorising the relationship between feminism and the plays more explicitly, accepting that feminist criticism, like all criticism, is a reconstruction of the play's meaning and asserting the specificity of a feminist response. This procedure differs from claiming Shakespeare's views as feminist in refusing to construct an author behind the plays and paying attention instead to the narrative, poetic and theatrical strategies which construct the plays' meanings and position the audience to understand their events from a particular point of view. For Shakespeare's plays are not primarily explorations of 'the real nature of women' or even 'the hidden feelings in the human heart'. They were the products of an entertainment industry which, as far as we know, had no women shareholders, actors, writers, or stage hands. His women characters were played by boys and, far from his plays being an expression of his idiosyncratic views, they all built on and adapted earlier stories.

The witty comic heroines, the powerful tragic figures, the opposition between realism and romance were the commonplaces of the literary tradition from which these tests emerged. Sex and sexual relations within them are, in the first analysis, sources of comedy, narrative resolution and *coups de théâtre*. These textual strategies limit the range of meaning which the text allows and circumscribe the position which a feminist reader may adopt *vis-à-vis* the treatment of gender relations and sexual politics within the plays. The feminist reader may resist the position which the text offers but resistance involves more than simple attitudinising.

II

In traditional criticism Shakespeare's plays are seldom regarded as the sum of their dramatic devices. The social location of the action, their visual dimension and the frequent claims they make for their own authenticity, invite an audience's engagement at a level beyond the plot. The audience is invited to make some connection between the events of the action and the form and pressure of their own world. In the case of sex and gender, the concern of feminists, a potential connection is presented between sexual relations as an aspect of narrative – who will marry whom and how? – and sexual relations as an aspect of social relations – how is power distributed between men and women and how are their sexual relations conducted? The process of interpretative criticism is to construct a social meaning for the play out of its narrative and dramatic realisation. However this is no straightforward procedure: the positions offered by the texts are often contradictory and meaning can be produced by adopting one of the positions offered, using theatrical production or critical procedures to close off others. The critic can use historical knowledge to speculate about the possible creation of meaning in the light of past institutions and ideologies but the gap between textual meaning and social meaning can never be completely filled for meaning is constructed every time the text is reproduced in the changing ideological dynamic between text and audience.

An interesting case in point is *Measure for Measure*, in which the conflicting positions offered by the text have resulted in critical con-

fusion among those who wish to fix its moral meaning as the authentic statement of a coherent author. The problems have centred
in large part on the narrative resolution in which the restoration of
order through marriages seems both an affront to liberal sensibili-
ties and an unsatisfactory suppression of the powerful passions
evoked throughout the action. There seems to be an irresolvable
gap between the narrative strategies – the bed-trick, the prince in
disguise plot – and the realism of the other scenes in which we see
'corruption boil and bubble till it o'errun the stew'.

The relevance of discussions of early modern sexuality and social
control is evident in the play's treatment of public regulation of
morality. Nevertheless such historically informed attention as the
play has received[25] has been in the attempt to close off its meaning
by invoking Jacobean marriage law or Christian theology in order
to determine the rightness or wrongness of Angelo's judgements,
the reason or lack of it in Isabella's defence of her chastity. These
arguments fail to convince, not because history is irrelevant but
because they cannot solve problems which arise in the first instance
from the production of meaning by the text.

The confusion in the narrative meaning is created because it
offers equal dramatic power to mutually exclusive positions. The
comic vitality of the low-life characters and their anarchic resistance
to the due processes of law dramatises the inadequacy of any
system of control which stops short of an order to 'geld and splay
all the youth of the city' (II.i.230). Nevertheless engagement with
them is complicated by the equal dramatic impact of the Duke's
disgust with their trade in flesh (III.ii.22–7). Similarly Isabella's
single-minded protection of her sexual autonomy is placed first by
the masochism of the sexual imagery in which it is expressed and
then by its juxtaposition with her brother's equally vividly expressed terror at the thought of death. Moral absolutes are rendered
platitudinous by the language and verse, particularly in the Duke's
summary where the jingling rhyme of the couplet mocks the very
morals it asserts.

This speech, at the mid point of the play, offers a summary of the
tension between narrative and social meaning. The moral absolutes
of the first part of the speech are set against the Duke's solution to
the problem. But the terms of the solution are moral and pragmatic:

> Craft against vice I must apply.
> With Angelo tonight shall lie

His old betrothed but despised.
So disguise shall, by th'disguised
Pay with falsehood false exacting
And perform an old contracting.
(III.ii.280–5)

Yet the ending of the play, for all its narrative manipulation, imposes not only a narrative solution but also a possible social resolution. Both the *coup de théâtre* of the Duke's reappearance and the language which accords his merciful authority the status of 'power divine' provide theatrical satisfaction for the finale which endorses the social implications of the Duke's judgement. Marriage is the solution to the puzzle of the bed-trick but it is also the solution to the disruptive power of Lucio who has offered troublesome alternatives to the main narrative line. The solution is imposed in this play by a figure from within the action, the all-powerful Duke, but it is no more inappropriate to the characters concerned than the finale of many another romantic comedy.

It is impossible to say how this resolution was regarded by Shakespeare's contemporaries. There is evidence to suggest that marriage was regarded as just such an instrument of effective social control and social harmony. However there is no reason why the elusive responses of past audiences need carry privileged status as the ultimate meaning of the text. The ideological struggle over sexuality and sexual relations which informs the text has emerged in different terms in the late twentieth century, and a liberal humanist reading of the text might present its social meaning as a despairing (or enthusiastic) recognition of the ineffectiveness of attempts at the control of such private, individual matters. A radical feminist production of the text could on the other hand, through acting, costume and style, deny the lively energy of the pimps and the bawds, foregrounding their exploitation of female sexuality. It might celebrate Isabella's chastity as a feminist resistance, making her plea for Angelo's life a gesture of solidarity to a heterosexual sister and a recognition of the difficulty of breaking the bonds of family relations and conventional sexual arrangements.

These different 'interpretations' are not, however, competing equals in the struggle for meaning. They each involve reordering the terms in which the text is produced, which of its conflicting positions are foregrounded, and how the audience response is controlled. In Jonathan Miller's production of the play, for example,

Isabella literally refused the Duke's offer of marriage and walked off stage in the opposite direction. Miller has been a powerful advocate for the right of a director to reconstruct Shakespeare's plays in the light of modern preoccupations, creating for them an afterlife which is not determined by their original productions.[26] As a theatre director, he is aware of the extent to which the social meaning of a play depends upon the arrangements of theatrical meaning; which is different from simply asserting alternative 'interpretations'. The concept of interpretation suggests that the text presents a transparent view on to the real life of sexual relations whether of the sixteenth or the twentieth century. The notion of 'constructed meaning' on the other hand, foregrounds the theatrical devices by which an audience's perception of the action of the play is defined. The focus of critical attention, in other words, shifts from judging the action to analysing the process by which the action presents itself to be judged.

This shift in the critical process has important implications for feminist criticism: the theatrical strategies which present the action to be judged resist feminist manipulation by denying an autonomous position for the female viewer of the action. Laura Mulvey and others have explored through the notion of scopophilia the pleasures afforded by particular ways of perceiving men and women in classic film narrative. Mulvey argues that in classic Hollywood films the techniques of lighting, focus and narrative pattern create women as the object, men as the bearers of the look: 'A woman performs within the narrative, the gaze of the spectator and that of the male characters in the film are neatly combined without breaking narrative verisimilitude'.[27] Theatrical production, of course, effects less complete control on the spectators' gaze than Hollywood cinema. Nevertheless the techniques of soliloquy, language and the organisation of the scenes limit the extent to which women characters are 'seen' in the action. One of the most common strategies of liberal mimetic interpretation is to imagine a past life, a set of alternatives and motivation for the characters. Yet the text much more frequently denies this free play of character, defining women as sexualised, seen vis-à-vis men.

The effect of this process can be seen in Measure for Measure where the women characters define a spectrum of sexual relations from Mistress Overdone (Overdone by her last husband), the elderly bawd, through Juliet who is visibly pregnant, to Isabella whose denial of sexuality is contained in the visual definition of her nun's habit. Mariana's ambiguous position as 'neither maid, widow nor wife' affords her no autonomy but is seen as problematic: indeed the narrative organisation of the latter part of the play is directed to reinstating her within the parameters of permitted sexual relations.

Mariana's introduction into the play shows how the text focuses the spectator's attention and constructs it as male.[28] She is introduced in tableau, the visual accompaniment to the boy's song. Her role in the action is defined not by her own activity but by her physical presence, itself contextualised within the narrative by the song's words:

> Take, O, take those lips away
> That so sweetly were forsworn;
> And those eyes, the break of day,
> Lights that do mislead the morn;
> But my kisses bring again, bring again;
> Seals of love, but seal'd in vain, seal'd in vain.
>
> (IV.i.1–6)

Isabella, for all her importance in the play, is similarly defined theatrically by the men around her for the men in the audience. In the scene of her first plea to Angelo, for example, she is physically framed by Angelo, the object of her demand, and Lucio the initiator of her plea. When she gives up after Angelo's first refusal, Lucio urges her back with instructions on appropriate behaviour:

> Give't not o'er so. To him again! entreat him,
> Kneel down before him, hang upon his gown!
> You are too cold.
>
> (II.ii.43–5)

As her rhetoric becomes more impassioned, her speeches longer, our view of her action is still dramatically mediated through Lucio whose approving remarks and comic asides act as a filter both for her action and for the audience's view of it.

Through Lucio and the provost the text makes us want her to win. However, the terms of her victory are also defined by the rhetoric and structure of the scene. A woman pleading with a man introduces an element of sexual conflict which is made explicit in the bawdy innuendo of Lucio's remarks (II.ii.123–4). The passion of the conflict, the sexualising of the rhetoric, and the engagement of the onstage spectators create a theatrical excitement which is necessary to sustain the narrative: it also produces the kind of audience involvement which makes Angelo's response make sense. Like Angelo we are witnesses to Isabella's performance so that we understand, if we do not morally approve of, his reaction to it. It is, moreover, rendered theatrically valid in the heart-searching soliloquy which closes the scene. His rhetorical questions 'Is this her fault or mine ... Can it be that modesty may more betray the sense / Than woman's lightness?' define the sexually appealing paradox of the passionate nun, and the audience is intellectually engaged in his quandary by his dilemma being put in the questioning form.

A feminist reading of the scene may wish to refuse the power of Angelo's plea, may recognise in it the double bind which blames women for their own sexual oppression. However to take up that position involves refusing the pleasure of the drama and the text, which imply a coherent maleness in their point of view.[29]

Isabella's dilemma is, by contrast, a pale affair. Her one soliloquy deals only in the abstract opposition of chastity against her brother's life. Her resounding conclusion 'Then Isobel live chaste and brother die: / More than our brother is our chastity' (II.iv.184–5) offers no parallel intellectual pleasures; it does not arise out of the passion of the preceding scene which was a conflict between Angelo and Isabella not Isabella and Claudio; its lack of irony or paradox offers no scope for audience play. It is simply the apparently irresolvable problem which the ensuing action, under the Duke's control, must seek to resolve. Isabella's action is determined in the text by her sexuality, and her space for manoeuvre is explicitly defined in Angelo's reminder of her circumscribed condition:

> Be that you are
> That is, a woman; if you be more, you're none;
> If you be one, as you are well expressed
> By all external warrants, show it now,
> By putting on the destined livery.
>   (II.iv.134–7)

Angelo's definition of a woman 'by all external warrants' is shared by the theatrical devices of the text. Any criticism which argues whether Isabella is a vixen or a saint places itself comfortably in the limited opening that the text allows for it; it takes up the argument about whether Isabella is to be more than a woman in giving up her brother or less than one in submitting to Angelo's lust. The text allows her no other role. The radical feminist 'interpretation' floated earlier would require a radical rewriting both of the narrative and of the way the scenes are constructed.

Feminist criticism of this play is restricted to exposing its own exclusion from the text. It has no point of entry into it, for the dilemmas of the narrative and the sexuality under discussion are constructed in completely male terms – gelding and splaying hold no terror for women – and the women's role as the objects of exchange within that system of sexuality is not at issue, however much a feminist might want to draw attention to it. Thus when a feminist accepts the narrative, theatrical and intellectual pleasures of this text she does so in male terms and not as part of the locus of feminist critical activity.

III

In *Measure for Measure* the pleasure denied is the pleasure of comedy, a pleasure many feminists have learned to struggle with as they withhold their assent from the social approval of sexist humour. A much more difficult pleasure to deny is the emotional, moral and aesthetic satisfaction afforded by tragedy. Tragedy assumes the existence of 'a permanent, universal and essentially unchanging human nature'[30] but the human nature implied in the moral and aesthetic satisfactions of tragedy is most often explicitly male. In *King Lear*, for example, the narrative and its dramatisation present a connection between sexual insubordination and anarchy, and the connection is given an explicitly misogynist emphasis.

The action of the play, the organisation of its point of view and the theatrical dynamic of its central scenes all depend upon an audience accepting an equation between 'human nature' and male power. In order to experience the proper pleasures of pity and fear, they must accept that fathers are owed particular duties by their daughters and be appalled by the chaos which ensues when those primal links are broken. Such a point of view is not a matter of consciously held opinion but it is a position required and determined by the text in order for it to make sense. It is also the product of a set of meanings produced in a specific way by the Shakespearean text and is different from that produced in other versions of the story.

The representation of patriarchal misogyny is most obvious in the treatment of Goneril and Regan. In the chronicle play *King Leir*, the sisters' villainy is much more evidently a function of the plot. Their mocking pleasure at Cordella's downfall takes the form of a comic double act and Regan's evil provides the narrative with the exciting twist of an attempt on Leir's life.[31] In the Shakespearean text by contrast, the narrative, language and dramatic organisation all define the sisters' resistance to their father in terms of their gender, sexuality and position within the family. Family relations in this play are seen as fixed and determined, and any movement within them is portrayed as a destructive reversal of rightful order (see I.iv). Goneril's and Regan's treatment of their father merely reverses existing patterns of rule and is seen not simply as cruel and selfish but as a fundamental violation of human nature – as is made powerfully explicit in the speeches which condemn them (III.vii.101–3; IV.ii.32–50). Moreover when Lear in his madness fantasises about the collapse of law and the destruction of ordered social control, women's lust is vividly represented as the centre and source of the ensuing corruption (IV.vi.110–28). The generalised character of Lear's and Albany's vision of chaos, and the poetic force with which it is expressed, creates the appearance of truthful universality which is an important part of the play's claim to greatness. However, that generalised vision of chaos is present in gendered terms in which patriarchy, the institution of male power in the family and the State, is seen as the only form of social organisation strong enough to hold chaos at bay.

The close links between misogyny and patriarchy define the women in the play more precisely. Goneril and Regan are not presented as archetypes of womanhood for the presence of Cordelia 'redeems nature from the general curse' (IV.vi.209). However Cordelia's saving love, so much admired by critics, works in the action less as a redemption for womankind than as an example of patriarchy restored. Hers, of course, is the first revolt against Lear's organising authority. The abruptness of her refusal to play her role in Lear's public drama dramatises the outrage of her denial of conformity and the fury of Lear's ensuing appeal to archetypal forces shows that a rupture of 'Propinquity and property of blood' is tantamount to the destruction of nature itself. Cordelia, however, is the central focus of emotion in the scene. Her resistance to her father gains audience assent through her two asides during her sisters' performances; moreover the limits of that resistance are clearly indicated. Her first defence is not a statement on her personal autonomy or the rights of her individual will: it is her right to retain a part of her love for 'that lord whose hand must take my plight'. Lear's rage thus seems unreasonable in that he recognises only his rights as a father; for the patriarchal family to continue, it must also recognise the rights of future fathers and accept the transfer of women from fathers to husbands. By the end of the scene, Cordelia is reabsorbed into the patriarchal family by marriage to which her resistance to Lear presents no barrier. As she reassures the king of France:

> It is no vicious blot, murder or foulness,
> No unchaste action or dishonoured step
> That hath deprived me of your grace and favour.
>   (I.i.228–31)

Her right to be included in the ordered world of heterosexual relations depends upon her innocence of the ultimate human violation of murder which is paralleled with the ultimate sexual violation of unchastity.

However, any dispassionate analysis of the mystification of real socio-sexual relations in *King Lear* is the antithesis of our response to the tragedy in the theatre where the tragic power of the play endorses its ideological position at every stage. One of the most important and effective shifts in the action is the transfer of our sympathy back to Lear in the middle of the action. The long sequence of Act II, scene iv dramatises the process of Lear's decline from the angry autocrat of Act I to the appealing figure of pathetic insanity. The psychological realism of the dramatic writing and the manipulation of the point of view, forges the bonds between Lear as a complex character and the sympathies of the audience.

The audience's sympathies are engaged by Lear's fury at the insult offered by Kent's imprisonment and by the pathos of Lear's belated attempt at self-control (II.iv.101–4). His view of the action is further emotionally secured by his sarcastic enactment of the humility which his daughters recommend:

> Do you but mark how this becomes the house:
> Dear daughter, I confess that I am old.
> Age is unnecessary. On my knees I beg
> That you'll vouchsafe me raiment, bed and food.
>   (II.iv.53–6)

As Regan says, these are unsightly tricks. Their effect is to close off the dramatic scene by offering the only alternative to Lear's behaviour as we see it. The dramatic fact becomes the only fact and the audience is thus positioned to accept the tragic as inevitable, endorsing the terms of Lear's great poetic appeal:

> O reason not the need! Our basest beggars
> Are in the poorest things superfluous.
> Allow not nature more than nature needs,
> Man's life is cheap as beasts.
> (II.iv.263–6)

The ideological power of Lear's speech lies in his invocation of nature to support his demands on his daughters; its dramatic power lies in its movement from argument to desperate assertion of his crumbling humanity as the abyss of madness approaches. However, once again, that humanity is seen in gendered terms as Lear appeals to the gods to

> touch me with noble anger,
> And let not women's weapons, water drops
> Stain my man's cheeks.
> (II.iv.275–7)

The theatrical devices which secure Lear at the centre of the audience's emotional attention operate even more powerfully in the play's denouement. The figure of Cordelia is used as a channel for the response to her suffering father. Her part in establishing the terms of the conflict is over by Act I; when she reappears it is as an emblem of dutiful pity. Before she appears on stage, she is described by a 'gentleman' whose speech reconstructs her as a static, almost inanimate daughter of sorrows. The poetic paradoxes of his speech construct Cordelia as one who resolves contradiction,[32] which is her potential role in the narrative and her crucial function in the ideological coherence of the text:

> patience and sorrow strove
> Who should express her goodliest. You have seen
> Sunshine and rain at once: her smiles and tears
> Were like a better way: those happy smilets
> That played on her ripe lip seemed not to know
> What guests were in her eyes, which parted thence
> As pearls from diamonds dropped.
> (IV.iii.17–23)

With Cordelia's reaction pre-empted by the gentleman, the scene where Lear and Cordelia meet substitutes the pleasure of pathos for suspense. The imagery gives Cordelia's forgiveness divine sanction, and the realism of Lear's struggle for sanity closes off any responses other than complete engagement with the characters' emotions. Yet in this encounter Cordelia denies the dynamic of the whole play. Lear fears that she cannot love him:

> for your sisters
> Have, as I do remember, done me wrong.
> You have some cause, they have not.
> (IV.vii.73–5)

But Cordelia demurs with 'No cause, no cause'.

Shakespeare's treatment of this moment contrasts with that of the earlier chronicle play from which he took a number of details, including Lear kneeling and being raised. In the old play the scene is almost comic as Leir and Cordella kneel and rise in counterpoint to their arguments about who most deserves blame.[33] The encounter is used to sum up the issues and the old play allows Cordella a much more active role in weighing her debt to Leir. In Shakespeare's text, however, the spectacle of suffering obliterates the past action so that the audience with Cordelia will murmur 'No cause, no cause'. Rather than a resolution of the action, their reunion becomes an emblem of possible harmony, briefly glimpsed before the tragic débâcle.

The deaths of Lear and Cordelia seem the more shocking for this moment of harmony but their tragic impact is also a function of thwarting the narrative expectation of harmony restored which is established by the text's folk-tale structure.[34] The folk-tale of the love test provides an underlying pattern in which harmony is broken by the honest daughter and restored by her display of forgiveness. The organisation of the Shakespearean text intensifies and then denies those expectations so as once more to insist on the connection between evil women and a chaotic world.

The penultimate scene opposes the ordered formality of the resolution of the Gloucester plot with the unseemly disorder of the women's involvement. The twice-repeated trumpet call, the arrival of a mysterious challenger in disguise, evoke the order of a chivalric age when conflict was resolved by men at arms. The women, however, act as disrupters of that order: Goneril attempts to deny the outcome of the tourney, grappling in an unseemly quarrel with Albany (V.iii.156–8) and their ugly deaths interrupt Edgar's efforts to close off the narrative with a formal account of his part in the story and Gloucester's death.

Thus the deaths of Lear and Cordelia are contrasted with and seem almost a result of the destructiveness of the wicked sisters. Albany says of them: 'This judgement of the heavens, that makes us tremble, / Touches us not with pity' (V.iii.233–4). The tragic victims, however, affect us quite differently. When Lear enters, bearing his dead daughter in his arms, we are presented with a contrasting emblem of the natural, animal assertion of family love, destroyed by the anarchic forces of lust and the 'indistinguished space of woman's will'. At this point in the play the most stony-hearted feminist could not withhold her pity even though it is called forth at the expense of her resistance to the patriarchal relations which it endorses.

The effect of these dramatic devices is to position the audience as a coherent whole, comfortably situated *vis-à-vis* the text. To attempt to shift that position by denying Lear's rights as a father and a man would be to deny the pity of Lear's suffering and the pleasurable reaffirmation of one's humanity through sympathetic fellow feeling. A feminist reading of the text cannot simply assert the countervailing rights of Goneril and Regan, for to do so would simply reverse the emotional structures of the play, associating feminist ideology with atavistic selfishness and the monstrous assertion of individual wills. Feminism cannot simply take 'the woman's part' when that part has been so morally loaded and theatrically circumscribed. Nor is any purpose served by merely denouncing the text's misogyny, for *King Lear*'s position at the centre of the Shakespeare canon is assured by its continual reproduction in education and the theatre and is unlikely to be shifted by feminist sabre-rattling.

A more fruitful point of entry for feminism is the process of the text's reproduction. As Elizabeth Cowie and others have pointed out,[35] sexist meanings are not fixed but depend upon constant reproduction by their audience. In the case of *King Lear* the text is tied to misogynist meaning only if it is reconstructed with its emotional power and its moral imperatives intact. Yet the text contains possibilities for subverting these meanings and the potential for reconstructing them in feminist terms.

The first of these lies in the text's historical otherness; for in spite of constant critical assertion of its transcendent universality, specific connections can be shown between Shakespeare's text and contemporary material and ideological conflict without presenting a merely reductive account of artistic production in terms of material circumstances.[36]

Discussing the 'gerontocratic ideal', for example, Keith Thomas has noted that 'The sixteenth and seventeenth centuries are conspicuous for a sustained desire to subordinate persons in their teens and twenties and to delay their equal participation in the adult world ... such devices were also a response to the mounting burden of population on an inflexible economy'.[37] This gerontocratic ideal was not without contradiction, for the very elderly were removed from economic and political power and 'essentially it was men in their forties or fifties who ruled'.[38] Moreover the existence of this ideal did not obviate the need for careful material provision for the elderly. There is a certain poignancy in the details of wills which specify the exact houseroom and the degree of access to the household fire which is to be left to aged parents.[39] However, this suggests that Lear's and his daughter's bargaining over the number of his knights need not be seen as an egregious insult and that the generational conflict within the nuclear family could not be resolved by recourse to a simply accepted ideal of filial piety.

As a corrective to prevailing gloomy assessments of the happiness of the early modern family, Keith Wrightson has produced evidence of individuals who show considerable concern to deal with family conflict in a humane and flexible fashion.[40] But it is equally clear from his evidence that family relations were the focus of a great deal of emotional energy and the primary source both of pleasure and pain. This is also borne out in Michael MacDonald's account of a seventeenth-century psychiatric practice in which, as today, women were more susceptible to mental illness than men:

> Not all the stress women suffered was caused by physical illness ... women were also more vulnerable than men to psychologically disturbing social situations. Their individual propensities to anxiety and sadness were enhanced by patriarchal custom and values that limited their ability to remedy disturbing situations... . Napier and his troubled patients also believed that oppression made people miserable and even mad, but the bondage they found most troubling subordinated daughters to parents, wives to husbands rather than peasants to lords.[41]

This discussion of social history cannot propose an alternative 'interpretation' of the text or assert its true meaning in the light of historical 'facts'. Rather it indicates that the text was produced within the contradictions of contemporary ideology and practice and suggests that similar contradictions exist within the play. These contradictions could fruitfully be brought to bear in modern criticism and productions. The dispute between Lear and his daughters is in part concerned with love and filial gratitude but it also dramatises the tense relationship between those bonds and the material circumstances in which they function. Lear's decision to publish his daughters' dowries is so 'that future strife / May be prevented now': the connection between loving harmony and economic justice is the accepted factor which underlies the formal patterning of the opening scene and is disrupted only by Cordelia's asides which introduce a notion of love as a more individual and abstract concept, incompatible both with public declaration and with computation of forests, champains, rivers and meads. Cordelia's notion of love gained precedence in modern ideology but it seriously disrupts Lear's discussion of property and inheritance. When Lear responds with 'Nothing will come of nothing' his words need not be delivered as an angry calling to account: they could equally be presented as a puzzled reaction to an inappropriate idea. Moreover Cordelia is not opposing hereditary duty to transcendent love – she does not reply 'There's beggary in the love that can be reckoned'. When she expands on her first assertion her legal language suggests a preference for a limited, contractual relationship: 'I love your majesty / According to my bond, no more nor less' (I.i.94–5). The conflict between the contractual model and the patriarchal model of subjects' obligations to their king was at issue in contemporary political theory[42] and Cordelia's words here introduce a similar conflict into the question of obligations within the family.

When in Act II Lear again bargains with his daughters, a similar confusion between affective relations and contractual obligations is in play. Lear asserts the importance of the contractual agreement made with his daughters, for it is his only remaining source of power. Since they are now in control, Goneril and Regan can assert an apparently benign notion of service which does not depend on contract or mathematical computation:

> What need you five and twenty? ten? or five?
> To follow in a house where twice so many
> Have a command to tend you?
>
> (II.iv.260–2)

The emotional impact of the scene, which is its principal power in modern productions, simply confuses the complex relations between personal autonomy, property and power which are acted out in this confrontation. The scene could be directed to indicate that the daughters' power over Lear is the obverse of his former power over them. His power over them is socially sanctioned but its arbitrary and tyrannical character is clear from his treatment of Cordelia. Lear kneeling to beg an insincere forgiveness of Regan is no more or less 'unsightly' than Goneril's and Regan's formal protestations to their father. Both are the result of a family organisation which denies economic autonomy in the name of transcendent values of love and filial piety and which affords no rights to the powerless within it. Such a production of meaning offers the pleasure of understanding in place of the pleasure of emotional identification. In this context Lear's speeches about nature and culture are part of an argument, not a *cri de coeur*; the blustering of his threats is no longer evidence of the destruction of a man's self-esteem but the futile anger of a powerful man deprived of male power.

Further potential for comically undermining the focus on Lear is provided by the Fool, who disrupts the narrative movement of the action, subverting if not denying the emotional impact of the scenes in which he appears. In an important sense the Fool is less an *alter ego* for Lear than for his daughters: like them he reminds Lear and the audience of the material basis for the change in the balance of power. However, where they exploit Lear's powerlessness with cruelty and oppression, he denies that necessity by his continued allegiance. In modern productions this important channel for an alternative view of events is closed off by holding the Fool within the narrative, using him as a means to heighten the emotional appeal of Lear's decline.[43]

The potential for subversive contradiction in the text is, however, restricted to the first part. Lear's madness and the extrusion of Gloucester's eyes heavily weight the action towards a simpler notion of a time when humanity must perforce prey upon itself like monsters of the deep, denying comic recognition of the material facts of existence. Yet even Cordelia's self-denying love or Gloucester's stoic resignation are denied the status of ideological absolutes. The grotesque comic lie of Gloucester's fall from Dover cliff is hardly a firm basis for a belief in the saving power of divine providence and Cordelia's acceptance of her father's claims on her is futile because it is unsupported by material power.

A production of the text which would restore the element of dialectic, removing the privilege both from the character of Lear and from the ideological positions which he dramatizes, is crucial to a feminist critique. Feminist criticism need not restrict itself to privileging the woman's part or to special pleading on behalf of female characters. It can be equally well served by making a text reveal the conditions in which a particular ideology of femininity functions and by both revealing and subverting the hold which such an ideology has for readers both female and male.

The misogyny of King Lear, both the play and its hero, is constructed out of an ascetic tradition which presents women as the source of the primal sin of lust, combining with concerns about the threat to the family posed by female insubordination. However the text also dramatises the material conditions which lie behind assertions of power within the family, even as it expresses deep anxieties about the chaos which can ensue when that balance of power is altered.

An important part of the feminist project is to insist that the alternative to the patriarchal family and heterosexual love is not chaos but the possibility of new forms of social organisation and affective relationships. However, feminists also recognise that our socialisation within the family and, perhaps more importantly, our psychological development as gendered subjects make these changes no simple matter.[44] They involve deconstructing the sustaining comforts of love and the family as the only haven in a heartless world. Similarly, a feminist critique of the dominant traditions in literature must recognise the sources of its power, not only in the institutions which reproduce them but also in the pleasures which they afford. But feminist criticism must also assert the power of resistance, subverting rather than co-opting the domination of the patriarchal Bard.

From *Political Shakespeare: New Essays in Cultural Materialism*, ed. Jonathan Dollimore and Alan Sinfield (Manchester: Manchester University Press, 1985), pp. 88–108.

NOTES

[This influential essay argues against the tendency – characteristic of much of the 'first wave' of feminist Shakespeare criticism – to take the plays as expressing Shakespeare's own views, and to worry about whether this made him pro-, proto- or anti-feminist. It demands instead that attention be paid to 'the narrative, poetic, and theatrical strategies which construct the plays' meanings and position the audience to understand their events from a particular point of view'. For Kathleen McLuskie, the plays work on a dynamic between sexual relations as an aspect of narrative and an aspect of social relations, and her reading of *Measure for Measure* proposes that its 'problem' status is generated by the tensions inherent in this dynamic. She outlines and tests possible ways of making sense of these problems from feminist points of view, especially in production, exemplifying her insistence that feminist critical and political practice need not and should not be monolithic.   Ed.]

1. See Michele Barrett, *Ideology and Cultural Production* (London: Croom Helm, 1979); Judith Williamson, *Decoding Advertisements* (London: Marion Boyars 1978); and Annette Kuhn, *Women's Pictures: Feminism and Cinema* (London: Routledge, 1982).

2. See the preface to Carolyn Lenz, Gayle Greene and Carol Neely (eds), *The Woman's Part: Feminist Criticism of Shakespeare* (Urbana, IL: Illinois University Press, 1980).

3. See Lenz, Greene and Neely, 'Women and Men in Shakespeare: a Selective Bibliography', ibid., pp. 314–36.

4. See especially Madelon Gohlke, '"I wooed thee with my sword": Shakespeare's Tragic Paradigms', ibid., pp. 150–70.

5. Janet Adelman, '"Anger's my meat": Feeding, Dependency and Aggression in *Coriolanus*', in David Bevington and J. L. Halio (eds), *Shakespeare's Pattern of Excelling Nature* (Newark, 1978), pp. 108–24.

6. Coppélia Kahn, 'Coming of Age in Verona', in Lenz, Greene and Neely, *The Woman's Part*, p. 171.

7. In particular Dorothy Dinnerstein, *The Mermaid and the Minotaur: Sexual Arrangements and Human Malaise* (New York: Harper and Row, 1977) and Nancy Chodorow, *The Reproduction of Mothering: Psychoanalysis and the Sociology of Gender* (Berkeley and Los Angeles, CA: California University Press, 1979).

8. Coppélia Kahn, 'Man's Estate', in *Masculine Identity in Shakespeare* (Berkeley and Los Angeles, CA: California University Press, 1981), p. 11.

9. Ibid., p. 1.

10. Linda Bamber, *Comic Women, Tragic Men: A Study of Gender and Genre in Shakespeare* (Stanford, CA: Stanford University Press), p. 1.

11. Ibid., p. 5.

12. Ibid., p. 15.

13 Ibid., p. 32.

14. Ibid., p. 39.

15. Marilyn French, *Shakespeare's Division of Experience* (London: Cape, 1982).

16. Ibid., p. 25.

17. Juliet Dusinberre, *Shakespeare and the Nature of Women* (London: Macmillan, 1975) p. 153. Dusinberre's understanding of feminism has been challenged by Martha Anderson-Thom, 'Thinking about Women and their Prosperous Art: a Reply to Juliet Dusinberre's *Shakespeare and the Nature of Women*', *Shakespeare Studies*, 11 (1978), 259–76.

18. William Haller and Malleville Haller, 'The Puritan Art of Love', *Huntington Library Quarterly*, 5, (1942) 235–72. Cf. K. Davies, '"The Sacred Condition of Equality": how Original were Puritan Doctrines of Marriage?', *Social History*, 5 (1977), 566–7.

19. Juliet Dusinberre, *Shakespeare and the Nature of Women*, p. 183.

20. Chapter 4, 'Husbands and Wives, Parents and Children' of Keith Wrightson, *English Society, 1580–1680* (London: Hutchinson, 1982) provides a comprehensively informed discussion of the controversy. See also Lawrence Stone, *The Family, Sex and Marriage in England, 1500–1800* (London: Weidenfeld and Nicolson, 1977); G. R. Quaife, *Wanton Wenches and Wayward Wives: Peasants and Illicit Sex in Early Seventeenth-Century England* (London: Croom Helm, 1969); Margaret Spufford, *Contrasting Communities: English Villages in the Sixteenth and Seventeenth Centuries* (Cambridge University Press, 1974).

21. Lenz, Greene and Neely, *The Woman's Part*, preface, p. ix.

22. Coppélia Kahn, 'Man's Estate', p. 20.

23. Linda Bamber, *Comic Women*, p. 43.

24. See, for example, Lisa Jardine's summary dismissal of feminist criticism in favour of historical criticism in *Still Harping on Daughters: Women and Drama in the Age of Shakespeare* (Brighton: Harvester, 1983), introduction, or Inga-Stina Ewbank reminding her audience at the bicentennial congress of the Shakespeare Association of America of Ibsen's distinction between 'feminism' and the truth about men and women: 'Shakespeare's Portrayal of Women: a 1970s View' in Bevington and Halio (eds), *Excelling Nature*, pp. 222–9.

25. See Ernest Schanzer, 'The Marriage Contracts in *Measure for Measure*', Shakespeare Survey, 13 (1960), 81–9, and replies by J. Birje-Patil, 'Marriage Contracts in *Measure of Measure*', *Shakespeare Studies*, 5 (1969), 106–11; S. Narajan, '*Measure for Measure* and Elizabethan Betrothals', *Shakespeare Quarterly*, 14 (1963), 115–19.

26. This idea was fully developed in Jonathan Miller's Eliot Lectures, 'The After Life of Plays', delivered at the University of Kent in 1978 [and later published as *Subsequent Performances* (London: Faber and Faber, 1986)].

27. Laura Mulvey, 'Visual Pleasure and Narrative Cinema', *Screen* 16, no. 3, p. 13. For a more extended discussion see Annette Kuhn, *Women's Pictures*.

28. Cf. Laura Mulvey's account of the way songs and close-up are used in order to fetishize women characters in Hollywood cinema (ibid., p. 13). The fact that Mariana was played by a boy does not alter the point: she is always played by a woman in modern representation.

29. Cf. the discussion of 'Reading as a Woman' in Jonathan Culler, *Theory and Criticism after Structuralism* (Ithaca, NY: Cornell University Press, 1982), pp. 43–63. The implication there is that positioning the reader as a woman is a matter of free choice and the position adopted is coherent and determines clear-cut readings.

30. Raymond Williams, *Modern Tragedy* (London: Chatto, 1966), p. 45.

31. See *The True Chronicle History of King Leir*, ed. Geoffrey Bullough, *The Narrative and Dramatic Sources of Shakespeare*, vol. VII (London: Routledge, 1973), pp. 337–402.

32. The imagery of ll. 12–14 gives this resolution a political tinge; resolution is seen as subjection.

33. See *The True Chronicle History of King Leir*, ed. Bullough, p. 393.

34. Freud in 'The Theme of the Three Caskets' accounts for the psychological power of the myth in terms of 'the three inevitable [*sic*] relations that a man has with a woman – the woman who bears him, the woman who is his mate and the woman who destroys him'. Lear's entrance with Cordelia dead in his arms is, for Freud, a wish-fulfilling inversion of the old man being carried away by death (*The Collected Papers of Sigmund Freud*, ed. Ernest Jones, vol. IV (London: Hogarth, 1925), pp. 244–56).

35. 'The problem of stereotyping is not that it is true or false, distorting or manipulated, but that it closes off certain production of meaning in the image' (Elizabeth Cowie, 'Images of Women', *Screen Education*, 23 (1977), 22).

36. Bullough (*Narrative and Dramatic Sources*, p. 270) has drawn attention to 'the remarkable historical parallel' of the case of Sir Brian Annesley whose daughter Cordell took steps to prevent her sister declaring their father insane so that she could take over the management of his estate. Cordell Annesley's solution was that a family friend should be entrusted with the old man and his affairs.

37. Keith Thomas, 'Age and Authority in Early Modern England', *Proceedings of the British Academy*, 62 (1976), 214.

38. Ibid., p. 211.

39. Discussed in Margaret Spufford, *Contrasting Communities*, p. 113.

40. Wrightson, *English Society*.

41. Michael MacDonald, *Mystical Bedlam: Madness, Anxiety and Healing in Seventeenth-Century England* (Cambridge: Cambridge University Press, 1981), pp. 39–40.

42. See Gordon Schochet, *Patriarchalism in Political Thought* (Oxford: Blackwell, 1975).

43. For example in the 1982–3 Royal Shakespeare Company production Antony Sher played the fool as a vaudeville clown but the theatrical inventiveness of his double act with Lear emphasized the closeness of their relationship with the fool as a ventriloquist's dummy on Lear's knee.

44. See Michele Barrett and Mary McIntosh, *The Anti-Social Family* (London: Verso, 1982).

2

Feminist Theory and the Editing of Shakespeare: *The Taming of the Shrew* Revisited

ANN THOMPSON

In the second half of 1992 I committed myself to two developments in my career that seemed to some of my friends incompatible. I went as visiting professor to the Center for Women's Studies at the University of Cincinnati for three months to teach a graduate course in Feminist Theory, and I signed a contract to become joint General Editor (with Richard Proudfoot) of the new Arden Shakespeare series, Arden 3. Women's Studies are still, even in the United States, a marginal, controversial area, existing precariously within academic institutions and vulnerable to financial cutbacks. Shakespeare Studies are at the center of English Studies, arguably one of the more conservative disciplines.

In so far as the academic study of 'English' has begun to change, with pressure from various quarters to enlarge the canon of texts, women's writing is seen as a direct threat to Shakespeare – for example, in the debate about 'political correctness' in the teaching of English that followed the publication of a survey of English degree syllabi in British polytechnics and colleges of higher education early in 1992.[1] This survey was widely reported in a distorted form in the right-wing popular press, which seized on the fact that Shakespeare was compulsory in only 50 per cent of the institutions covered. A. N. Wilson's article on 'Shakespeare and the Tyranny of Feminism' (London *Evening Standard*, 4 February 1992) can be taken as representative of the generally hysterical reaction with its claim that the novels of Margaret Atwood, Toni Morrison and Alice Walker are compulsory reading for more students in British higher education than the plays of William Shakespeare. This is of course a ludicrous exaggeration, and the survey itself made no assumptions about any necessary antagonism between Shakespeare and women writers, but, while the same abbreviation serves (confusingly, in my notes) for both, W.S. (women's studies) is the opposition, W. S. (William Shakespeare) the establishment.

So what can feminist theory have to do with the editing of Shakespeare? Even within women's studies the role of feminist theory is problematic. There is still considerable hostility to it for two basic reasons:

1. It is seen (in its institutionalised form) as the exploitation, appropriation, and even de-radicalisation of the women's liberation movement. Through women's studies, feminism becomes co-opted into the white male establishment, and its energies are misdirected into narrow scholastic battles.
2. It is seen as élitist because it is inaccessible to most women. It is in conflict with the popular and historical feminist stress on the personal, the experiential.

The first of these objections was discussed by Mary Evans in her 1982 essay 'In Praise of Theory'.[2] She argued that feminist theory has not been appropriated or co-opted because women's studies cannot merely be 'added on' to the existing academic agenda without challenging and changing everything else. She quoted Maurice Godelier's paraphrase of Marx:

> We might say that the dominant ideas in most societies are the ideas of the dominant sex, associated and mingled with those of the dominant class. In our own societies, a struggle is now under way to abolish relations of both class and sex domination, without waiting for one to disappear first. ('The Origins of Male Domination', *New Left Review* 127 [1981], 3–17)

Feminist theory challenges patriarchal ideology and questions how 'ideas' themselves are produced, assessed and distributed in our society. Given the overwhelming dominance of the male sex in the editing of Shakespeare, Evans's argument implies a prima facie case for feminist intervention.

The second of the objections was the focus of Sarah Fildes's 1983 essay 'The Inevitability of Theory'.[3] She traced the emphasis on the personal element in popular feminism to the absence of other discussions of women's lives: feminists have been obliged to make use of sources such as diaries, autobiographies, even novels, as the only available forms of data on the experiences of women, which were otherwise ignored by the traditional academic disciplines. (One might also mention the importance of the personal in the influential consciousness-raising movement.) But the personal can be claustrophobic, a dead end in which feeling is privileged over analysis or action. Theory opens onto a larger, more objective picture. Moreover, it is not optional but inevitable: there is no escape from theory, as there is no escape from ideology. While you accept the status quo, theory can remain unconscious, implicit, but, once you begin to resist or challenge, theory has to become conscious and explicit. In the present context it is clear that a major aspect of women's responses to Shakespeare over time has been the personal one, in particular the desire to identify with female characters and to praise or blame the author accordingly.[4] Without detracting from the validity of such responses, feminist theory can facilitate an analysis of how Shakespeare has been mediated and reproduced for women readers (and audiences) through the male editorial tradition.

For, as Gary Taylor says, 'Women may read Shakespeare, but men edit him.'[5] Apparently, no edition of the complete works has ever been prepared entirely by a woman. Mary Cowden Clarke wrote in the preface to her 1860 edition of Shakespeare's works, 'I may be allowed to take pride in the thought that I am the first of his female subjects who has been selected to edit his works', but she did most of the work in collaboration with Charles Cowden Clarke (who was incidentally her husband, not her brother, as Taylor calls him both here [p. 196] and in *Reinventing Shakespeare*).[6] In fact, the first edition published in New York by Appleton was ascribed simply to 'M.C.C.', but the 1864 London edition published by Bickers was ascribed to 'Charles and Mary Cowden Clarke', as were subsequent reprints. In any case the claim was a mistaken one: the distinction of first female editor must unfortunately go to Henrietta Bowdler, whose edition of the works (far from complete, by definition) was first published anonymously in 1807 and then under the name of her brother, Thomas Bowdler, in 1818. The most important female editor in the twentieth century was undoubtedly Alice Walker, who succeeded R.B. McKerrow on the old-spelling edition sponsored by Oxford University Press in the 1930s 'under the condition that her work be vetted by a board of male scholars headed by W. W. Greg';[7] she never finished it.

The situation is not much different today. A survey of current editions of single plays reveals the following statistics: in the New Arden series (henceforth to be known as Arden 2), which has published all the plays except *The Two Noble Kinsmen*, only one play has been edited by a woman: Agnes Latham's *As You Like It* (1975). In the Penguin series, which has published all the plays except *Cymbeline* and *Titus Andronicus*, only three plays have been edited by women: Anne Righter (Barton)'s *The Tempest* (1968), M. M. Mahood's *Twelfth Night* (1968), and Barbara Everett's *All's Well That Ends Well* (1970). In the Oxford series only one of the nineteen plays published so far has been edited by a woman: Susan Snyder's *All's Well That Ends Well* (1993). In the New Cambridge series only three of the twenty-five plays published so far have been edited by women: my own *Taming of the Shrew* (1984), Elizabeth Story Donno's *Twelfth Night* (1985), and M. M. Mahood's *Merchant of Venice* (1987). It is still the case, as Taylor says, that, 'when they do edit, token women are almost always confined to the comedies, usually to plays which present few textual problems'.[8] In addition, it is notable that none of these female editors, from Henrietta Bowdler in 1807 to M. M. Mahood one hundred and eighty years later, would have been publicly recognized as a feminist. (I include myself here, since I had not published anything relevant at the time my edition was commissioned.) Would it have made any difference? Would more female editors have produced editions significantly different from those produced by male editors? On the existing evidence one would probably have to answer this question in the negative, but I would want to draw a distinction between female editors and feminist editors – between what has happened in the past and what might happen in the future. Presumably no one today would dispute that more female editors are desirable (like more female judges or more female members of Parliament or Congress), but what specific contribution might feminist editors make? ...

[A brief survey of recent developments in the theory and practice of textual criticism has been cut   Ed.]

I shall now attempt a brief survey of how a feminist approach to editing might make specific differences in the three main areas of an editor's responsibility: the text, the introduction and the commentary.

THE TEXT

Editors of Shakespearean texts have always had to choose between possible readings, and it is arguable that a feminist editors might make a different set of choices. In the case of plays that survive in two or more early printed versions, editors have to choose which version they see as more 'authoritative'. This choice will depend on a number of factors including, of course, an argument about the provenance of each text, but an awareness of gender issues can contribute to such a choice in the present and help to explain the reasons behind editorial decisions made in the past. At the most obvious level editorial choices can strengthen or weaken the roles of female characters. As long ago as 1965, Nevill Coghill argued in 'Revision after Performance'[9] that, if the folio text of *Othello* is an authorial revision, one of the author's aims was to make the role of Emilia more important, particularly towards the end of the play. This did not have much impact at the time, but it was taken up again in 1982 by E. A. J. Honigmann, who added the observation that several of the folio-only passages are more 'sexually specific' than the equivalent passages in the quarto, 'that is, they add images or turns of thought that throw new light on sexual behaviour or fantasy, notably reinforcing the play's central concern with normal and abnormal sexuality'.[10] D. C. Greetham would say that the intellectual climate in 1982 was more receptive to revisionism than that in 1964 partly because of the work of the literary theorists. I would add that the higher level of gender awareness was partly due to the work of feminists.

Another example of discussion of the potential for editorial choice in this area is Steven Urkowitz's essay 'Five Women Eleven Ways: Changing Images of Shakespearean Characters in the Earliest Texts',[11] in which he demonstrates that the parts of Queen Margaret in *2* and *3 Henry VI*, Anne Page in *The Merry Wives of Windsor*, Juliet and Lady Capulet in *Romeo and Juliet*, and Gertrude in *Hamlet* differ significantly between the early quartos and the folio. Also relevant is Beth Goldring's essay 'Cor.'s Rescue of Kent',[12] in which she argues that *Cor.* as a speech prefix at a crucial point in the opening scene of *King Lear* could stand for Cordelia and not, as editors have assumed, for Cornwall.

Othello, King Lear and the *Henry VI* plays are all textually complex, but editors of apparently straightforward, folio-only plays also have to make choices. They are sometimes confronted with passages of speech that seem at first sight meaningless and need to be reassigned, relineated, repunctuated, or more substantially emended before they can be made to yield any sense. In addition to their reliance on relatively objective criteria (such as theories about the provenance of the folio copy and the degree of likely scribal and compositorial error), editors must of course attempt to understand the context of each letter, word, sentence or speech and to relate what is happening at the microlevel of the language to larger patterns of coherence at the macrolevels of plot, character, theme or message. We have all learned from the literary theorists that such an understanding is bound to be limited and subjective: we cannot stand outside the ideological baggage we carry, though we can at least attempt to be aware of the preconceptions and prejudices that may affect our interpretations.

In 'Textual and Sexual Criticism' Gary Taylor discusses a crux in *The Comedy of Errors* that he claims has defeated past editors, partly because they were men who accepted the double standard of sexual behaviour that the speaker (Adriana in II.i) is complaining about. Thus, a gender-conscious male editor, sympathetic to the aims of feminism, can expose the sexist assumptions of previous male editors. It seems to me highly likely that feminist editors will discover many more examples of this phenomenon, and I am personally indebted to Taylor's work, but I am less happy about the last section of his essay in which he represents the process of editing itself through sexual metaphors, claiming that male editors favor 'lightning strikes of ingenuity' rather than slow, painstaking efforts. He concludes:

> Editors always engage in a particular kind of intercourse with an author's discourse: they engorge the text, and simultaneously intrude themselves into it. The male editorial tradition has preferred cruxes which offer opportunities for a quick, explosive release; if an emendation does not provide such a quick fix, it leaves editors feeling dissatisfied. But a crux like this one presents us with 'falshood and corruption' which can only be overcome by 'often touching':

prolonged exploratory attentiveness. Neither of these methods should have a monopoly on the text. A good editor, like a good lover, should be capable of both.[13]

While this is clever in its use of phrases quoted from the passage under discussion ('falshood and corruption', 'often touching') and, I believe, the author is at heart well-intentioned toward feminist scholarship, it leaves us, like Taylor's more famous metaphor of editors as 'the pimps of discourse', with the impression that texts are female and editors (still) male.[14]

THE INTRODUCTION

Male editors who have misunderstood the nature of the problem in the passage from *The Comedy of Errors* discussed by Taylor have also of course failed to pay any attention in their introductions to the larger issue of the double standard of sexual behaviour in the play, which is endorsed most strongly by the female characters (Luciana in III.ii, the Abbess in V.i) and which has been highlighted by feminist critics. Male editors have solemnly assured their readers that Prince Hal in the *Henry IV* plays undergoes a 'comprehensive' education through his visits to the Boar's Head tavern, which enable him to achieve a 'universal' or 'representative' knowledge of his subjects, not noticing that this has involved an extremely limited experience of women. (Hal himself remarks on this deficit when he is required to become a wooer at the end of *Henry V* – one instance among many of Shakespeare being less blind to women's issues than his editors.) Male editors assume that sex is Ophelia's only problem: one remarked in 1982 that 'her tragedy of course is that Hamlet has left her treasure with her' and that she has nothing left to do but 'bewail her virginity'.[15] A successor quoted these remarks approvingly in 1987, adding complacently that as a virgin Ophelia dies 'unfulfilled'.[16]

A feminist editor of Shakespeare will, in fact, usually find that in their introductions her male predecessors have neglected, distorted and trivialised topics that are of interest to women. She must interrogate the assumptions made about gender in the text itself and in the previous transmission and elucidation of the text, drawing on feminist studies of the ways in which Shakespeare has been reproduced and appropriated by patriarchal cultures. An interesting example of this is Elaine Showalter's essay 'Representing Ophelia:

Women, Madness and the Responsibilities of Feminist Criticism'.[17]
She sets out to 'tell Ophelia's story' not so much from the text of
Hamlet but from the 'afterlife' of the character as represented in
painting, literature and psychiatry as well as in the stage history.
Ophelia has become the type, or icon, of female insanity, and her
story changes independently of theories about the play in so far as it
is determined by attitudes toward women and madness more generally. Hence, Showalter's focus is on 'the Ophelia myth' that has
accrued around the play and that affects our interpretation of it.

One could adopt a similar strategy in an edition of *Cymbeline* by
investigating 'the Imogen myth', whereby the play's heroine
became, during the Victorian period, 'the most lovely and perfectly
delineated of all Shakespeare's characters' and 'the immortal
godhead of womanhood'.[19] What precisely was it about Imogen
that brought forth these superlatives at a time when the play as a
whole was not held in very high esteem? It turns out, briefly, that
she is specifically praised for her total femininity (which cannot be
concealed under male disguise), for the domesticity of her figurative
language (she refers twice to her needle) and her actions such as
cooking for her brothers and Belarius: as the actress Helen Faucit
put it, 'For the first time, the cave is felt to be a home'.[20] She is also
commended for her purity (unlike the problematic Isabella in
Measure for Measure, she calls out for help as soon as she recognises the language of seduction), her complete obedience to her
husband even when he orders her death, and for the magnanimity
with which she gives up her right of succession to the kingdom once
her long-lost brothers are found. 'Conjugal tenderness' is said to be
her dominant quality, and she is often described as 'matronly':
perhaps it is not surprising that three of the most celebrated performers of the role – Helen Faucit, Ellen Terry and Peggy Ashcroft
– all played Imogen when they themselves were fifty or more.

This approach could also inform and enliven a stage history,
often a rather dull section of an introduction consisting of a dutiful
list of names, dates and places with little to interest non-antiquarian
readers. With *Cymbeline*, for example, one can trace how the idealisation of the heroine could only have been achieved by radical
cutting and expurgation of the text, beginning with David Garrick's
version in 1761. Explicit sexual references and references to all but
the most 'innocent' parts of the human body were routinely
omitted. In the wager scene (I.iv), for example, it became standard
for Iachimo to assert that he would 'win the love' of Imogen rather

than that he would enjoy her 'dearest bodily part', and in the scene in which he returns to Rome (II.iv) it became standard to omit Posthumus's blunt challenge to him to prove 'that you have tasted her in bed'. Posthumus's misogynistic soliloquy at the end of this scene was often cut, as were Iachimo's references to prostitutes in his scene with Imogen (I.vi). The purpose of Cloten's pursuit of the heroine was altered in so far as references to his intent to rape her were omitted. After his fight with Cloten (IV.ii), Guiderius usually entered carrying Cloten's sword, not his head, and Imogen's speech on awakening from her drugged sleep later in this scene was shorn of its references to the body's leg, foot, thigh, and so on. She certainly did not daub her cheeks with the dead man's blood. Despite all this, Imogen's part remained central to the play, though the dynamics of it shifted according to whether the actor-manager of the time was playing Posthumus (like Garrick and John Philip Kemble) or Iachimo (like Macready and Irving). In thus attempting a gender-conscious approach to the study of stage history, a feminist editor can also build on the work of Irene Dash, whose book *Wooing, Wedding, and Power: Women in Shakespeare's Plays*[21] considered the ways in which female roles in a number of texts have been altered and abridged in a male-dominated theatrical tradition.

THE COMMENTARY

Mary Cowden Clarke took a swipe at the male editorial tradition when she dismissed most footnotes as 'mere vehicles for abuse, spite and arrogance'. Any editor who has plowed through the eighteenth-century commentaries will have some sympathy with the charge. As in the introduction, so in the commentary, a modern feminist editor can generate a refreshing amount of interesting new material simply by performing a critique of her male predecessors' work. The typical rhetorical stance of the male editor is aloof, patronising and overtly or covertly misogynistic. The feminist editor will again find that the editors are frequently more sexist than the text, both in what they discuss and in what they fail to discuss. I shall limit myself to two examples of each category.

To begin with sins of commission, towards the end of *The Comedy of Errors* the Abbess questions Adriana about the possible cause of her husband's apparent madness and establishes that it is due to 'the venom clamors of a jealous woman' (V.i.69),[22] Adriana having dared to complain to her husband about his relationship with a prostitute. This conclusion is reached after some very leading questioning, in which Adriana is made to convict herself of excessive and violent scolding. Her sister Luciana objects to the Abbess's verdict and defends Adriana, asserting, 'She never reprehended him but mildly' (87), and she asks her, 'Why bear you these reproofs and answer not?' (89), to which Adriana replies, 'She did betray me to my own reproof' (90). This last line is paraphrased by a 1972 editor[23] as meaning 'She tricked me into recognising my own faults' – a paraphrase that is quoted without comment (and presumably approvingly) by a 1987 editor.[24] Surely this is simply incorrect? The line means, 'She tricked me into criticising myself', and the context (not to mention the rest of the play) establishes that the criticism is not justified. Adriana is not 'recognising her own faults' but accusing herself of faults she does not possess. This misreading can, like Taylor's textual example, be attributed to the unthinking sexist assumption on the part of male editors that Adriana is indeed the one who is at fault in this context. The way they present their reading as an apparently straightforward paraphrase means it will all too easily be accepted by readers who are themselves conditioned by patriarchal attitudes and who assume the editor speaks with authority in such a matter.

My other example is from *Othello*. (Can one imagine anyone advising *him* not to criticize his wife for her infidelity but, rather, to put up with it quietly and even accept that it is all his own fault? Can one imagine male editors finding it natural to endorse such a position?) The problem here is with Desdemona's sensuality, and it was, sadly, a female editor in 1957 who, as Gary Taylor demonstrates,[25] rejected the quarto reading of I.iii.251, in which Desdemona says her heart is subdued to the 'utmost pleasure' of Othello, preferring the less physical folio reading 'very quality'. The same editor argued in her commentary that, when Desdemona complains that if Othello goes to Cyprus without her, 'The rites for why I love him are bereft me' (I.iii.257), *rites* has nothing to do with conjugal rites. A male editor in the following year, whose textual theory committed him to following the quarto, printed 'utmost plesure' in I.iii but explicitly expressed his approval of a later quarto reading at II.i.80, in which Cassio prays that Othello's 'tall ship' may soon arrive in Cyprus so that he can 'swiftly come to Desdemona's arms'.[26] This editor commented unfavourably on the more physical folio reading that Othello may 'Make love's quick

pants in Desdemona's arms' on the grounds that it is 'out of character for Cassio and his usual attitude to Othello and Desdemona'.
Both these editors seem to use their authority in their commentaries
to take as much sex out of the play as they can.

As for sins of omission, I'll begin with *As You Like It*, in which it
has always struck me that the famous 'seven ages of man' speech
(II.vii.137–66) conspicuously excludes women. After the Duke's in-
troductory reference to 'this wide and universal theatre' and
Jacques's opening 'All the world's a stage, / And all the men and
women merely players', the speaker limits his focus to just one half
of mankind – 'each man in his time plays many parts' – and proceeds to delineate the schoolboy, the specifically male lover, the
soldier, the justice, and so on. No editor remarks on this. Indeed, all
eight pages of commentary on the speech in the recent New
Variorum edition[27] celebrate Shakespeare's ability to portray 'representatives of the entire human race'. A feminist editor might note
the invisibility of women here and perhaps relate it to the absence
of actual women on the English Renaissance stage, a convention
about which this play is notably selfconscious, especially in its
epilogue.

My other example is from *King Lear*. At the beginning of IV.iii in
editions that conflate the quarto and folio texts, a Gentleman explains that the army that has arrived from France to support Lear is
being led by Cordelia, not by the king of France, whose absence is
rather vaguely explained by 'something he left imperfect in the
state' (3), which needs his attention. Editors do have something to
say about this passage (which is in the quarto text but not in the
folio), the standard explanation for the king's absence being that
Shakespeare is cautious about making what is after all French military intervention look too much like a foreign invasion. This issue
has been debated by recent textual critics who have disputed
Shakespeare's need to 'censor' his work in this way: see, for
example, Gary Taylor's essay 'Monopolies, Show Trials, Disaster
and Invasion: *King Lear* and Censorship'.[28] But a feminist editor
might add that it is also crucial for the emotional effect of Lear's
reunion with Cordelia in IV.viii and V.iii that her husband not be
present. One might even express concern at the way in which the
play's ending encourages us to endorse Lear's appropriation of
Cordelia regardless of her wishes or her other ties, ignoring our
sense that she was right to refuse just such an appropriation in the
opening scene.

Finally, it is hard to know whether to laugh or cry when one comes to examine the traditional editorial procedures for dealing with obscenity in Shakespearean texts, an area that gives rise to sins of both kinds. Some editors simply try to evade the issue altogether, from Pope, who cut many of the lines Shakespeare gave to the sexually outspoken Princess in *Love's Labour's Lost*,[29] to modern editors of *As You Like It*, who fail to comment on the sexual innuendo in Rosalind's speeches.[30] In both cases the fact that a woman is speaking is significant: Shakespeare's heroines (including Desdemona in my earlier examples) are more frank and enthusiastic about sex than his male editors think 'ladies' should be.

Frequently, editors use coy phrases such as 'bawdy quibble', 'double entendre', or the even more quaint 'sexual equivoque' without spelling out what precisely is going on. They go to extraordinary lengths to avoid using 'rude' words themselves, as can be illustrated from the English lesson scene in *Henry V* (III.iv). One 1965 editor informed his readers that *le foot* and *le count* are 'similar in sound to the French equivalent of English "four-letter" words'.[31] A 1968 editor volunteered the information that *foutre* means 'coition' and that *con* means 'female organ'.[32] The year 1976 saw a regression from this brave outspokenness with an editor who remarked that the scene in general exhibits 'some gentle humour in a number of mispronunciations' and that *foot* and *count* are 'close approximations to obscene words'.[33] A modern feminist editor would surely make less of a fuss about printing *fuck* and *cunt* and commenting on the kind of humor that is being generated in this scene between two women.

The sexual politics of *The Taming of the Shrew* have always been controversial. It is the only one of Shakespeare's plays to have provoked a theatrical reply or sequel in his lifetime in the form of John Fletcher's *The Woman's Prize, or The Tamer Tamed* (c. 1611), in which Petruchio, now a widower, marries again and has the tables turned on him by his second wife. (The implicit homage of such a sequel may have been one of the factors in Shakespeare's decision to collaborate with Fletcher in his last three plays from around 1612–14: *Cardenio*, *Henry VIII* and *The Two Noble Kinsmen*.) While *The Shrew* has been a popular play in the theatre for four hundred years, its stage history offers numerous examples of ambivalence on the part of adaptors and producers toward its subject matter. As early as *The Taming of a Shrew*, the problematic quarto

text published in 1594 and generally known as *A Shrew*, Katherina
is given an aside in the wooing scene (the equivalent to II.i in the
traditional treatment of the folio version):

> *She turnes aside and speakes*
> But yet I will consent and marrie him,
> For I methinkes have lived too long a maid,
> And match him too, or else his manhood's good.
> (sc.V, 40–2)[34]

Thus, it is made explicit, as it never is in *The Shrew*, that Katherina
can see some positive advantage in marrying and that she is going
to enjoy competing with her partner. But later the brutality of the
taming is played up when, in the equivalent of IV.iii, we get the
stage direction '*Enter Ferando* [Petruchio] *with a peece of meate
uppon his daggers point.*'

Similarly, Catherine has an aside in the midst of the exchange of
insults in this scene in Garrick's version (which held the stage from
1754 to 1844 in England and to 1887 in the United States):

> A Plague upon his Impudence! I'm vexed –
> I'll marry my Revenge, but I will tame him.
> (14)[35]

And at the end of the scene she confirms this hint of a reversal of
roles and adds further motivation in a closing soliloquy:

> Sister Bianca now shall see
> The poor abandon'd Cath'rine, as she calls me,
> Can hold her Head as high, and be as proud,
> And make her Husband stoop unto her Lure
> As she, or e'er a Wife in Padua.
> As double as my Portion be my Scorn;
> Look to your Seat, Petruchio, or I throw you.
> Cath'rine shall tame this Haggard; – or if she fails,
> Shall tye her Tongue up, and pare down her Nails.
> (16–17)

Garrick has here transferred some of Petruchio's taming
metaphors to Catherine in an attempt to redress the balance
between hero and heroine, but it also seems that it was he who
first made a whip an obligatory stage property for Petruchio. Thus,
from the beginning the theatrical tradition has simultaneously
apologised for and exaggerated the play's misogyny.[36]

Male editors have also felt uneasy about *The Shrew*. In 1904 one found Petruchio's order to Katherina in the last scene to take off her cap and tread on it particularly offensive: 'Though not intended to humiliate her, but rather to convince his sceptical friends, it always strikes me as a needless affront to her feelings . . . offered at the very moment when she is exhibiting a voluntary obedience'.[37] Another in 1928 wrote, 'There have been shrews since Xantippe's time . . . and it is not discreet for an editor to discuss, save historically, the effective ways of dealing with them . . . but . . . one cannot help thinking a little wistfully that the Petruchian discipline had something to say for itself'. He immediately withdrew this by remarking that Petruchio's method 'was undoubtedly drastic and has gone out of fashion . . . Let it suffice to say that *The Taming of the Shrew* belongs to a period, and it is not ungallant, even so'.[26] A more recent editor writing in 1981 revealed his embarrassment about the play by having a great deal to say in his introduction about shrews as little furry animals and almost nothing to say about sexual politics. Both this editor and another one in 1982 contrived to take no notice whatever of feminist critics, who had by then already produced some stimulating new readings of the play.[39]

It is not an exaggeration to say that being commissioned to edit *The Taming of the Shrew* around 1979 and the experience of working on the play over the subsequent three or four years contributed to my becoming a feminist in a public, professional sense as well as in a private capacity. (I was simultaneously beginning to develop the first courses on women writers and feminist criticism at the University of Liverpool.) I don't want to dwell on the final product, which was published in 1984, but I did try, especially in my introduction and commentary, to consider issues neglected by other editors and in particular to treat *The Shrew* as a 'problem play' whose darker side has been acknowledged, consciously or unconsciously, throughout its stage and critical history. Perhaps I did not, by today's standards, go far enough. I was present at a paper given by Annabel Patterson at the World Shakespeare Congress in Tokyo in August 1991 during which, after some positive remarks about my edition, she said as much. I reflected then that some of the defects could be attributed to my lack of self-assurance, both as an editor and as a feminist, while others were due to the need to compromise with the wishes of the general editors of the series and behind them the publishers. Rather than conduct a backward-looking autocritique, what I shall do in the final section of this essay is consider briefly what I would do differently if I were editing *The Shrew* today, ten years after it was published.

I doubt if I would want to make any changes in the text itself, though I would of course need to engage with the choices and arguments of subsequent editors, notably those of Stanley Wells and Gary Taylor in the Oxford *Complete Works* and *Textual Companion*.[40] The 1594 quarto text of *A Shrew* is so different at the level of linguistic detail from *The Shrew* that no editor of the latter play would be likely to emend the text with readings taken from the former, but I would want to re-examine my position on *A Shrew* itself and on the relationship between the two versions in the light of work published recently by Graham Holderness and Bryan Loughrey in the introduction to their reprint of *A Shrew*[41] and by Leah Marcus in her essay 'The Shakespearean Editor as Shrew-Tamer'.[42] These discussions challenge the orthodox position, established by all three of the 1980s editions, that *A Shrew* is a later text than *The Shrew* and is to some extent derived from it. They also argue that *A Shrew* is a more 'progressive' text than *The Shrew* in its sexual politics. Marcus contrasts the continuing use of the additional Christopher Sly episodes in the stage history of *The Shrew* with their suppression by editors and traces a depressing history of a virtual conspiracy to associate the greater realism and the greater commitment to patriarchy of *The Shrew* with the 'authentic Shakespeare', while *A Shrew* with its 'significant ideological differences' is banished from the canon.

I think the ideological differences are less clear-cut than these authors claim, and their textual arguments for the chronological precedence of *A Shrew* are not immediately convincing. A substantial counter argument is advanced in Stephen Roy Miller's *A Critical, Old-Spelling Edition of 'The Taming of A Shrew, 1594'*,[43] which seems to me, after a very thorough analysis of the evidence, forcefully to re-establish the view that *A Shrew* is a deliberate (though not always totally competent) adaptation of *The Shrew*. Marcus misrepresents the editorial tradition when she says that editors have suppressed the additional Sly episodes when all recent editions print them, albeit in appendices. Nevertheless, her work and that of Holderness and Loughrey is interesting, perhaps especially to literary theorists, in representing a poststructuralist and postrevisionist attitude to the fundamental indeterminacy of all texts. The solution proposed by Marcus for editors – that they should print complete versions of both texts – is not likely to appeal to publishers of regular Shakespeare series, but Miller's edition and the text provided by Holderness and Loughrey will allow those interested to read the plays intertextually.

In line with what I have said here, I might wish to be even more explicit in my commentary about obscenity in the play, especially in the wooing scene (II.i) and in the final scene (V.ii), though I was gratified to read in a recent essay by Thomas L. Berger that my commentary was the most explicit on these matters of the six editions of *The Shrew* he examined.[44]

But the major changes would come in the introduction. Many things would need updating, but I would want to do that along specifically feminist lines. In discussing more recent stagings, for example, I'd pay particular attention to those that have made some distinct point about the play's sexual politics. Two such productions were those at the Everyman Theatre in Liverpool in 1987 and at the Royal Shakespeare Theatre in Stratford-upon-Avon in 1992. (The latter production transferred to the Barbican Theatre in London in 1993.) The Liverpool production, directed by a woman, Glen Walford (who incidentally used my text), gave the play a North African setting, which was apparently intended to emphasise the restrictions on the women who appeared partially veiled. While this was effective to some extent, it also allowed the overwhelmingly white British audience to feel a sense of racial and religious superiority, complacent in their assurance that the Western Christian tradition is more progressive in these matters than the Eastern Islamic tradition. The Stratford production, directed by Bill Alexander, was (I would say significantly) more interesting for its treatment of the Induction and the subplot than for its treatment of the main plot. (Leah Marcus should have seen it.) It used an extended and thoroughly modernised version of the Christopher Sly episodes featuring a group of thoughtless yuppies who remained onstage right through the play and participated by being required to play minor roles from time to time, usually as servants. In the subplot Tranio became a potentially serious rival to Lucentio in the wooing of Bianca. The main plot was disappointingly conventional (apart from the casting of a blonde Katherina and a small Petruchio), with hero and heroine falling in love fairly obviously at first sight, though the playing of the scene on the road back to Padua (IV.v) as a straight love scene was novel. In general, however, this production seemed more interested in class issues than in gender issues – the first postfeminist *Shrew*?

Turning to the critical tradition, I would be delighted to find much more material now than ten years ago. In the early 1980s I was able to treat feminist criticism as relatively univocal, partly because the field was then dominated by the North American approach, which had developed out of psychoanalytic criticism and which was exemplified by Coppélia Kahn's essay 'The Taming of the Shrew: Shakespeare's Mirror of Marriage'[45] and Marianne Novy's essay 'Patriarchy and Play in The Taming of the Shrew'.[46] Now I would want to explore the pluralism of feminist approaches and, in particular, the extent to which they have been influenced by American New Historicism and British cultural materialism. This would involve a more historical treatment of the play itself: I'd put it in the context of actual sexual politics in the 1580s and 1590s, drawing on recent work by critics such as Karen Newman in her chapter 'Renaissance Family Politics and Shakespeare's Taming of the Shrew' in Fashioning Feminity and English Renaissance Drama,[47] and Lynda E. Boose in her essays 'Scolding Brides and Bridling Scolds: Taming the Woman's Unruly Member[48] and 'The Taming of the Shrew: Good Husbandry and Enclosure'.[49] At the same time I'd want to pay more attention to the history of women's responses to the play over the last four hundred years, drawing on my own recent work in this field and on books such as Women's Re-Visions of Shakespeare, edited by Marianne Novy.[50]

While feminist critics have been becoming more historical, they have accused New Historicist critics in particular of treating issues of sexuality almost entirely in terms of power to the exclusion of gender: see Lynda E. Boose, 'The Family in Shakespeare Studies; or – Studies in the Family of Shakespeareans; or – The Politics of Politics';[51] Carol Thomas Neely, 'Constructing the Subject: Feminist Practice and the New Renaissance Discourses'[52] and my own essay 'Are There Any Women in King Lear?'[53] A contemporary edition of The Shrew would need to take on these debates as they impinge upon critical discussions of the play. It would also need to engage with the ongoing debate within feminist criticism itself between what one might call 'apologist' criticis, who want to 'save' Shakespeare or even co-opt him as a protofeminist, and the more negative, or pessimistic, critics, who see him as quite irredeemably patriarchal. (In the former camp one might put Irene Dash[54] and Linda Bamber, author of Comic Women, Tragic Men;[55] in the latter camp one might put Peter Erickson, author of Patriarchal

Structures in Shakespeare's Drama[56] and Marilyn Williamson, author of *The Patriarchy of Shakespeare's Comedies.*)[57]

There are of course anxieties that focus around this latter position: if we conclude that Shakespeare's views on gender would class him with the reactionaries were he alive today, does that mean we shall stop reading or teaching him? This brings me back to 'Shakespeare and the Tyranny of Feminism': feminism as censorship. The very fact that criticism of *The Taming of the Shrew* has enjoyed a positive renaissance in recent years mainly because of the contributions of feminist critics, while other early comedies such as *The Two Gentlemen of Verona* and *The Comedy of Errors* remain relatively neglected, does not bear out the charge. (One might also cite the feminist-inspired debates that are revivifying study of more problematic misogynists such as John Milton and D. H. Lawrence.) Personally, however, I am prepared to admit I have no intention of re-editing *The Taming of the Shrew*: having toyed with *Cymbeline* for a while, I'm now working on the Arden 3 edition of *Hamlet*.

From *The Margins of the Text*, ed. D. C. Greetham (Ann Arbor: University of Michigan Press, 1997), pp. 83–103.

NOTES

[This essay explores the relation between feminist theory and the editing of Shakespeare, with reference to that institutional and cultural politics which see two 'W. S.'s – William Shakespeare and 'Women's Studies' – as the establishment and the opposition respectively. Against this pessimistic, exclusionary cultural politics, however, Ann Thompson offers an argument against separatism, and for engaging with Shakespeare and the institutional power he is set up to represent. She insists that feminism has had a revivifying effect on Shakespeare criticism, rather than censoring or impoverishing it, as some conservative commentators claim. The substance of the essay shows how a feminist approach to editing might make a difference to three key areas: text, introduction, commentary. Her stance is anti-essentialist: while female editors may preserve the status quo, it is feminist editing that will make a difference.

Omitted at the point indicated is a short section outlining recent developments in editing and theory; I am grateful to Professor Thompson for allowing me to make this cut.   Ed.]

1. The survey was carried out by Tim Cook of Kingston University for *PACE*, the newsletter of SCEPCHE, the Standing Conference on English in Polytechnics and Colleges of Higher Education. SCEPCHE

subsequently merged with CUE, the Council for University English, to become CCUE, the Council for College and University English, and the publication is now known as the CCUE newsletter.

2. *Feminist Review*, 10 (1982), 61–74.

3. *Feminist Review*, 14 (1983), 62–70.

4. See my essay 'Pre-Feminism or Proto-Feminism? Early Women Readers of Shakespeare', *The Elizabethan Theatre*, 14 (1996), 195–211.

5. Gary Taylor, 'Textual and Sexual Criticism: a Crux in the Comedy of Error', *Renaissance Drama*, 19 (1988), 195.

6. *Reinventing Shakespeare* (New York: Weidenfield and Nicolson, 1989), p. 206.

7. Taylor, 'Textual and Sexual Criticism', 197.

8. Ibid.

9. In his book *Shakespeare's Professional Skills* (Cambridge: Cambridge University Press, 1965).

10. E. A. J. Honigmann, 'Shakespeare's Revised Plays: *King Lear* and *Othello*', *Library*, 4 (1982), 162.

11. In *Images of Shakespeare*, ed. Werner Habicht, D. J. Palmer and Roger Pringle (London: Associated University Press, 1988), pp. 292–304.

12. In *The Division of the Kingdom*, ed. Gary Taylor and Michael Warren (Oxford: Clarendon Press, 1983), pp. 143–51.

13. Taylor, 'Textual and Sexual Criticism', 221.

14. Taylor uses the phrase 'pimps of discourse' in the general introducion to the Oxford *Textual Companion* (Clarendon press, 1987), p. 7. It becomes more explicitly gendered on p. 60, where he gives an analogy from Harold Pinter's *The Homecoming* in which Lenny the pimp talks of a woman 'falling apart with the pox': when a listener asks 'How did you know she was?' Lenny replies, 'I decided she was.' Taylor continues, 'An editor, in emending, decides a text is diseased.'

15. The Arden *Hamlet*, ed. Harold Jenkins (London: Methuen, 1982), pp. 152, 151.

16. The Oxford *Hamlet*, ed. G. R. Hibbard (Oxford: Oxford University Press, 1987), p. 51.

17. In *Shakespeare and the Question of Theory*, ed. Patricia Parker and Geoffrey Hartman (London: Methuen, 1985), pp. 77–94.

18. Louis Lewes, *The Women of Shakespeare*, trans. Helen Zimmem (London: Hodder Brothers, 1895), p. 340.

19. A. C. Swinburne, *A Study of Shakespeare* (London: Chatto and Windus, 1880), p. 227.

20. Helen Faucit, *On Some of Shakespeare's Women, by One who has Impersonated Them* (London: Blackwood, 1885), p. 251.

21. Irene Dash, *Wooing, Wedding, and Power: Women in Shakespeare's Play* (New York: Columbia University Press, 1981).

22. Quotations and references are from *The Riverside Shakespeare*, ed. G. Blakemore Evans (Boston, MA: Houghton Mifflin, 1974).

23. The New Penguin *Comedy of Errors*, ed. Stanley Wells (Harmondsworth: Penguin, 1972), p. 176.

24. The New Cambridge *Comedy of Errors*, ed. T. S. Dorsch (Cambridge: Cambridge University Press, 1987), p. 99.

25. Taylor, 'Textual and Sexual Criticism', 199. The edition in question is the New Shakespeare *Othello*, ed. Alice Walker (Cambridge: Cambridge University Press, 1957).

26. The Arden *Othello*, ed. M. R. Ridley (London: Methuen, 1958).

27. The New Variorum *As You Like It*, ed. Richard Knowles (New York: Modern Language Association, 1977).

28. In *Division of the Kingdoms*, pp. 75–119.

29. See Dash, *Wooing, Wedding, and Power*, pp. 14–20.

30. See Juliet Dusinberre, 'As *Who* Liked It?' *Shakespeare Survey*, 46 (1993), pp. 9–21.

31. The Signet *Henry V*, ed. John Russell Brown (New York: New American Library, 1965).

32. The New Penguin *Henry V*, ed. A. R. Humphreys (Harmondsworth: Penguin, 1968).

33. The Macmillan *Henry V*, ed. Brian Phythian (London: Macmillan, 1976).

34. Quotation and reference from the text given in Geoffrey Bullough (ed.), *Narrative and Dramatic Sources of Shakespeare* (London: Routledge and Kegan Paul, 1964), I:77.

35. *Catherine and Petruchio* (London: Cornmarket Press Facsimile, 1969), p. 14.

36. For further discussion of these and other examples, see '*The Taming of the Shrew* on Stage', in the introduction to my edition (Cambridge: Cambridge University Press, 1984), pp. 17–24.

37. The Arden *Taming of the Shrew*, ed. R. Warwick Bond (London: Routledge, 1904), p. lviii.

38. The New Shakespeare *Taming of the Shrew*, ed. Sir Arthur Quiller-Couch (Cambridge: Cambridge University press, 1928), pp. xxxvi–xxxvii.

39. The 1981 editor was Brian Morris, the Arden *Taming of the Shrew* (London: Routledge); the 1982 editor was H. J. Oliver, the Oxford *Taming of the Shrew* (Oxford: Oxford University Press).

40. *Complete Works* (Oxford: Clarendon Press, 1986) and *Textual Companion* (Oxford: Clarendon Press, 1987).

41. *A Shrew* (Hemel Hempstead: Harvester-Wheatsheaf, 1992).

42. *English Literary Renaissance*, 22 (1992), pp. 177–200.

43. Published by Oxford University Press/The Malone Society in 1998.

44. Berger's essay 'Looking for Sex in All the Wrong Places', a contribution to the seminar on editing at the International Shakespeare Conference at Stratford-upon-Avon in August 1992, is as yet unpublished.

45. *Modern Language Studies*, 5 (1975), pp. 88–102.

46. *English Literary Renaissance*, 9 (1979), pp. 264–80.

47. *Fashioning Femininity and English Renaissance Drama* (Chicago: Chicago University Press, 1991), pp. 33–50.

48. *Shakespeare Quarterly*, 42 (1991), pp. 179–213.

49. In *Shakespeare Reread*, ed. Russ McDonald (Ithaca, NY: Cornell University Press, 1994), pp. 193–225.

50. For my own work, see note 4. See also *Women Reading Shakespeare, 1660–1900*, edited by Ann Thompson and Sasha Roberts (Manchester University Press, 1997). Novy's book was published by the University of Illinois Press (1990).

51. *Renaissance Quarterly*, 40 (1987), pp. 707–42.

52. *English Literary Renaissance*, 18 (1988), pp. 5–10.

53. In *The Matter of Difference*, ed. Valerie Wayne (Hemel Hempstead: Harvester–Wheatsheaf, 1991), pp. 117–28.

54. Dash, *Wooing, Wedding, and Power.*

55. *Comic Women, Tragic Men* (Stanford, CA: Stanford University Press, 1982).

56. *Patriarchal Structures in Shakespeare's Drama* (Berkeley: University of California Press, 1985).

57. *The Patriarchy of Shakespeare's Comedies* (Detroit, IL: Wayne State University Press, 1986).

3

Women's Alternative Shakespeares and Women's Alternatives to Shakespeare in Contemporary British Theatre

LIZBETH GOODMAN

This is an essay about some of the women who play, or choose not to play, Shakespeare's women in contemporary British theatre. In looking at a variety of different kinds of feminist reinterpretations of Shakespeare, not only in theory but also in practice, it becomes clear that such factors as the performer's relationship to Shakespeare's women and issues such as social and economic support for new work by women must inform discussion of women's roles in (and in creating alternatives to) the Shakespearean canon.

Feminist critics from varying cultures, critical schools and perspectives have begun re-viewing and partially dismantling the Shakespearean canon, in particular, deconstructing canonical images and structures. In this essay, only the most immediate element of deconstructing the canon is of concern: the practical effects of the construction of alternative Shakespeares and of women's alternatives to alternative Shakespeares.

British theatre has left a legacy of practical obstacles for the female performer today: employment opportunities are obviously limited by perpetuation of a canon built around Shakespeare, whose parts for women are comparatively few and composed largely of supporting rather than leading roles. The tendency to reproduce the Shakespearean canon at the expense of new writing has obvious negative effects, such as relatively low levels of funding for young writers and new plays, and limited availability of space for these plays in the seasonal programmes of the major subsidised national companies: the National Theatre and the Royal Shakespeare Company.

In regard to the limitations which perpetuation and re-production of the traditional canon has imposed upon women in the British theatre, feminist playwright and performer Bryony Lavery has observed, 'The theatre seems too much like a great museum run by male curators. The glass exhibition cases are opened up and historic exhibitions taken out and shown to us all, if we can afford the entrance fee. . . . There are far too many good women actors for the amount of space in those glass cases. There is too much to say today to listen to the voices of the museum ghosts. . . . I'm tired of my role as a cleaner in this museum. Most of the rubbish is dropped by men.'[1] Lavery's observation can be applied to the canonisation of Shakespeare. The question posed is not *how* to play Shakespeare but *whether* to play Shakespeare. The related and larger question is whether women writers may have something to say which is not contained in and cannot be extrapolated from a Shakespearean text: something which deserves funding, encouragement, performance and review; whether strong female performers have the potential to create, in the act of performing, characters that move beyond the status quo and add up to more than the sum of their parts.

Nowhere is the gender-based hierarchy of theatre studies brought out more strongly than in performance of Shakespeare. Most parts are played by men, except in the rare all-women's or mixed-cast experimental production, and most directors are men (with only a few notable exceptions such as Deborah Warner, Janet Suzman and Phyllida Lloyd). Shakespeare can still be played – very successfully – by all-male casts, as in the 1991–2 international touring production of *As You Like It* directed by Declan Donnellan for Cheek by Jowl.[2] They also enrich the study of gender roles in the theatre. All-female productions of Shakespeare might do the same but are not considered similarly 'authentic' to Shakespeare. The mainstage rehearsal space for any Shakespeare performance is still likely to allow only a subordinate place for women and will in this sense be similar in many respects to a men's club or – in Lavery's terms – to a museum, in which most powerful roles (in performance and in terms of direction and production) are held by men. In fact, the upper echelons of direction, production and administration of the national subsidised companies in Britain are, as they have always been, occupied almost exclusively by men.[3]

Sue Parrish and Sue Dunderdale found that out of the 620 plays produced in the major British repertoire companies and venues in 1982–3, only 42 (less than 6.8 per cent) were written by women. Of these, 22 were written by Agatha Christie. Of the 42, 14 were produced in studios, none by Agatha Christie.[4] Therefore, only 6 plays (less than 1 per cent of plays produced on main stages) were written by women other than Agatha Christie. A 1990 survey, conducted by researchers for a Channel Four television series on women as 'Ordinary People' shows that, of 435 plays produced by the National Theatre, only 10 were written by women.[5] Thus, for all the talk about revolutions in the British theatre, and for all the very real progress that has been made, it is evident that the area of Shakespearean performance remains one of the last bastions of patriarchal control over performance and over the perpetuation of the British acting tradition.

Since there is a limited and steadily decreasing amount of funding available to all British theatre, the more that is spent on Shakespeare, the less that remains to be spent on the alternatives. But then, what exactly are the alternatives? In Britain, 'alternative theatre' (which can be compared to the American off-off-Broadway circuit) is often confused and conflated with terms such as 'experimental theatre' and 'fringe theatre'. But the term 'alternative theatre' more accurately refers only to theatres (companies, productions, or venues) which fall outside the subsidised and commercial (West End) theatre sectors.

It is not a haggling over terminology which is of interest here, but rather a more generalised understanding of what it means to be considered alternative to the British theatre tradition. Such an understanding must be reached by consideration of women's perceived relationships to the concept of alternatives to Shakespeare, to the traditional canon, and to the term 'alternative' itself. It is thus necessary to turn to a contemporary resource: the performers who create and recreate Shakespeare's women in British theatre today. These performers inevitably hold widely differing views of their relationships to the Shakespearean canon, ranging from a sense of

complicity with it to a need for distance, or even denial, of its legitimacy as an inheritance.

INHERITING FALSE FATHERS? PERFORMERS' APPROACHES TO THE SHAKESPEAREAN PATRIMONY

Deborah Levy, in her play *Pax*, creates the character of the 'Hidden
Daughter' who rejects her inheritance from 'false fathers'. In some
sense, this notion of the false inheritance or inappropriate legacy of
words and images from a patriarchal tradition is also relevant to a
study of feminist performance of alternative Shakespeares, in that
many of the varied approaches thereto include, or react against, just
such an idea.

The perspectives of contemporary players of Shakespeare's
women on the British stage are anything but uniform. It becomes
clear in evaluating the views and statements of women in British
theatre – whether in personal conversation, public lectures, or any
of the available published interviews and reviews – that despite
diferences in age, class and political perspectives, many share a
recognition of the alternative status of their own views vis-à-vis
those of the so-called gatekeepers of the canon. The nature of this
perception of difference, however, varies greatly from individual to
individual.

The two performers chosen for this brief study are Fiona Shaw
and Tilda Swinton: women who can be compared in some ways
(for instance, both are known for important cross-dressing roles),
and yet who must be contrasted in most respects. These women
speak from very different perspectives, which is not surprising,
given that they come from quite different backgrounds (Shaw is
Irish and Swinton a descendant of the British upper middle class).
Both have worked on the most 'alternative' fringe stages as well as
on the main stages of the RSC and the Royal National Theatre.
Fiona Shaw is best known for her creative interpretations of women
in the classics; Tilda Swinton for her alternative roles. Both are
known for their film roles as well as theatre work (Shaw was fea-
tured in *My Left Foot*, *Mountains of the Moon* and *Three Men and
a Little Lady*; Swinton in several of the films of Derek Jarman, including *Caravaggio*, *The Last of England*, the recent *Edward II*,
Sally Potter's new film of Virginia Woolf's *Orlando* and in the

television work of John Byrne). While these tag descriptions of Shaw's and Swinton's work may facilitate discussion, what is most interesting about the comparison is the way in which the tags or labels will *not* fit.

Fiona Shaw purposefully sets out to confound simplistic descriptions and draws on her Irish heritage as an 'alternative' to the British tradition. In her own words, 'The history of the British theatre has little to do with me, because I am Irish.'[6] The distinction between Irish and English tradition is generally recognised, but that between Irish and British tradition and history much less so. In this statement, Shaw reminds us that Ireland has its own rich history and tradition separate from those of England (as do Scotland and Wales). In locating herself outside the English or so-called British tradition, Shaw effectively marginalises herself, and does so in a liberating way: her self-exclusion from that tradition thereby declares 'outsider' status and provides the right to a 'backdoor' entrance into the canon, or at least into performance thereof. In denying her part in the British Empire, she frees herself to experiment with its associated traditions.

Shaw also excludes herself from the expectations normally associated with modernity in performance, in one tongue-in-cheek observation: 'The history of the eighteenth century is very familiar, as I effectively grew up with that in Ireland.'[7] This sense of Shaw's distance from Englishness and modernity is employed to define her stance as a performer of Shakespeare today. Shaw's comments are an exercise in identity politics: they partially distance her 'self' in performance from the Shakespearean canon and the British acting tradition. At the same time, however, Shaw is strongly in favour of contemporary reinterpretations of Shakespeare and argues that overemphasis on 'women and Shakespeare', as on the theory of acting, may only distract the performer from the focus of her work – performing. Instead, she argues for emphasising rhythm, presentation, power. The contradiction is apparent: in denying the importance of gender in performance, she opens the way to an active critique of gender stereotypes. Shaw's work continually shifts the boundaries of gender representation by showing that such boundaries are most pliable when they are not constantly reinforced by self-reflection.

A case in point was her 1989 interpretation of Shakespeare's Rosalind in Tim Albery's production of *As You Like It*. Shaw's Rosalind was among the strongest modern portrayals of a

Shakespearean female character, despite her disclaimers at
relationship with Englishness, modernity, and the relation
gender to performance. Rosalind is, of course, among the best-
known and most-frequently 'reclaimed' of Shakespeare's crossdressing women. In an earlier and much-discussed production,
Shaw played Celia to Juliet Stevenson's Rosalind, a casting which
allowed Shaw to develop (by contrast) her ideas of what Rosalind
could be.[8] Shaw's Rosalind, in the Albery production, was self-
possessed, strong but not 'masculine' even when dressed in
breeches: she was androgyny powerfully, and somehow erotically,
personified.

A publicity picture used to promote this production illustrates
Shaw's erotic androgyny: the photo shows Shaw seated, embraced
by but not embracing Orlando (Adam Kotz). Both are on the
ground, but neither is in a supplicant position. Nor do the two seem
equal. Shaw is mud-splattered, Kotz is clean. Shaw is barefoot, Kotz
wears shoes. Their hair is the same length and is combed back in
similar styles. Shaw's features are more angular, her pose more possessed. Orlando's expression is more exaggerated, yet Rosalind's
(Shaw's) is more engaging.

Body language in this isolated pose is indicative of the presentation of gender relationships in the play as a whole. This Orlando
embraces Rosalind and (it seems) the idea of her, while she seems to
embrace another idea. His eyes are rapturously closed, his smiling
mouth wide open. Her eyes are open and directed into the distance,
her mouth nearly closed in a grin. Orlando's body is directed at
Rosalind's, and hers is angled slightly, with one foot pressed to the
ground and the other loose but positioned for movement. In the
tangle of arms, his are on top, touching hers, while her right hand
touches her own grounded leg, and she curls the fingers of her left
hand carelessly, as if unconscious of the overarching embrace.

In performance, perhaps more than in a publicity still, Shaw's
presence is compelling. The gaze of the audience is literally redi-
rected at her, whether she plays woman or man. She embodies a
contradiction: a strong person for whom a single gender cannot be
read into either costume or gesture. Similarly, as Shen Te in
Deborah Warner's 1989 National Theatre production of Brecht's
The Good Person of Sichuan, Shaw played both woman and man,
cross-dressing and thereby breaking down the borders between
genders, while somehow managing to avoid stereotypical presentation of 'feminine' and 'masculine' characteristics. The character of

Shen Te was reshaped into something both more and less human, ending in a powerful and believable presentation of a character in the context of a situation which, so soon after the Tiananmen Square massacre, had very real implications. The text was not altered, the action not curtailed. The play was not anachronistically set. This was not an alternative Brecht, any more than Albery's *As You Like It* was alternative Shakespeare. Yet Shaw's roles in both productions *were* alternative: that is, they offered alternatives to a dichotomy in the representation of gender, and instead presented an intriguing ambiguity. In *As You Like It*, such a presence manipulated the expectations of the audience: the transformation from 'female' to 'male' which is key to Rosalind's role is deflated in its importance when both sexes seem to be embodied in one performer.

The unique power of Shaw's presence stems from her performance of two genders and her ability to project an individual woman out of both. She appears not as a woman dressed as a man but as herself. It is not the costume which makes Shaw's Rosalind into a man; rather it is Shaw's personality which enlivens and supports both parts. It has been argued that women have long been cast as 'other' in terms of representational conflation of the actress with her costume.[9] Shaw's characterisation of Rosalind illustrates one way in which performers today may reclaim the power to wear the costume, rather than be subsumed into it. Her costume is not a sign representing her but rather a disguise she uses to subvert expectation. The process of creating alternatives as enacted by Shaw is built upon a recognition of a working dynamic between gender and power, which informs her characterisations of both female and male parts, and which is stressed in performance, where acting (in practice) takes priority over the (feminist) theory of performance. Shaw's presentation of androgyny contributes to a greater act of subversion that takes into account her personal context and ambivalence about elements of the British tradition, and thereby liberates her, as a performer, to create alternatives that are authentic both to the requirements of Shakespeare and to herself.

By contrast, Tilda Swinton takes a very different view of the dramatic possibilities of Shakespeare's female characters:

> There are, as we know, very few deterministic women characters in the classics, in the sense of women who actually determine their own destinies. Some of the most interesting roles for women in

Shakespeare, for instance, involve dressing up as boys. Rosalind, Viola, Portia ... but actually, I don't think that those roles should be played by women at all. I don't think those plays work today; the point is that the play was written for boys to play the women's parts. So in *As You Like It*, (as I see it) Rosalind can never be successfully played by a woman today: when Orlando falls in love with what we can patently see really is a boy (and it is a boy: albeit a boy playing a girl playing a boy) and Orlando thinks he's in love with this boy, then we have a real frisson. That's political. That's profound. To really stick a knife in modern Shakespeare, I think that *As You Like It* played with women reveals itself as rather a silly play: beautiful, nice poetry, lovely images, but it doesn't add up to much.

The battle when working with texts is the battle to get those texts to really work as plays. Plays really work as they were originally intended to work, and Shakespeare's plays were intended for men and boys. They weren't written for women. It would probably make life a great deal easier for actresses if Shakespeare were only played by men; then women would be free to play roles which mean something to them, which were written for them.[10]

Swinton is deliberately provocative in this statement, and in another interview she admitted that she has always wanted to play Hamlet. Here, two points should be considered: there are powerful feminist interpretations of Shakespeare's women (Fiona Shaw's Rosalind included), and the implications of a statement such as 'Shakespeare may be better played by men' are not necessarily negative and indeed potentially positive. Such a statement, taken out of context, might be read as support for any number of standard misogynist views of women's roles (on and off stage). But Swinton is adamant that her choice of so-called alternative roles is a choice *for* powerful roles in spite of the dominant press emphasis on what she chose *against*:

In terms of the politics of choice: when you study my work – even when I study my work – on the face of it, it looks like a choice has been made, I suppose one has been made, in terms of relationship to career structure; you could say I actually chose against a certain course. . . . All this also applies to choosing roles, and in that sense there is a running commentary on my relationship to the established repertoire, but it's a negative commentary – not in terms of performance, but in terms of focus. . . . For example, when I did *Man to Man*, one of the basic lines of press inquiry was based on the titillation of the fact that I was 'the one who doesn't', 'the one who left the

RSC'. That was the initial impact of all the hype. Only after that was there any interest in what I *did*.[11]

Furthermore, Swinton attributes some of the 'press titillation' not only to her career decisions as such but also to her status as a young woman from the British upper middle class: 'There was a shock that someone patently from the class into which I was born, with the credentials and the proportions, someone who could quite easily have been seen to be perfect fodder for RSC life membership, chose against it, or at least questioned it. I suppose there is a personal-political element underlying the reaction: the sniff of sacrilege. That in itself was a press story.'[12]

With Swinton's personal status vis-à-vis her 'press identity' thus established as context, her earlier comments regarding the value of Shakespeare for the woman performer are recast in a more positive light. The idea is not that women cannot play Shakespeare well, but rather that they can do more, and might better move on to more challenging roles: perhaps those written for them by other women.

When women define themselves *as* the mainstream, the value system which insists upon and defines a differentiation between the mainstream and the alternative begins to fall apart. Such a disintegration or subversion of values is illustrated by this extract on the topic of women vis-à-vis mainstream and alternative theatre, from another interview with Swinton: 'It all boils down to this: I've never been conscious of taking an alternative stance. My position is not alternative to me. . . . As far as I'm concerned, there's nothing "alternative" about my work at all. If I were to say that I'm taking an alternative stance, that's saying that I consider myself less powerful than someone else, less powerful than I could be. The work that I'm doing is the work that I need to do in order to be at my most powerful and most effective.'[13]

Swinton is dissatisfied with the definitions assigned to her, imposed upon her by producers, critics, audiences. She responds by offering her alternative definitions. She considers herself neither more nor less than 'master' of her own theatrical possibilities, and is thus free to transfigure herself (or her concept of self, and thereby her presentation of self in performance), and to translate her own role from the object to the subject position, at least within the playing space. When a woman, and especially a performer, thus reacts to the limitations of an acting tradition, she actively declares herself an agent of change, an act*or*.

If Swinton is not 'alternative to self,' it is because she defines herself as the norm (at least for herself, when she herself is acting). She discards the traditional measure of artistic value and creates her own. So did Shaw, in her self-distancing from the British tradition. In declaring and affirming her Irishness, Shaw defines a new norm, a unique starting place for the development of identity and for the presentation of self in performance. These two women have many more differences than similarities. It is, however, their challenge to dominant value systems which allows for comparison between them.

ORGANISING AND PERFORMING THE OPPOSITION: ALTERNATIVE THEATRE AND ALTERNATIVES TO SHAKESPEARE

Thus far, individual writers and performers have been discussed vis-à-vis their relationships with the Shakespearean canon, whether in terms of complicity with the canon or denial of the value and relevance thereof. There is another approach which is worth examining: the creation of collective feminist alternatives to Shakespeare. Three notable but little-documented projects can be seen as British feminist alternatives to Shakespeare: they are Monstrous Regiment's production of *Shakespeare's Sister* (1980 and 1982), the Royal Shakespeare Company's Women's Project (1984–7), culminating in the 1986 production of *Heresies*, and Women's Theatre Group's productions of *Lear's Daughters* (1987 and 1988).

Monstrous Regiment was formed as a feminist theatre collective in 1975 by a small group of performers who were disillusioned with the limited opportunities available to women in both mainstream and fringe theatre. In the company's words, they were 'a group of professional actors who wanted to make exciting political theatre based on women's experience: tired of seeing that experience marginalised or trivialised, we wanted to take it out of the wings and place it at the centre of the stage'.[14] One of the earliest British feminist theatre groups and one of the few original groups still operating in Britain, the Regiment was set up as a permanent collective committed to feminist and socialist ideals. Key founding members included Gillian Hanna, Mary McCusker, Chris Bowler and Sue Beardon. Writers who worked with the Regiment early on included Bryony Lavery, Caryl Churchill, Sue Todd and Michelene Wandor.

Performers who have worked with the Regiment since 1976 are too numerous to list, but include women (and men) from the gamut of British theatre: from Paola Dionisotti (known for her work with the RSC) to Sue Todd (known for directing the RSC Women's Project, as well as for work with the early women's Street Theatre Group, among others) to Ann Mitchell (known primarily for work in fringe, feminist theatre), to Caryl Churchill (whose early collaborative work with the Regiment, in both *Vinegar Tom* and the co-written cabaret *Floorshow*, was influential in her development as a playwright).[15] The link to the RSC is important: both Dionisotti and Todd were later involved in formation of the RSC Women's Project. Deborah Levy has worked with Women's Theatre Group in addition to the RSC and several other feminist companies. Similarly, Bryony Lavery has worked extensively with Monstrous Regiment and Women's Theatre Group.

Monstrous Regiment has been, in effect, a forum where many of the founders of the contemporary British 'women in theatre movement' met to share work and exchange ideas.

Initially, the Regiment had no permanent artistic director, and all policy decisions were made democratically. This structure has changed in recent years due to the financial necessity of decreasing numbers of fulltime staff, but the working practices developed in the early years of the collective can still be seen to shape the Regiment's work. Monstrous Regiment has always taken account of contemporary political and social events in its work, has striven for a transcultural perspective, and has informed all its projects with an awareness of changes in feminist theory and practice. *Shakespeare's Sister* was one such project.[16]

The idea of 'Shakespeare's Sister' is familiar from Virginia Woolf's *A Room of One's Own*, in which Woolf imagines that Shakespeare may have had a sister, who would have died unknown, not for lack of talent but rather because she was a woman. Shakespeare's Sister has since been a relatively popular figure in feminist writing which seeks to review the canon in search of a legacy of women writers, and the phrase has taken hold in more popular cultural forms, such as rock and punk music.

Monstrous Regiment described the play in this way in their press release: 'Shakespeare's Sister is a tragic fantasy figure created by Virginia Woolf in *A Room of One's Own*. She is a gifted woman, born in the wrong age and of the wrong sex and therefore never allowed the chance of self fulfilment. *Shakespeare's Sister* takes this image and explores it in relation to marriage today, measuring it against views of contemporary women. The play is a new departure for Monstrous Regiment in that it uses bizarre and surreal theatrical techniques. It is funny and disturbing, familiar and sad, showing us how little things have changed in the treatment of women and in their view of themselves.'[17] This was not a play about Shakespeare, nor even an alternative Shakespeare, but rather a women's alterative to Shakespeare: a theatrical representation of women's lives. While the play was chosen by the Regiment partially because of its feminist political content, it is important to note that the play was not originally produced with a British audience in mind. Still, Monstrous Regiment saw the play's relevance to British, and particularly British feminist, audiences.

Shakespeare's Sister was developed from improvisations based on research, interviews and newspaper articles about the status of women in Parisian society in the 1980s. The collaborative process of the play's development was similar, in some respects, to those of *Heresies* and *Lear's Daughters* (though both of those plays were scripted, the process of developing the script involved extensive input from performers in both cases). The act of choosing and producing the play was a radical transcultural act of reclamation: the fictional character created by an English woman (Woolf), claimed internationally by feminist critics and historians (primarily in America), recreated for the stage by a French theatre company, and reclaimed by a British socialist-feminist company for production for a British audience. Similarly, the major impact of the RSC Women's Project was not generated by the play it eventually produced but rather by the project itself and by its development in relation to individual women engaged in re-viewing and playing Shakespeare. The RSC Women's Project, like Monstrous Regiment, chose to produce women's alternatives to Shakespeare rather than alternative Shakespeares.

The RSC Women's Project was formed in 1984–5 and disbanded in 1987. The Project was inspired primarily by three performers working for the Royal Shakespeare Company – Fiona Shaw, Juliet Stevenson and Lindsey Duncan – with input from several other women who were performing for the RSC, and from directors, writers and administrators from a range of other theatre groups and associations, including Sue Todd and Angela Carter. The Project is most significant in that it represents the only avowedly feminist theatre company to date which can be considered mainstream, in that it was generated from within the Royal Shakespeare Company and was thus subsidised as part of one of the established 'Theatres National'.

The history of the RSC Women's Project is little documented and must be pieced together from statements made from memory by the individuals involved, and from reviews and collected press cuttings from the Project's only full production: Deborah Levy's *Heresies* in 1986. In fact, even the name of the group is debatable: it seems that the larger ideas and initiatives were known as the Women's Project (now commonly associated with the production of *Heresies),* and the women themselves were known as the RSC Women's Group.

The following information regarding the origins of the Project has been extracted from a long interview with Genista McIntosh, who was employed during the Project's gestation, first as an independent agent, and then as administrator for the RSC. McIntosh recalled,

> I think that what happened is that at a certain time in that company's life in Stratford, there was a company meeting at which some of those women challenged Terry Hands, Artistic Director, about there being so little work and provision for women in the company ... in terms of insufficient positive discrimination for performers, directors, writers, designers, technicians, etc. They threw down a gauntlet to Terry, which he took up, primarily by saying that if that's how they felt, they should do something about it and he wouldn't stand in their way.
>
> They started to work. Initially, there were no limits imposed on their imaginative sweep. . . . Another round of discussions began about the *kind* of work that a Women's Group should do.[18]

It is precisely the issue of the kind of work which was done which is of interest to this discussion of women's alternatives to Shakespeare. *Heresies*, like *Shakespeare's Sister*, was not an all-women's production: it involved male performers as well. It was inspired by women and developed through a long workshop process run by women. It was written by a woman and directed by a woman. Also like *Shakespeare's Sister, Heresies* was not explicitly about Shakespeare and was certainly not derivative of any one play. That kind of direct approach to altering the Shakespearean canon came only later, for instance in the acclaimed 1987–8 productions by the Women's Theatre Group of *Lear's Daughters*.[19]

The earlier work of both Monstrous Regiment and the RSC Women's Project took a less direct approach to the Shakespearean canon, examining images and ideas which were less obviously associated with Shakespeare's plays, but more closely associated with the power of the Shakespearean image: that of the bard, the male genius, the patriarchal figure overshadowing the development of contemporary theatre. Such work suggested that it was the Shakespearean image, rather than the plays, which had the most interesting impact on the lives and work of living women. The RSC Women's Project recognised a significant gap in opportunities for women performers.

In McIntosh's words, 'Within that group, there was a feeling about appropriation of Shakespeare having provided relatively few major opportunities for women. The very domination of the repertoire by Shakespeare inevitably limited the opportunities for women; and it was this which was originally meant to be challenged. . . . There was the natural emphasis on restructuring or deconstructing Shakespeare to provide more opportunities for the women in the company.'[20] The Project experienced a setback in morale when two key members (Shaw and Stevenson) left the group to pursue other projects. Accounts of this event differ substantially, but all note that these professional career moves were questioned, not on professional grounds, but rather on personal/political grounds. This kind of conflict of interests and perspectives can be seen to be fairly characteristic of the British feminist theatre movements of the seventies and eighties, and even of the early nineties. Personal career development was (and is) sometimes seen as disloyal to the collective project, a view which adds an element of tension to the act of choosing roles and thus helps to explain the divergence of views between women, like those discussed earlier, who come from different class backgrounds and different generations, and who therefore bear radically dissimilar relationships to British socialist–feminist ideals, and specifically to the notion of the collective and the definition of feminism.

This tension resulted in the remaining members of the Women's Project pulling closer together and beginning to focus their energies on bringing the project to fruition in a production: 'At this point, Sue Todd reactivated her relationship with Deborah Levy: she and Deborah had worked together previously, I believe it was in the Monstrous Regiment. . . . At any rate, it turned out that Deborah had already been working on a play which fits the Project's ideals: a partially written piece which was highly experimental in form. That play was *Heresies*, which was the Project's only production.'[21]

Briefly, *Heresies* was an ambitious project concerned with several overlapping themes, including the nurturing role often played by women, represented in terms of the notion of a 'women's creativity'. The central figure of the large cast was an architect, a figure which was developed in *Pax* and in some of Levy's earlier work, based on a polysemous image of a female builder.

Both *Pax* and *Heresies* are, at one level, plays about building images of women from pieces of narrative and bits of information, much like Virginia Woolf's construction of the character of Shakespeare's sister, and like Monstrous Regiment's re-creation of her in modern guise. Like Woolf and the Regiment's re-production of *Shakespeare's Sister*, *Heresies* emphasises the value of many women working without recognition. Appropriately, *Heresies* was also a collaborative project to some extent. Though Levy wrote the script in full, she worked extensively with the performers before creating the characters who eventually shaped the play.

The play conveys the voices of individual women, all of whom try to create something: most importantly, a sense of self for public presentation. It is most interesting that the collective structure of the Women's Project which informed and influenced Levy's script for *Heresies* was seen by the critics as a weakness rather than a strength. Many mixed reviews of the play in performance reflect a certain cynicism about the feminist collective as an effective structure for the production of 'good theatre'.[22] Overall, the most common criticism of the play suggested that it was 'over-ambitious', due, perhaps, to an over-emphasis on collaboration. Yet this focus on project over play is appropriate to Levy's conception of the role of the play. She describes her style of writing, of piecing together her plays, as a process of 'structuring the audience's attention' with regard to the actual theatre space, and with awareness of the audience's active role in making the play, as similar to the playwright's 'presence', and as opposed to the notable absence of the critic. In Levy's words, 'the only thing the artist has going for her is that she is present and therefore potentially receptive, able to tap into what is around, and to make of it something new'.[23]

Levy is critically aware of context. So was the RSC Women's Group as a whole. The Group was particularly determined that their production should be performed in a particular kind of space, with a particular place in the public realm of 'structured attention': that is, on a main stage. Interestingly, though, *Heresies* was staged in the Pit, the RSC's London studio space for alternative work. Since *Heresies*, there have been no more all-women's productions at the RSC. More to the point, there has never been a woman director employed to work on the RSC main stage in London (though Buzz Goodbody did a main stage production of *As You Like It* in 1973 in Stratford). There was not another main stage production directed by a woman until 1988, when Di Trevis also directed in Stratford, though Deborah Warner's acclaimed production of *Titus Andronicus* was staged at the Swan in Stratford-upon-Avon (a major venue, though not a 'main stage') in 1987.

Such practical and material considerations are immediate to the task of placing a production like *Heresies* into its proper context. Just as the character of Shakespeare's Sister took on a new dimension when performed in English, and in England, by the socialist–feminist group Monstrous Regiment, so *Heresies* was perceived as actually heretical when produced by a group of women within the Royal Shakespeare Company. In this context, it is particularly interesting to consider *Lear's Daughters*, produced only a few years after *Heresies*, in smaller venues and with very limited resources.

Lear's Daughters was written by Elaine Feinstein and Women's Theatre Group and was specifically envisioned as a feminist rewriting of Shakespeare. As is the case with much group-devised work, it is difficult to say who actually 'wrote' the working script for the play.[24] *Lear's Daughters* was commissioned in 1987 by Women's Theatre Group; Elaine Feinstein was offered the commission as writer, to work with members of the company, which at that time consisted of Gwenda Hughes, Janys Chambers, Hilary Ellis, Maureen Hibbert and Hazel Maycock. All company members contributed to the workshops, and thus to the rewriting of the working script.

The play is a landmark in feminist 'reinventing' of Shakespeare. It takes as its premise the notion that, to a female reader (and more specifically to a feminist reader), all of history as presented in standard texts may resemble a genealogy of 'false fathers'. When these false fathers are produced on stage, the fathers come to life, and the necessary feminist reaction is the creation of new mothers (just as, in theory, the 'false universal' must be deconstructed and replaced within feminist criticism). *Lear's Daughters* questions the mainstream casting of Shakespeare as the 'fit father' of the literary-dramatic canon. The focus is not on Lear but on his daughters, on the women who are affected by the events of the play: the Queen (who does not appear in the original), the three princesses, the Nanny (a new character: another mother figure), and the androgynous Fool).

The play is billed as 'the story of women growing up in the kingdoms of their fathers'. The gaze of the audience-spectator of the play is directed not only at the women in the story of Lear but at Lear's daughters as they might be seen today.

> three daughters, locked in a room
> with
> two mothers, dead or gone missing
> and a
> Father, waiting outside
> three princesses, sitting in a tower
> with
> two servants, behind the door
> and a
> King holding the crown.

The daugher role and sister role are prioritised, and the mother role implied as part and parcel of both. The father in this stark picture figures as a threat, a shadow of vague and impersonal power, although (or perhaps because) he is neither seen nor heard; he is the embodiment of the 'absent father' image of today's no-longer-nuclear families. The mother is also noticeable in her absence, but she is represented in the figure of another character, Nanny, and also in the grotesque image of the mother-figure – to whom the three princesses direct their speeches and actions in mimed sequences – represented by a tea towel hastily draped over a saucepan (metonymically representing the 'other' missing crown). Nanny is both mother and servant, in the words of the play, 'the mother who is paid'. Fool is costumed and directed as a highly androgynous figure; s/he is the only character in the play who is even partially 'male', and therefore, as if by rights, wears the managerial hat. Fool is both servant and stage manager.

The princesses are carefully balanced against each other in terms of character and color (multi-racial casting is common to much of the Women's Theatre Group's work). In the first production, Cordelia was played by a blond, white woman, while Regan and Goneril were played by black women. This heightened the sense of petty favouritism which Lear expressed for Cordelia (a factor which is emphasised in the play in scenes which suggest that some sexual attraction may have motivated the favouritism and frightened young Cordelia into a permanently childlike and vocally reticent state). By contrast, Regan and Goneril seem (quite literally, given the racial counterplay) to be children of different fathers, or mothers. In the second production, however, all three sisters were played by black performers while both Nanny and Fool were played by white women. Fool was played in both productions by a white woman in whiteface wearing black and white: half of her suit of clothes designated as male and half as female. Lear himself is never seen. The implication was communicated in the second production, however, that he and (or) his dead wife or one of his mistresses – if indeed the daughters are of different mothers – must be (have been) black. The servants are white. These points are represented physically but not explored (this is not color-blind, but rather determinedly color-conscious casting).

The question of lineage informs the story of *Lear's Daughters* in sexual as well as racial terms. Little is known of the dead Queen, except that she suffered in childbirth. The promiscuity of Lear is common knowledge. His paternity, like his patriarchal right, is not questioned. The daughters' relationship with their father is one of fear and awed respect, notably tinged with embarrassment on the part of Cordelia, and with jealousy on the part of the other two. Theoretical questions of otherness, agency and difference are thus enacted in this story of daughters, literally locked in the attic, growing together and apart in isolation from their mother and in a combination of fear and desire in relation to their father, and by extension – as he is the only man they have ever known – to men in general. Each sister symbolically insists upon her right to her own vision and version of the story. Each also seeks to wear the crown. In the final image of *Lear's Daughters*, the crown is thrown into the air and caught by all three daughters at once. The shrinking spotlight highlights the black and white of hands on gold just before the final blackout.

SWEEPING UP: ON A CLEAR STAGE

Feminist interpretation of Shakespeare creates a space for a critical deconstruction and re-evaluation of mainstream values, as well as a physical space appropriate to the feminist project of reshaping and re-viewing gender roles. As Janelle Reinelt has observed,

'Historicizing gender relations is a powerful way to change the field itself because it explicitly challenges the notion of transhistorical male and female modes of being and recovers a marginalized alternative narrative of women as active subjects determining the concrete course of human events.'[25] The theatre is the frame and impetus for active representation of ideas and language in three dimensions, in the public sphere. Crucial differences between women, and even between feminists, complicate any attempt to define 'women's theatre' or to locate its place in the history of representation. The critical perception of the female gaze, or the woman's view of self and self in performance, is still seen by many, and even by some women performers themselves, as alternative and therefore in danger of continual attack. This, in theatrical terms, sometimes renders it difficult to evaluate women's work (in the theatre as in other sectors) in relation to standard (academic) measures. But Jill Dolan suggests that the theatre is an appropriate site for the deconstruction of gendered forms of representation, not in spite of the difficulties here mentioned, but *because* of them. She writes, 'The stage, then, is a proper place to explore gender ambiguity, not to cathartically expunge it from society, but to play with, confound and deconstruct gender categories. If we stop considering the stage as a mirror of reality we can use it as a laboratory in which to reconstruct new, non-genderized identities. And in the process, we can change the nature of theatre itself'.[26]

Gender ambiguity is the essential point of interest in Shakespeare, at least in terms of representation of women. The woman performer in Shakespeare is intrinsically, radically, perhaps definitionally alternative to the boy-man for whom the parts were written. She may choose to play those parts as a woman, or as a woman playing a man playing a woman, or not at all. She may choose to play them as if they were written for a woman, even specifically for her. She may choose to play them as if she is part of the circumstances of their production, or by reminding herself that she stands outside those circumstances, or by denying the relevance of any such considerations. She may see herself as a performer of alternative Shakespeares or as an *actor* in the process of creating alternatives to Shakespeare.

All these perspectives incorporate one basic idea: that of including self in performance. All may be bases for radical reorganisation of the operative set of values or structures by and through which women's work in the theatre (and in other spheres) is evaluated. As the process develops and the boundaries shift, this radical inclusion of women may become part of the value system itself, and women's work may then be judged, not according to some predefined and imposed alternative scale of values, but rather according to criteria authentic to individual and collective perspectives, contexts, and ways of seeing. Then theory may have a firmer base in practice.

> Imagine a Theatre for Women somewhere in Warwickshire, by a river, well subsidized ...
> Imagine a National Theatre somewhere in London, say by a river, well subsidized, putting on NEW plays ... [27]

Or even better, imagine a theatrical climate in which this and other alternatives are all possible; a stage on which there is room for all.

From *Cross-Cultural Performances: Differences in Women's Re-Visions of Shakespeare*, ed. Marianne Novy (Champaign–Urbana: University of Illinois, Press, 1993), pp. 206–26.

NOTES

[Tackling questions of cultural power and canonical status, Lizbeth Goodman examines the material practices of British theatre that both sustain Shakespeare's privileged place and marginalise new work, examining the consequences of this situation for women writers, performers and directors. She elicits the views of female theatre practitioners who are at the cutting edge of alternatives to Shakespeare/alternative ways of doing Shakespeare, tracing their diverse class and national locations and career trajectories, and the political consequences of their theatrical choices. The discussion revolves around some key issues for recent gender criticism, notably interpreting the body in performance, and the relation between the gender of the performer and that of the role.   Ed.]

1. Bryony Lavery, 'But Will Men Like It?' *Women and Theatre: Calling the Shots*, ed. Susan Todd (London: Faber and Faber, 1984), pp. 30–1.

2. The production, with an all-male multiracial cast, toured from July 1991 to March 1992. Another all-male British production of *As You Like It* was produced by the Royal National Theatre, directed by Clifford Williams, with Anthony Hopkins and Derek Jacobi, first performed at the Old Vic Theatre, 3 October 1967.

3. A study in 1986–7 showed that only 4.5 per cent of artistic directors were women and 27.5 per cent of senior administrators were women: 'Updated Survey of Sex of Artistic Directors and Administrators Currently Working in Repertory Theatres in England and Wales',

Contacts, 76 (1986/7). In 1983, the figures were even lower, particularly for the Theatres National (the RSC, the National Theatre and the Royal Court Theatre): Sue Dunderdale and Sue Parrish, report for Conference of Women Theatre Directors and Administrators, 1982/3, published in *Drama*, 152 (1984).

4. Statistics compiled by Sue Dunderdale for the Conference of Women Theatre Directors and Administrators (CWTDA), published in *Drama*, 152 (1984). Also see Sir Kenneth Cork, 'Theatre is for All: the Inquiry into Professional Theatre in England' [a.k.a. 'The Cork Report'] (London: Arts Council of Great Britain, 1986), 44; and Caroline Gardiner, 'What Share of the Cake: the Employment of Women in the English Theatre' (London: The Women's Playhouse Trust, 1987).

5. Findings from the survey were printed in the series booklet: *Ordinary People: Why Women Become Feminists*, ed. Derek Jones (London: Channel Four Television, 1990).

6. Fiona Shaw, a talk given at the DIVINA International Conference on 'The Changing Representation of Women in the Theatre', Turin, 4–5 June 1990; Shaw spoke as part of the British panel (also including Charlotte Keatley, Gabriella Giannachi and Lizbeth Goodman). The conference report appears in *New Theatre Quarterly*, 7 (Feb. 1991), pp. 97–9.

7. Ibid.

8. *As You Like It*, directed for the Royal Shakespeare Company by Adrian Noble in 1985. This production is discussed at length in Carol Rutter, *Clamorous Voices*, ed. Faith Evans (London: The Women's Press, 1988), pp. 97–121.

9. Lesley Ferris, *Acting Women: Images of Women in the Theatre* (London: Macmillan, 1989).

10. Lizbeth Goodman, 'Subverting Images of the Female: an Interview with Tilda Swinton', *New Theatre Quarterly*, 6 (Aug. 1990), 222. This interview was compiled from a series of taped and untaped sessions, June–October 1989.

11. Ibid., 221. The reference is to Manfred Karge's *Man to Man*, performed by Swinton at the Royal Court Theatre, January 1988.

12. Ibid., 221.

13. Ibid., 222.

14. From the Monstrous Regiment company brochure (1985). Also see the first Monstrous Regiment book: *Monstrous Regiment: A Collective Celebration*, ed. Gillian Hanna (London: Nick Hem Books, 1991), which includes four of the company's plays published for the first time.

A long interview with Gillian Hanna appears in *New Theatre Quarterly*, 6 (Feb. 1990), pp. 432–56.

15. *Floorshow* was co-written by Caryl Churchill, Bryony Lavery and Michelene Wandor in 1977–8. A complete list of contributors to and participants in Monstrous Regiment productions is included in the company brochure (1985).

16. *Shakespeare's Sister*, based on an original production devised by Théâtre de l'Aquarium, Paris. Translated by Gillian Hanna for Monstrous Regiment. This version was first performed at the Institute of Contemporary Arts, London, for three weeks in December 1980: directed by Hilary Westlake, designed by Gemma Jackson, with a cast including Gilllian Hanna and John Slade. Revived by the Regiment for a second (national touring) production in 1982: directed by Jan Sargent, designed by Gemma Jackson, with Patricia Donovan, Tony Guilfoyle, Gillian Hanna, Ann Haydn, Stephen Ley and Mary McCusker.

17. Monstrous Regiment, press release for *Shakespeare's Sister* (1980); unpublished, in the Monstrous Regiment company files. Reviews are also collected in the company archives.

18. From an unpublished interview with Genista McIntosh, who was Senior Administrator and artistic director-elect at the time of the interview, 2 May 1990. McIntosh has since been appointed Executive Director of the National Theatre.

19. *Lear's Daughters*, by Elaine Feinstein and Women's Theatre Group, in *Herstory*, vol. 1, ed. Gabrielle Griffin and Elaine Aston (Sheffield: The Academic Press, 1991). NB: in 1992, Women's Theatre Group changed its name to The Sphinx.

20. Unpublished interview with Genista McIntosh.

21. Ibid.

22. Reviews are collected in full in the Royal Shakespeare Company archives.

23. Deborah Levy, 'Structuring the Audience's Attention', an unpublished seminar paper delivered to the Graduate Women and Literature Seminar, St John's College, Cambridge, 7 February 1990.

24. The authorship of the play is contentious, as the script which Feinstein contributed was significantly reworked in devising and rehearsal by the company. As a result, Feinstein's name appears on only some of the press releases and reviews for the show. The complicated question of 'copyright' for this and other British feminist plays is examined in detail in my book *Contemporary Feminist Theatres* (London: Routledge, 1993).

25. Janelle Reinelt, 'British Feminist Drama: Brecht and Caryl Churchill', unpublished conference paper, delivered at a conference on 'Brecht: Thirty Years After', Toronto, Autumn 1986.

26. Jill Dolan, 'Gender Impersonation Onstage: Destroying or Maintaining the Mirror of Gender Roles', in *Women and Performance*, 2:2 (1985), 10.

27. Lavery, 'But Will Men Like It?', p. 31.

4

Gender and Nation: Anticipations of Modernity in the Second Tetralogy

JEAN E. HOWARD AND PHYLLIS RACKIN

The wooing scene in *Henry V* has proved popular with recent audiences; but, as Lance Wilcox has observed, Shakespeare's representation of Henry's courtship repeatedly identifies his conquest of Katherine as a kind of rape.[1] Unprecedented in Shakespeare's earlier plays, the identification of rape as a model of masculine dominance illuminates the dark underside of the emergent conception of marriage as the proof of manhood and the necessary basis for patriarchal authority – the production of rape as the gatekeeper for the gender hierarchy. For if the ideology of patrilineal inheritance made cuckoldry a dangerous crime, the ideology of masculine performance makes rape a necessary one. The first criminalised women as potential cuckold-makers, the second disempowers them as potential victims.

'Performative masculinity', the term we have used to designate the emergent conception of male identity, is adapted from an article by Susan Jeffords: 'Performative Masculinities, or, "After a Few Times You Won't be Afraid of Rape at All"'.[2] Jeffords' remarkably prophetic analysis was published in the Spring–Summer 1991 issue of *Discourse*, well before the eruption of the Tailhook scandal,[3] the furious public response to President Clinton's promise to end American military discrimination against gay and lesbian soldiers, and the widely publicised systematic rape of civilian women by soldiers in Bosnia. Jeffords' title comes from a 1986 film, *Opposing Force*, in which the setting is a mock prisoner of war camp established by the American Air Force to train pilots for survival in enemy captivity. The heroine, the first woman to be trained in the camp, is raped by a superior officer, who claims, in the words of Jeffords' title, that the rape is a necessary part of her training for military service. 'You're frightened now,' he explains. 'But after a few more times you won't be afraid of rape at all.'

Two of the many strengths of Jeffords' analysis are her insistence upon making distinctions between historically different versions of patriarchy and her focus upon war as the arena in which the terms of the gender hierarchy are renegotiated.[4] Situating her own analysis in the present, she documents both the widespread practice of raping civilian women in recent wars and the equally widespread exploitation of the threat of rape by modern governments as an excuse for excluding women from combat duty. She argues that in both cases biological sexual difference becomes the ground for re-establishing a gender hierarchy destabilised by the modern ideology of universal citizenship in civil society. '"Equal citizenship",' she explains, 'has come to be a part of the way that a dominant gender system presents itself in the US. But in tandem with this abstraction of equality is an insistence on what are viewed as the concrete differences of biology, drawing attention ... to the body as the site of difference'.[5]

Jeffords' analysis goes a long way towards explaining not only the specific examples of sexual persecution we mentioned (Tailhook, Bosnia, gay-bashing) but also the current obsession with women's bodies, the increasingly pornographic representations of the relationships between men and women in popular culture and the preoccupation with bodies (reified as 'the body') and sexuality in much contemporary literary scholarship. However, the beginnings of the process Jeffords describes can be traced at least as far back as Shakespeare's *Henry V*, a play that responds remarkably well to the sort of analysis she proposes, a fact which probably helps to explain both its popularity in recent productions and the attention it has received in recent feminist criticism.

More than any of Shakespeare's earlier English histories, *Henry V* defines the roles of men and women in terms that clearly prefigure the performative masculinity and embodied female vulnerability that Jeffords identifies as ideologically motivated responses to our own historical situation. Military conquest provides the arena and sexual conquest the warrant for establishing the male protagonist's authority, and female characters are defined primarily in terms of their sexuality. The logic of sexual difference in *Henry V* is now so familiar that it is easy to miss how innovative it was at the end of the sixteenth century. As Tania Modleski has observed, 'contemporary [i.e. late twentieth-century] texts devoted to analyzing "the enduring appeal of battle" tend to focus obsessively on the issue of sexuality – to the point indeed of excluding almost every other factor'.[6] Although the re-enactment of historical battles is one of the chief attractions in Shakespeare's history plays, it is only in *Richard III* and *Henry V* that rape is associated with military invasion. Significantly, these are also the only Shakespearean histories in which marriage represents the desired conclusion of the action, and the only ones in which no woman appears, or is even mentioned as appearing, on the fields of battle. All these differences mark the emergence, at the ends of the two tetralogies, of a recognisably modern model of masculine identity and male dominance.

In the plays where the logic of patrilineal feudal succession is privileged, rape is never associated with military conquest or valorised as the 'natural' instinct of men. Instead, it serves to separate 'low' men from their betters. The only references to rape in the Henry VI plays are associated with Jack Cade's rebellion, where it is identified with the dangers of a world turned upside down. The quarto version of *Henry VI, Part II* contains an account of a rape committed by one of Cade's followers and Cade's enthusiastic approval of the act. Although this incident is absent from the folio text, Cade's own proposal that 'There shall not a maid be married, but she shall pay to me her maidenhead ere they have it' (*Henry VI, II*: IV.vii.121–3) appears in both versions. In this inversion of *droit de seigneur*, the supposed right of a feudal lord to take the virginity of his vassal's bride,[7] as in the Gothic barbarians' rape of Lavinia in *Titus Andronicus* and Caliban's attempt to rape Miranda in *The Tempest*, the historical actuality of class and colonial oppression is displaced and denied. The function of rape as a means by which the powerful control the less powerful is elided; the would-be perpetrators are foreign barbarians and plebeian rebels. Prospero colonises the island, but he never rapes a native woman.[8] The Romans capture Tamora, but they do not rape her. Cade's warning to his followers about the tyranny of the nobility, who 'break your backs with burthens, take your houses over your heads, ravish your wives and daughters before your faces' (IV.viii.29–31) reflects the

social reality of a world where female labourers were always vulnerable to sexual exploitation at the hands of their masters, but this
is the only reference to that fact in all of Shakespeare's history
plays.[9] In each case, a socially or racially inferior man is represented
as attempting to deprive another man of his rightful property, and
the desire to rape signals the bestiality of its perpetrator. Not only a
dishonor to the victim and to the men to whom she rightfully
'belongs', it also criminalises the rapist.

A similar conception of rape persists in *Richard III*, the first play
where rape is mentioned among the dangers of war. It is the villain
who introduces the threat of rape, and the rapists are stigmatised
not only as ignoble but also as unmanly. Their leader, according to
Richard, is a 'milksop' who has been 'Long kept in Britain [i.e.
Brittany] at our mother's cost' (V.iii.324–5). The potential rapists
are beggars, bastards and foreigners, all of which means that they
are not real men:

> If we be conquered, let men conquer us,
> And not these bastard Britains [i.e. Bretons], whom our fathers
> Have in their own land beaten, bobb'd, and thump'd,
> ...
> Shall these enjoy our lands? Lie with our wives?
> Ravish our daughters?
> (*Richard III*: V.iii.332–7)

In *Henry V*, by contrast, the hierarchies of status and nation are
supported rather than threatened by sexual violence. Not only
masculinity but nationality and military prowess are now grounded
in embodied sexual difference. Describing the departure of the
English fleet 'holding due course to Harflew' (III.Ch.17), the Chorus
to Act III explains that England has been left

> Guarded with grandsires, babies, and old women,
> Either past or not arriv'd to pith and puissance;
> For who is he, whose chin is but enrich'd
> With one appearing hair, that will not follow
> These cull'd and choice-drawn cavaliers to France?
> (III.Ch. 20–4)

Apparently, the only people who are qualified for membership in
the English army are sexually mature men. Their qualifications are
shown by the appearance of hair on their chins and proved by their
ability to rape women – an ability which is specifically articulated at

the gates of the French city which the Chorus identifies as the army's destination.[10] In this moment of threatened sexual violence, which is powerfully articulated in Branagh's updated film version of the play but already explicit in Shakespeare's text, it is the heroic English king who voices the threat of rape. Moreover, in this play, unlike *Richard III*, it is English soldiers who will do the raping and French women who will be the victims.

Like *Henry V*, *Richard III* represents a royal marriage as the desired conclusion of the historical action. Here, as in their association of rape with military conquest, both plays prefigure modern conceptions of masculine authority, and here too *Henry V* is significantly more modern than *Richard III*. Although both plays end by announcing that victories won on the battlefield will be ratified in marriage and both marriages serve to insure the bridegroom's sovereignty, the bride-to-be in *Richard III* is a disembodied name, while the French princess in *Henry V* is brought on stage as a sexualised object of theatrical display and erotic desire. In this connection Richard Loncraine's recent film version of *Richard III*, starring Ian McKellen, offers an interesting parallel when it includes Elizabeth of York among the dramatis personae and also shows Richmond making love to her on the night before the Battle of Bosworth Field – in an interpolated scene which gives new meaning to Richmond's oversleeping on the morning of the battle and his declaration that he had 'the sweetest sleep and fairest-boding dreams / That ever ent'red in a drowsy head' (V.iii.227–8). In Shakespeare's script, Richmond dreams about the ghosts of Richard's victims, who exhort him to victory in the coming battle, and Elizabeth never appears on stage. *Henry V* is the only Shakespearean history play where male authority is demonstrated in modern terms, by the hero's sexual conquest of a desirable woman; and it is not surprising that modern critics have admired the wooing scene as a final demonstration of Henry's 'humanity' or that Loncraine and McKellen found it necessary to embellish their version of the earlier play by showing how the founders of the House of Tudor consummated their marriage. In *Richard III*, the courtship of Lady Anne provided a remarkable display of Richard's masculine power, but Richard's power, unlike that of Richmond – and unlike that of Henry V – is never depicted as legitimate. In *Henry V*, for the first time in Shakespeare's English histories, male heterosexual dominance achieves its modern status as the 'natural' basis of legitimate masculine authority.

Richard III and *Henry V* are also the only Shakespearean history plays in which battlefields are designated as exclusively male terrain, and here too both plays signal their modernity, for, as Jeffords points out, the sexual logic of performative masculinity requires the exclusion of women from military combat.[12] Women's exclusion from combat is not a universal practice, grounded in nature and ratified by immemorial custom; but the pressure of modern gender ideology tends to erase or minimise historical facts that threaten to contradict it, even for professional historians. Noting the 'blindness of historians to women's military roles' Barton Hacker points out that 'when military history emerged during the latter part of the nineteenth century, armies were not what they had been even a few decades earlier. . . . Women's absence from late nineteenth-century armies debarred them from military history in its formative stages, and ever since has obscured the meaning of their presence in other armies at other times'.[13] A history of women's roles in medieval and early modern armies has yet to be written, for just as military histories tend to ignore the roles of women, histories of women tend to ignore their roles as soldiers. Despite their absence from military history, women were present in large numbers as 'a normal part of European armies ... until well into the nineteenth century'.[14] Many were noncombatants – wives, prostitutes, sutlers, and serving women who accompanied the soldiers.[15] But some of these women also fought, like the Frisian woman described by Froissart who 'fought in the front rank and died pierced with arrows' in 1396 or the woman who carried the Flemish banner in a battle against Charles VI in 1382.[16] For the most part, common women, like the common men in early armies, were nameless in historical records, but there were numerous accounts of aristocratic women warriors. As Philippe Contamine points out, 'The participation of armed ladies ... was considered, when everything is taken into account, as fairly normal, given the fact that many feudal customs gave them a formal right to succession'.[17]

In the first tetralogy and *King John*, Shakespeare's representations of medieval battles exploit the historical fact of women's presence. In *King John*, as in history, Elinor of Aquitaine is a 'soldier' (I.i.150) who leads her own forces in France.[18] In the Henry VI plays, Shakespeare follows his historical sources in making Margaret a better general than her husband and in representing Joan as leading the French army to repeated victories; and he improves on their accounts by having Joan defeat the Dolphin and fight the great Talbot to a draw in single combats spectacularly performed on stage. As many recent critics have been quick to notice, however, the figure of the woman warrior was already a source of anxiety when the Henry VI plays were first performed – a cultural contradiction expressed in numerous and conflicting references to Amazons in contemporary texts as well as the circulation of the story that Queen Elizabeth had appeared at Tilbury dressed in armor and explaining that although she had 'the body of a weak and feeble woman', she had 'the heart and stomach of a king, and of a king of England too'. Shakespeare's representations of Joan and Margaret seem clearly designed to exploit the shock value of the appearance of a woman warrior.[19] In *Henry VI, Part III* the Duke of York tells Margaret that her warlike behaviour is completely antithetical to women's nature: 'Women are soft, mild, pitiful, and flexible,' he explains, 'Thou stern, obdurate, flinty, rough, remorseless.' He also denounces Margaret as an 'Amazonian trull', linking the masculinity of the female warrior with the sexual promiscuity of the harlot (I.iv.141–2, 114). The same associations colour Shakespeare's characterisation of Joan, who is both the leader of the Dolphin's army and his 'trull' (*Henry VI, Part I*: II.ii.28).[20] However, although their behaviour is clearly marked as sexually transgressive, neither of these warrior women is ever subjected to the danger – or even the threat – of rape. Margaret's charms are twice described as 'ravishing' (*Henry VI, Part I*: V.v.15; *Henry VI, II*: I.i.32); but no one ever attempts – or contemplates attempting – to ravish Margaret. The notoriously sensationalised violence in *Henry VI, Part III* includes the abuse of a corpse, the flourishing of a decapitated head, and the murders of two children, all performed on stage, but it does not include any references to rape.

The conflation of military conquest with rape helps to produce a naturalised categorical difference between male and female. As York tries to explain, the violence of the battlefield should be a male monopoly. In the Henry VI plays and *King John* this is not yet the case. As we noted earlier, York speaks as the victim of Margaret's violence in one of the most brutal scenes in those plays, when she taunts him with a napkin stained in the blood of his murdered child and has him crowned with a paper crown. York responds with a long and eloquent denunciation of Margaret's brutality, explaining that women are not supposed to behave this way. At the end, it will be recalled, he breaks down in tears, and Northumberland, Margaret's henchman, also admits that he can 'hardly ... check [his] eyes from tears' (*Henry VI, III*: I.iv.151). Margaret, however, is unmoved: she orders York killed, delivers the *coup de grâce* herself, and ends the scene with the grisly joke: 'Off with his head, and set it on York gates, / So York may overlook the town of York' (I.iv.179–80).

Like Joan's single combats with Talbot and the Dolphin, Margaret's murder of York is Shakespeare's invention; both appealed to a contemporary appetite for representations of Amazonian women. As York's complaint makes clear, the figure of the woman warrior was already a cultural anomaly, but, as Shakespeare's embellishments of his historical sources make equally clear, she was also an object of fascinated interest. The twentieth-century editor of the Arden edition of *Henry VI, Part III*, by contrast, seems oblivious to her attractions. Carefully noting that 'Margaret is not present, according to the chronicles, in this scene,' he seems to find the spectacle of female violence so intolerable that he attempts to obliterate the stage-Margaret's presence ('Margaret *is* not present') rather than simply recording the historical Margaret's absence (in which case he would, presumably, have written, '*was* not present').

Shakespeare's own erasure of the woman warrior is one of the projects of the later plays. In the second tetralogy, female soldiers no longer appear on stage, but in *Richard II*, we learn that 'distaff-women manage rusty bills' [that is, pikes, or long spears] in arms against the king (III.ii.118); and *Henry IV, Part I* begins with the abbreviated account of the battlefield mutilation of the English soldiers' corpses by the Welsh women. In these plays, women's presence on the battlefield is briefly told rather than extensively shown, the distaff-women are not generals, the violence the Welshwomen commit is a gendered act of sexual mutilation, and, of course, they are foreigners. Mortimer's Welsh bride wants to 'be a soldier too' and follow her husband 'to the wars' (III.i.193), but Hotspur's English wife has no such unruly desires. By the time we get to *Henry V*, even the French women are safely contained at home. The gendered distinction between hearth and battlefield is now fully in place, and no woman appears – or is mentioned as appearing – in any army. Entirely confined to domestic settings and domestic roles, female characters serve only as the objects of male protection and the occasions for masculine competition.

Consider again the transformation of Mistress Quickly. The first thing we hear about her in *Henry V* is that she is now married to

Pistol. In what looks very much like a parodic anticipation of a modern war movie, the quondam Quickly bids her new husband a fond farewell as he departs for France. 'Prithee, honey-sweet husband,' she implores, 'let me bring thee to Staines [i.e. to a town on the road to Southampton, where the army will embark for France]. He refuses, explaining that his *'manly* heart doth ern' (II.iii.1–3, italics added) and ordering his clinging bride to keep the home fires burning in terms which designate as his property the tavern that was hers in both parts of Henry IV. 'My love, give me thy lips,' he says. 'Look to *my* chattels and *my* moveables' (II.iii.47–8, italics added).

Domesticated and dependent, the female characters in *Henry V* are both economically and sexually vulnerable. Pistol goes on to admonish his newly acquired wife, who has been running the tavern as long as we have known her, 'the [word] is "Pitch and pay"; / Trust none' (II.iii.49–50). Pistol is a lying braggart, but the economic dependency of women receives better testimony in Act IV, when the upright common soldier Williams admonishes his king (and Shakespeare's audience) that when soldiers die there will be 'wives left poor behind them' and 'children rawly left' (IV.i.139–41). The aristocratic women in the play are equally helpless. The French princess Katherine, her lady-in-waiting and her mother the queen are all confined to the enclosed space of the palace, and their roles in the play are limited to the provision of sexual titillation for the audience and a bride for the soldier hero.

As we noted earlier, Quickly's domestication implies an effort to contain the threat represented by her economic independence – and that of her counterparts in Shakespeare's audience. What is also striking in *Henry V* is that the proto-bourgeois project of domestication is now universalised, and the forces of modernity are, for the first time, privileged. Beginning with the non-élite, entrepreneurial London woman in the anachronistically modern tavern, the new model of wifely dependence reaches across the English channel and up to the highest place in the social hierarchy to provide a precedent for the domestication of the future bride of Henry V, a woman who was also, by her later marriage to Owen Tudor, the great-great-grandmother of Elizabeth I. The gendered resemblances between the French princess and the English tavern-keeper are numerous, superseding social and national difference to affirm the universality of the sexualised difference between men and women. In the person of the princess, the entire French nation will assume the role of a married woman, the *feme covert* whose identity was legally subsumed in that of her husband and whose property became his possession.

Before Henry can assume the title of *Héritier de France*, however, the patrilineal right that authorises the Dolphin's claim to that title must be discredited. In striking contrast to the earlier history plays, the vestigial ideology of chivalry and hereditary nobility is now identified with the French and gendered feminine, while the modern culture of personal achievement and national identity is now identified as masculine and English. In *Henry V* it is not the virile English king but the effete French Dolphin who inherits Hotspur's obsession with horses. A descendent of the effete courtier who infuriated Hotspur at the Battle of Holmedon, the Dolphin is also a descendent of Hotspur himself, for just as Henry takes on Hotspur's heroic honour, the Dolphin takes on his exaggerated devotion to his horse. In the Dolphin's declaration, 'my horse is my mistress' (III.vii.44), in the inflated language in which he describes his infatuation, and in his revelation that he 'once writ a sonnet in his praise' (III.vii.39), chivalry itself becomes the object of satire. Moreover, the Dolphin's identification of the horse as male provides a significant contrast to Hotspur's comparison of the effeminate courtier at Holmedon to a bridegroom. In *Henry V*, the status of a bridegroom provides the final proof of Henry's masculine authority, and the Dolphin's effeminating passion for his horse is associated with deviance from an emergent heterosexual norm.

The quarto version of *Henry V* assigns the Dolphin's part in the Agincourt scenes to the Duke of Bourbon. The folio attribution of these lines to the Dolphin helps to discredit the grounding of political authority in patrilineal right and thus to prepare for Henry's assumption of the Dolphin's hereditary title to the French throne. Whichever version is accepted, however, the satirical portrait of a Frenchman in love with his horses serves to discredit the feudal ideal of chivalry, and throughout the Agincourt scenes the culture of hereditary status distinctions is identified with the French and discredited. Before the battle, the French Constable contemptuously predicts 'our superfluous lackeys and our peasants / Who in unnecessary action swarm / About our squares of battle, were enow / To purge this field of such a hiding foe' (IV.ii.26–9). Moreover, the chief representative of the French at Agincourt is Montjoy, a proud

French herald who comes to the English camp so often that his appearance becomes a kind of joke (IV.iii.128). After the battle of Agincourt, Montjoy returns again, 'his eyes ... humbler than they used to be', to beg permission (IV.vii.67)

> That we may wander o'er this bloody field
> To book our dead, and then to bury them;
> To sort our nobles from our common men.
> For many of our princes (woe the while!)
> Lie drown'd and soak'd in mercenary blood;
> So do our vulgar drench their peasant limbs
> In blood of princes, and [their] wounded steeds
> Fret fetlock deep in gore, and with wild rage
> Yerk out their armed heels at their dead masters,
> Killing them twice.
>
> (IV.vii.72–81)

What distresses the French herald is the failure of chivalry: the horses turn against their masters; the peasants are drenched in the blood of princes. Like this speech, the prominence given the French herald in the Agincourt scenes identifies the French with the culture of hereditary entitlement. The English herald, like his French counterpart, is associated with the books that recorded the names of the noble. The notes he gives his king after the battle list the names and titles of the noblemen killed in both the armies but only the number of the 'other men' who died. However, his role in the scene is minimal; he himself is nameless, he has only one line to speak, and his only function is to provide the king with lists of the dead. The English cause at Agincourt is defined by the king himself, who associates it with the emergent values of manhood and personal achievement. Unlike the French herald, Henry declares that he wants his common subjects to mingle their blood with his:

> For he to-day that sheds his blood with me
> Shall be my brother; be he ne'er so vile,
> This day shall gentle his condition;
> And gentlemen in England, now a-bed,
> Shall think themselves accurs'd they were not here;
> And hold their manhoods cheap whiles any speaks
> That fought with us upon Saint Crispin's Day.
>
> (IV.iii.61–7)

A high moment in patriotic modern productions of the play, Henry's promise to his soldiers still helps to enforce the ideological regime it helped to produce: it denies social distinctions and relies on gender distinctions to identify England as the prototype of the modern nation state, a place where men are men and women are women, but all men are brothers. These are blatantly ideological claims whose 'truth' is established only by enormous cultural effort. They are none the less claims that have come to underpin the modern nation state and its attendant gender ideologies.

Like Henry's speech at Agincourt, the fact that the common woman of the English tavern provides a prototype for the role of the French woman in the royal palace identifies the project of modernisation with English imperialism. Just as the scenes in Quickly's tavern have already done in both parts of *Henry IV* and continue to do in *Henry V*, the scenes in Katherine's palace provide comic relief from the serious, masculine business of war. Both women bring considerable property to their new husbands – Pistol becomes the landlord of the tavern, Henry the lord of the French – but here again Quickly does it first. Even Katherine's language – a mangled English that is riddled with inadvertent sexual double entendres – has a prototype in Quickly's malapropisms.

Although Henry's claim to France requires the erasure of national difference, it is also identified as a specifically English project: the national identity that must be obliterated is French; the language the French princess must learn to speak is English. Describing the full-blown imperialism of the nineteenth century, Benedict Anderson characterises it as 'a certain inventive legerdemain ... required to ['affirm the identity of dynasty and nation'] and permit the empire to appear attractive in national drag'.[21] Anderson's suggestively gendered language has a remarkable prototype in Shakespeare's play, for the contradictions implicit in Henry's proto-imperialist project can be resolved only by reference to the imagined body of the French princess, which mystifies territorial expansion and naturalises dynastic marriage as heterosexual conquest. Here, as in later imperialist discourse, the territory to be conquered is imagined as the body of a woman, and the project of imperial expansion is conceived as a distinctively male activity. In learning English, the French princess is symbolically stripped of her clothing. The naked body which provides a 'natural' basis for the differences between male and female roles in modern society is the subject of Katherine's language lesson, which is almost entirely devoted to words for the parts of her body. The only exception is 'la robe', introduced at the end so both the French women can mispronounce its English translation. The English word *gown* becomes in the mouths of the Frenchwomen 'le count' (in the folio) or 'le coune' (in the quarto), thus ending the scene with an uproarious sexual joke that unambiguously specifies the purpose of the entire exercise. The scene, moreover, is designed not only to name Katherine's body but also to exhibit it – in Shakespeare's own version of 'national drag' – for the best way for the boy actor who played Katherine's part to make the French words comprehensible to an English audience would be to point, as he named each of the body parts, to the place on his own body where it was (or was imagined to be).

Both Katherine's language lesson and the scenes in the London tavern interrupt the historical narrative of Henry's French conquest, but in both cases the irrelevance of the comic interlude is only apparent. Act II begins with the Chorus's announcement that the English army is departing for France:

> The King is set from London, and the scene
> Is now transported, gentles, to Southampton;
> There is the playhouse now, there must you sit,
> And thence to France shall we convey you safe,
> And bring you back, charming the Narrow Seas
> To give you gentle pass; for if we may,
> We'll not offend one stomach with our play.
> (II.Cho.34–40)

That looks like the end of the Chorus, but another two lines, which sound like an afterthought, immediately follow: 'But till the King come forth, and not till then, / Unto Southampton do we shift our scene.' Many editors have speculated that the Chorus's final couplet and the London scene it introduces were, in fact, revisions to an original playscript that did not include them; but whatever their respective dates of composition, the tavern scene seems clearly designed to follow, and provide an implicit comment on, the opening Chorus in its entirety.

'Now all the youth of England are on fire', the Chorus began, 'and honor's thought / Reigns solely in the breast of every man' (II.Cho.1–4). No sooner does the Chorus finish than Nym and Bardolph take the stage and we learn about another contest for masculine honour, this one centring on the possession of the hostess, whom Pistol has just married despite her previous betrothal to Nym. Both England and France have already been personified as women (I.ii.155–65, 227) and defined as the subjects of masculine competition; but Pistol reinforces the connection when he parodically echoes the imagery the Chorus has just used, declaring that his 'cock is up, / And flashing fire will follow' (II.i.52–3). He also names what is at stake in both contests when he agrees at the end of the scene to settle his quarrel with Nym by paying the money he owes him, but only 'as manhood shall compound' (98). At the end of the play, Pistol loses his wife to venereal disease in the same scene where he loses his honour to Fluellen's cudgel (V.i). The name he uses for the disease, that bespeaks his wife's sexual promiscuity – 'malady of France' (82) – reiterates the association between the imperial dominance of the English nation and the domestic dominance of the English husband: a chaste wife would not have contracted the 'French' disease.

Honour and manhood are also at stake in Henry's determination to conquer France, a conquest that he defines in a curiously gendered simile. 'Or there we'll sit,' he declares,

> Ruling in large and ample empery
> O'er France and all her almost kingly dukedoms,
> Or lay these bones in an unworthy urn,
> Tombless, with no remembrance over them.
> Either our history shall with full mouth
> Speak freely of our acts, or else our grave,
> Like Turkish mute, shall have a tongueless mouth,
> Not worshipp'd with a waxen epitaph.
>   (I.ii.225–33)

Although this speech comes in Act I, before there has been any talk of marrying Katherine, Henry already thinks of France as a woman ('her') and defines his conquest as the necessary validation of his manhood. If he fails, he says, his grave, 'like Turkish mute, shall have a tongueless mouth.' This allusion to the bodily mutilation that deprives a eunuch in a seraglio of his manhood[22] also recalls Westmerland's description in *Henry IV, Part I* of the mutilation of the English soldiers following their defeat on a Welsh battlefield. The image of the waxen epitaph recalls the traditional textual basis of masculine authority but renders it ephemeral: the image of the Turkish mute implies a new, universal basis for that authority in embodied sexual difference but insists on its vulnerability. As the Turkish mute demonstrates, a body can be altered.

The victory Henry requires conflates military conquest with male sexual potency, and leads ineluctably, by the logic of performative masculinity, to the imagery and actuality of rape that Jeffords identifies as salient features of the modern discourse and modern practice of war.[23] The exclusion of women from the battlefield and their relegation to the roles of civilian victims in *Henry V* looks ahead to the increasing cultural insistence that because men and women have different bodies they have different roles to play in life. The language lesson, with its sexualisation of the imagined woman's body, hints at what was to become a dominant ideology of a gender hierarchy naturalised in embodied sexual difference.[24] The play also looks to the future when – in a connection unprecedented in Shakespeare's earlier history plays – military conquest is associated by the leaders of both the opposing armies with rape.

The association appears to be intentional, for the speech Henry delivers at the gates of Harfleur is Shakespeare's invention. Holinshed briefly describes the 'distresse' the inhabitants of Harfleur suffered when the English took the city, but there is no reference to rape in his account.[25] In Shakespeare's version, however, Henry warns the besieged citizens that unless they surrender, 'the flesh'd soldier, rough and hard of heart ... shall range / With conscience wide as hell, mowing, like grass / Your fresh fair virgins and your flow'ring infants.' He repeats the threat twice more: 'your pure maidens', he warns, will 'fall into the hand / Of hot and forcing violation'. 'Look to see / The blind and bloody soldier with foul hand / [Defile] the locks of your shrill-shriking daughters' (III.iii.11–14, 20–1, 33–5).[26]

The terms in which the victims are described, '*your* fresh fair virgins', '*your* pure maidens', and '*your* shrill-shriking daughters', clearly identify Henry's warning as a threat, through their property, to the *men* of Harfleur, an identification that is echoed later when Bourbon exhorts his fellow Frenchmen to return to battle.

> Shame and eternal shame, nothing but shame!
> Let us die! In once more! Back again!
> And he that will not follow Bourbon now,
> Let him go hence, and with his cap in hand
> Like a base pander hold the chamber-door
> Whilst [by a] slave, no gentler than my dog,
> His fairest daughter is contaminated.
>
> (IV.v.10–16)

Although Bourbon's warning lacks the pornographic redundancy and vivid details of Henry's threats to the citizens of Harfleur, it belongs to the same discourse. In both cases, as in Pistol and Nym's fight for possession of the hostess, the contest for manhood and honour takes the form of a contest for the sexual possession of women.

In *Henry V*, in fact, the entire French kingdom is represented as a woman to be conquered by the masculine force of the English army, a conceit that is implied by the placement of Katherine's language lesson immediately after Henry's speech at Harfleur and literalised in the final scene when Henry claims the French princess for his bride.[27] In terms that resonate with his threats at Harfleur, he jokes with the Duke of Burgundy that because 'love is blind and enforces', he, being a blind lover, 'cannot see many a French city for one fair French maid that stands in my way'. The French king replies obligingly that 'the cities [are] turn'd into a maid; for they are all girdled with maiden walls that war hath [never] ent'red (V.ii.300–1, 317–19, 321–3). In what might appear to be, but is certainly not, a *non sequitur*, Henry replies with the blunt question, 'Shall Kate be my wife?' and, having received the desired response, reiterates the connection one more time:

> I am content, so the maiden cities you talk of may wait on her; so the maid that stood in the way for my wish shall show me the way to my will.   (324–8)

Branagh's film nicely captures the threat of sexual violence overshadowing Henry's future bride, but although Henry describes his courtship in the language of rape and warfare, it is important to emphasise that the marriage is not a rape. Burgundy's description of France in the final scene as an unhusbanded garden that can be saved only by union with England implies a necessary ideological distinction between the benevolent rule of a husband and the destructive conquest of a rapist: both Katherine and France, he implies, need to be husbanded by Henry.[28] It is, however, even more important to Henry that the marriage take place, for it is only by legal possession of Katherine that he can acquire legitimate authority over France and, through it, over England.

From the beginning of the play Henry has defined the conquest of France as the means by which he will secure the royal legitimacy that he could not inherit from his usurping father. Lacking a legitimate patrimonial title to the name of king, Henry secures it by matrimonial conquest. 'No king of England, if not king of France' (II.ii.193): it is only by marrying Katherine that he can legitimate both titles. The final concession Henry requires from the French

king is that he name him, in writing, in both French and Latin, as
his son and the heir to France. 'Let that one article rank with the
rest', Henry demands, 'And thereupon give me your daughter'
(V.ii.346–7).[29] The contract by which Henry finally acquires the
royal father who can legitimise his identity as king has all the familiar attributes of what Gayle Rubin has identified as the traffic in
women; but Katherine also has all the traditional attributes of a
rape victim. Sexualised from the moment of her first appearance on
stage, her destiny is already inevitable – it has already been described, in fact, in the immediately preceding scene when Henry
told the citizens of Harfleur what would happen to their daughters
when his soldiers conquered the city.[30] The courtship scene at the
end of the play comes as close as it can to enacting the predicted
rape. First characterised in language that associates her with the
conquered cities of France, Katherine is then subjected to a symbolic rape when Henry forces her to endure his kiss. From that
moment on, she has not another word to say. Silenced, like
Philomel and like Shakespeare's own Lavinia, Katherine provides
the proof of Henry's manhood as well as the legitimation of his
identity as king. The modernity of this conflation probably helps to
explain the emphasis that the Harfleur speech, the language lesson,
and the wooing scene have received in recent criticism. It also helps
to explain the effectiveness and accessibility of Kenneth Branagh's
Henry V, a film which reveals how thoroughly Shakespeare's play
anticipates the terms in which we have come to think out sexuality
and its relationship to male and female identities. Shakespeare and
his audiences did not, however, take the sex–gender arrangements
of *Henry V* for granted. They had to travel a long way to get there.

In Shakespeare's earlier history plays, where masculine authority
is still conceived as the product of patrilineal succession, royal marriages never turn out well. The marriage of Henry VI, for instance,
is repeatedly characterised as a 'fatal' mistake, the reason for his
loss, first, of manhood and royal authority and finally of the crown
he inherited from his father. In fact, the narratives in the earlier
plays can never reach their desired conclusions until female characters are banished from the stage of history. But once personal performance displaces patrilineal genealogy as the basis for male
authority, the narrative reaches its desired conclusion when the
hero acquires a wife. At the end of *Henry VI, Part I*, Joan is hustled
off the stage to be burned at the stake. In *Henry V* Shakespeare lit-
eralises the Pauline injunction, 'It is better to marry than to burn' (I

Corinthians 7.9) when another French woman is hustled on to the stage to provide a bride for the conquering English hero and a focus for the sexual fantasies of the audience.

Naturalised in the discourse of biological sexual difference, the supposedly instinctive desire of men to rape and the assumed physical vulnerability of women to be raped have provided a remarkably durable rationale for male heterosexual privilege. The images of rape that characterise Henry's acquisition of a wife establish, almost at the moment of its conception, the connection between the nascent bourgeois ideal of heterosexual marriage and the savage fantasies of rape that attend it.[31]

From *Engendering a Nation: A Feminist Account of Shakespeare's English Histories* (London: Routledge, 1997), pp. 195–215.

NOTES

[Jean E. Howard and Phyllis Rackin argue that the second tetralogy of Shakespearean history plays depicts not a historical time prior to the Wars of the Roses, but the early modern world in which the plays were produced – a moment which is often considered to be the threshold of modernity. In these plays, the construction of royal masculinity both redefines monarchy and validates an emergent form of masculinity for Shakespeare's audience. The extract here, from the final pages of the book, moves from an exploration of the violent heterosexual masculinity of war, via a consideration of the gender ideologies that require combat to be a men-only activity, to an account of the participation of women in battle in the first tetralogy, and their confinement to a feminine domestic space in the second. The authors conclude by stressing the extent to which Henry's attitude to France and to Katherine both anticipates and installs modern regimes of gender ideology.   Ed.]

1. Lance Wilcox, 'Katherine of France as Victim and Bride', *Shakespeare Studies*, 17 (1985), 61–76.

2. Susan Jeffords, 'Performative Masculinities, or, "After a Few Times You Won't be Afraid of Rape at All"', *Discourse*, 13 (1991), 102–18.

3. The Tailhook scandal resulted from an attempted cover-up at the highest levels of the American navy of sexual assaults upon women by naval officers at their 1991 convention in Las Vegas, Nevada.

4. Susan Jeffords, *The Remasculinization of America: Gender and the Vietnam War* (Bloomington, IN: Indiana University Press, 1989).

5. Jeffords, 'Performative Masculinities', pp. 108–9.

6. Tania Modleski, *Feminism without Women: Culture and Criticism in a 'Postfeminist' Age* (New York: Routledge, 1991), p. 61.

7. Michael Hattaway (ed.), *The Second Part of King Henry VI* (Cambridge: Cambridge University Press, 1991), p. 189n.

8. Native men had far fewer opportunities to rape European women than European male colonisers had to rape native women. Moreover, the North American woodland tribes that English settlers encountered in Virginia and New England did not have a rape culture, unlike their European colonisers. Mary Rowlandson's account of her four-month captivity by Indians is a vivid case in point. Rowlandson's insistence that although she was starved and beaten, she was never sexually threatened by her captors reveals a profound difference between her own culture and that of the Indians: Rowlandson had assumed, and she knew that her readers would assume, that she would 'naturally' be raped by her captors. See *A Narrative of the Captivity and Restauration of Mrs Mary Rowlandson* (1682).

9. A comparison between Shakespeare's text and its source at this point is instructive. Shakespeare's account of Jack Cade's rebellion draws heavily on accounts of the even earlier Peasants' Revolt in the time of Richard II. Cade's fleeting reference to the sexual oppression by the nobility is the only trace of a detailed account that Holinshed supplies as a possible explanation for the beginnings of the rebellion: Parliament having passed a levy on every man and woman above the age of sixteen, a tax gatherer came to the house of John Tiler, the man who, as leader of the revolt, was to assume the name of Jack Straw. Tiler had 'a fair young maid to his daughter', but Tiler's wife informed the officer that the girl was not yet of age to be taxed. Holinshed notes that the tax 'monie was in common speech said to be due for all those that were undergrowne, bicause that yoong persons as well of the man as of the womankind, coming to the age of fourteen or fifteene yeares, have commonlie haire growing foorth about those privie parts, which for honesties sake nature hath taught us to cover and keepe secret. The officer therefore not satisfied with the mothers excuse, said he would feele whether hir daughter were of lawfull age or not, and therewith begin to misuse the maid, and search further than honestie would have permitted.' The cries of the outraged mother bring her husband home, whereupon he kills the officer and the rebellion begins. An alternative explanation, also supplied by Holinshed, states that the rebellion was started by 'one Thomas Baker' after 'one of the kings servants named John Leg, with three of his fellowes, practiced to feele young maids whether they were undergrowne'. Raphael Holinshed, *Chronicles of England, Scotland and Ireland*, 6 vols (1587), 2:735–6.

The only vestige of these accounts in Shakespeare's text is the fleeting reference to sexual oppression in the list of unsubstantiated charges against the nobility that Cade uses to stir the mob to rebellion.

The anonymous play *The Life and Death of Jacke Strawe* (1593), by contrast, opens with a confrontation between Strawe and the tax collector over the very incident that Holinshed describes. Strawe denounces the collector for his 'abuse [of] the poor people of the Countrie. / But chiefest of all vilde villaine as thou art, / To play so unmanly and beastly a part, / As to search my daughter thus in my presence' (I.i.25–8).

10. Diane Wolfthal shows in '"A Hue and a Cry": Medieval Rape Imagery and its Transformation', *Art Bulletin*, 75 (1993), 39–64, that 'Northern European [pictorial] images of rape undergo a change in tone and content over the course of the fifteenth and early sixteenth centuries. Early renderings more clearly condemn the rapist' (57). In later paintings, 'the "victim" is shown as a willing, in fact, an eager partner', and the rape is shown 'simply as an amorous affair, with no hint of violence'. 'Beginning in the late fifteenth century,' women 'in Northern European art ... are increasingly depicted as seductresses. Even models of chastity become temptresses. For example the heroine Tomyris, traditionally represented fully clothed, is by the turn of the century shown nude' (60). Moreover, while earlier representations of rapes tend to focus on the victims, 'the rapist is now the focus' (62).

11. *Henry V* is also more modern in its focus on the king's character. Richmond's character is not an issue in *Richard III*, but the issue of Henry's character is foregrounded in both parts of *Henry IV* as well as *Henry V*, and it is represented in prototypical modern terms. Both the dispute with Williams in IV.i and its resolution in IV.iii, for instance, are based on the public/private binary, which divides 'Henry the king' from 'Henry the man'. The modernity of this issue is attested by the fact that the enigma of Henry's characterisation has dominated modern critical discussions of the plays.

12. Jeffords, 'Performative Masculinities'. The same restrictions apply, of course, to theatrical representations. On 18 March 1993, the *Philadelphia Inquirer* reported a lawsuit to force the American National Park Service to permit women to participate in re-enactments of Civil War battlefields. The plaintiff in the suit was able to produce documentation on about 125 women who actually enlisted during the war under male aliases, but the officials of the Park services told her, 'We don't allow women in uniform here', and informed her that she could only participate if she removed the uniform and took the part of one of the 'local farm women or visiting ladies seeking loved ones'.

13. B. C. Hacker, 'Women and Military Institutions in Early Modern Europe: a Reconnaissance', *Signs*, 6 (1981), 643–71 (645).

14. Ibid., 643.

15. Ibid.; Philippe Contamine, *War in the Middle Ages*, trans. Michael Jones (Oxford: Basil Blackwell, 1984), p. 241.

16. Contamine, *War in the Middle Ages*, p. 242.

17. Ibid., p. 241.

18. Like many other women, the historical Elinor also fought in the Crusades. See ibid., p. 241; Jessica Amanda Salmonson, *The Encyclopaedia of Amazons: Women Warriors from Antiquity in the Modern Era* (New York: Doubleday, 1992), p. 79; and Amy Kelly, *Eleanor of Aquitaine and the Four Kings* (New York: Vintage, 1957), p. 45.

19. Gabrielle Bernhard Jackson, 'Topical Ideology: Witches, Amazons, and Shakespeare's Joan of Arc', *English Literary Renaissance*, 18 (1988), 40–65(54).

20. As Simon Shepherd points out in *Amazons and Warrior Women: Varieties of Feminism in Seventeenth-Century Drama* (Brighton: Harvester, 1981), 'the connection of Amazons with lust has a long history' (p. 16). See also Ania Loomba, *Gender, Race, Renaissance Drama* (New York: St Martin's Press, 1989), p. 47, and S. C. Shapiro, 'Amazons, Hermaphrodites, and Plain Monsters: The "Masculine" Woman in English Satire and Social Criticism, 1580–1640', *Atlantis*, 13 (1987), 65–76.

21. Benedict Anderson, *Imagined Communities: Reflections on the Origin and Spread of Nationalism* (London: Verso, 1983), p. 83.

22. Gary Taylor (ed.), *Henry V* (Oxford: Oxford University Press, 1984), p. 133n.

23. Jeffords, 'Performative Masculinities'.

24. As Thomas Laqueur has argued, the dominant gender ideology at the time this play was written was not yet grounded in embodied sexual difference, for the Galenic conception of male and female bodies as essentially homologous meant that biological sex did not yet 'provide a solid foundation for the cultural category of gender but constantly threatens to subvert it'. Thomas Laqueur, *Making Sex: Body and Gender from the Greeks to Freud* (Cambridge, MA: Harvard University Press, 1990), p. 124.

25. Holinshed, *Chronicles*, 3:73–4.

26. Here too Shakespeare anticipates some of the modern narratives of performative masculinity described by Jeffords in 'Performative Masculinities'. She points out that in the 1986 film *Opposing Force* 'As viewers we are asked to watch the performance of rape from the point of view of the man who is not raping, the "friend"' (113), but the enemy–friend binary is, by the logic of performative masculinity, constantly subject to redefinition as benevolent male figures become rapists and rapists reform (111–15).

27. See Wilcox, 'Katherine of France as Victim and Bride'. The same trope is suggested in the representation of England in I.ii.158 as a 'mourning widow', subject to invasion by the Scot 'with ... fullness of his force' (150), but it is much less fully and consistently developed. Lines 155 and 158 use feminine pronouns for England, but the 'her' in line 163 did not appear until the eighteenth century. The folio has 'their', and the quartos have 'your'.

28. Barbara Hodgdon, *The End Crowns All: Closure and Contradiction in Shakespeare's History* (Princeton, NJ: Princeton University Press, 1991), pp. 201–3.

29. This transaction transforms the crown into private property that the king can leave to Henry even though the Dolphin is his son (ibid., p. 203). This is in sharp contrast to the negative representations in earlier plays, such as *Richard II* and *Henry VI, Part III*, of royal attempts to interrupt the line of patrimonial succession by bequeathing the crown to usurpers.

30. Wilcox, 'Katherine of France as Victim and Bride', 66.

31. For many other examples of this coupling, see Susanne Wofford, 'The Social Aesthetics of Rape: Closural Violence in Boccaccio and Botticelli' in D. Quint *et al.* (eds), *Creative Imitation: New Essays on Renaissance Literature in Honour of Thomas M. Greene* (Binghamton, NY: State University of New York Press, 1992). Wofford demonstrates that 'the representation of scenes of violence against women' as wedding entertainment or on wedding gifts 'is attested to rather widely in early modern culture' (194 *et passim*). Especially striking is her description of the popularity of rape scenes as decorations on the wedding chests (*cassoni*) used in fifteenth-century Florentine marriages. Catherine Belsey has found an interesting counterpart to the *cassoni* in a needlework panel representing Tereus and Procne which dates from the end of the sixteenth century (private communication).

5

How to Read
The Merchant of Venice
without being Heterosexist

ALAN SINFIELD

It has been recognised for a long time that *The Merchant of Venice* is experienced as insulting by Jewish people, who constitute a minority in Western Europe and North America. So powerful, though, is the reputation of Shakespeare's all-embracing 'humanity' that this scandal has often been set aside. Nevertheless, in 1994 a newspaper article entitled 'Shylock, Unacceptable Face of Shakespeare?' described how directors were acknowledging that the text requires radical alterations before it can be produced in good faith.[1] David Thacker at the Royal Shakespeare Company was changing some of Shylock's most famous lines and moving scenes around. And Jude Kelly at the West Yorkshire Playhouse was presenting a Portia ready to embrace racist attitudes in her determination to be worthy of her father and a Jessica weeping inconsolably at the end as she laments her loss of her Jewish heritage.

For some commentators, it is a sign of the deterioration of our cultures that minority out-groups should feel entitled to challenge the authority of Shakespeare. Christopher Booker, writing in the *Daily Telegraph* in 1992, complained bitterly about an English Shakespeare Company production of *The Merchant* set in 1930s Italy, with Shylock as a suave, sophisticated modern Jewish businessman confronted by fascists. 'In other words,' Booker writes, 'the producer has given up on any distasteful (but Shakespearean) idea of presenting

Shylock as an archetypal cringing old miser. He really had to be more sympathetic than the "Christians".' To Booker this was 'bleatings about racism', whereas 'Shakespeare so wonderfully evokes something infinitely more real and profound ... a cosmic view of human nature which is just as true now as it was in his own day'.[2]

The problem is not limited to Jewish people. The Prince of Morocco is made to begin by apologising for his colour – 'Mislike me not for my complexion,' he pleads (II.i.1), taking it for granted that Portia will be prejudiced. And he is right, for already she has declared her distaste: 'if he have the condition of a saint, and the complexion of a devil, I had rather he should shrive me than wive me' (I.ii.123–5); and after Morocco has bet on the wrong casket she concludes: 'Let all of his complexion choose me so' (II.vii.79). And how might gay men regard the handling of Antonio's love for Bassanio, or the traffic in boys that involves Launcelot, the disguised Jessica, the disguised Nerissa and the disguised Portia?

The question of principle is how readers not situated squarely in the mainstream of Western culture today may relate to such a powerful cultural icon as Shakespeare. In a notable formulation, Kathleen McLuskie points out that the pattern of 'good' and 'bad' daughters in *King Lear* offers no point of entry to the ideas about women that a feminist criticism might want to develop; such criticism 'is restricted to exposing its own exclusion from the text'.[3] This challenge has caused some discomfort: must exclusion from Shakespeare be added to the other disadvantages that women experience in our societies? But it has not, I think, been successfully answered. In this essay I pursue the question as it strikes a gay man.

I ANTONIO vs PORTIA

As W. H. Auden suggested in an essay in *The Dyer's Hand* in 1962, *The Merchant of Venice* makes best sense if we regard Antonio as in love with Bassanio.[4] In the opening scene their friends hint broadly at it. Then, as soon as Bassanio arrives, the others know they should leave the two men together – 'We leave you now with better company. ... My Lord Bassanio, since you have found Antonio / We two will leave you' (I.i.59, 69–70). Only Gratiano is slow to go, being too foolish to realise that he is intruding (I.i.73–118). As soon as he departs, the tone and direction of the dialogue switch from formal banter to intimacy, and the cause of Antonio's sadness emerges:

> Well, tell me now what lady is the same
> To whom you swore a secret pilgrimage –
> That you to-day promis'd to tell me of?
> (I.i.119–21)

Bassanio moves quickly to reassure his friend and to ask his help: 'to you Antonio / I owe the most in money and in love' (I.i.130–1). The mercenary nature of Bassanio's courtship, which troubles mainstream commentators who are looking for a 'good' heterosexual relationship, is Antonio's reassurance. It allows him to believe that Bassanio will continue to value their love, and gives him a crucial role as banker of the enterprise.

Whether Antonio's love is what we call sexual is a question which, this essay will show, is hard to frame, let alone answer. But certainly his feelings are intense. When Bassanio leaves for Belmont, as Salerio describes it, he offers to 'make some speed / Of his return'. 'Do not so,' Antonio replies:

> And even there (his eye being big with tears),
> Turning his face, he puts his hand behind him,
> And with affection wondrous sensible
> He wrung Bassanio's hand, and so they parted.
> (II.viii.37–8, 46–9)

The intensity, it seems, is not altogether equal. As Auden observes in his poem 'The More Loving One', the language of love celebrates mutuality but it is unusual for two people's loves to match precisely:

> If equal affection cannot be,
> Let the more loving one be me.[5]

Antonio the merchant, like Antonio in *Twelfth Night* and the Shakespeare of the sonnets, devotes himself to a relatively casual, pampered younger man of a higher social class.

In fact, Antonio in the *Merchant* seems to welcome the chance to sacrifice himself: 'pray God Bassanio come / To see me pay his debt, and then I care not' (III.iii.35–6). *Then* Bassanio would have to devote himself to Antonio:

> You cannot better be employ'd Bassanio,
> Than to live still and write mine epitaph.
> (IV.i.117–18)

As Keith Geary observes, Antonio's desperate bond with Shylock is his way of holding on to Bassanio;[6] when Portio saves Antonio's life, Lawrence W. Hyman remarks, she is preventing what would have been a spectacular case of the 'greater love' referred to in the Bible (John 15:13), when a man lays down his life for his friend.[7]

That theme of amatory sacrifice contributes to an air of homoerotic excess, especially in the idea of being bound and inviting physical violation. When Bassanio introduces Antonio to Portia as the man 'To whom I am so infinitely bound', she responds:

> You should in all sense be much bound to him,
> For (as I hear) he was much bound for you.
> (V.i.135–7)

At the start, Antonio lays open his entire self to Bassanio:

> be assur'd
> My purse, my person, my extremest means
> Lie all unlock'd to your occasions.
> (I.i.137–9)

Transferring this credit – 'person' included – to Shylock's bond makes it more physical, more dangerous and more erotic:

> let the forfeit
> Be nominated for an equal pound
> Of your fair flesh, to be cut off and taken
> In what part of your body pleaseth me.
> (I.iii.144–7)

In the court, eventually, it is his breast that Antonio is required to bare to the knife, but in a context where apparent boys may be disguised girls and Portia's suitors have to renounce marriage altogether if they choose the wrong casket, Shylock's penalty sounds like castration. Indeed, Antonio offers himself to the knife as 'a tainted wether of the flock'; that is, a castrated ram (IV.i.114).

The seriousness of the love between Antonio and Bassanio is manifest, above all, in Portia's determination to contest it. Simply, she is at a disadvantage because of her father's casket device, and wants to ensure that her husband really is committed to her. The key critical move, which Hyman and Geary make, is to reject the sentimental notion of Portia as an innocent, virtuous, 'Victorian' heroine. Harry Berger regards her 'noble' speeches as manipulations: 'Against Antonio's failure to get himself crucified, we can place Portia's divine power of mercifixion; she never rains but she pours.' Finally, she mercifies Antonio by giving him back his ships.[8]

Antonio's peril moves Bassanio to declare a preference for him over Portia:

> Antonio, I am married to a wife
> Which is as dear to me as life itself,
> But life itself, my wife, and all the world,
> I would lose all, ay sacrifice them all
> Here to this devil, to deliver you.

Portia, standing by as a young doctor, is not best pleased:

> Your wife would give you little thanks for that
> If she were by to hear you make the offer.
> (IV.i.278–85)

It is to contest Antonio's status as lover that Portia, in her role of young doctor, demands of Bassanio the ring which she had given him in her role of wife. Antonio, unaware that he is falling for a device, takes the opportunity to claim a priority in Bassanio's love:

> My Lord Bassanio, let him have the ring,
> Let his deservings and my love withal
> Be valued 'gainst your wife's commandement.
> (IV.ii.445–7)

The last act of the play is Portia's assertion of her right to Bassanio. Her strategy is purposefully heterosexist: in disallowing Antonio's sacrifice as a plausible reason for parting with the ring, she disallows the entire seriousness of male love. She is as offhand with Antonio as she can be with a guest:

> Sir, you are very welcome to our house:
> It must appear in other ways than words,
> Therefore I scant this breathing courtesy.
> (V.i.139–41)

She will not even admit Antonio's relevance: 'I am th'unhappy subject of these quarrels', he observes; 'Sir, grieve not you, – you are welcome not withstanding', she abruptly replies (V.i.238–9). Once more, self-sacrifice seems to be Antonio's best chance of staying in the game, so he binds himself in a different project: *not* to commit his body again to Bassanio in a way that will claim a status that challenges Portia:

> I once did lend my body for his wealth,
> Which but for him that had your husband's ring
> Had quite miscarried. I dare be bound again,
> My soul upon the forfeit, that your lord
> Will never more break faith advisedly.
> (V.i.249–53)

Portia seizes brutally on the reminiscence of the earlier bond: 'Then you shall be his surety' (V.i.254). Antonio's submission is what she has been waiting for. Now she restores Bassanio's status as husband by revealing that she has the ring after all, and Antonio's viability as merchant – and his ability to return to his trade in Venice – by giving him letters that she has been withholding.

A gay reader might think: well, never mind; Bassanio wasn't worth it, and with his wealth restored, Antonio will easily find another impecunious upper-class friend to sacrifice himself to. But, for most audiences and readers, the air of 'happy ending' suggests that Bassanio's movement towards heterosexual relations is in the necessary, the right direction (like Shylock's punishment, perhaps). As Coppélia Kahn reads the play, 'In Shakespeare's psychology, men first seek to mirror themselves in a homoerotic attachment ... then to confirm themselves through difference, in a bond with the opposite sex – the marital bond.'[9] And Janet Adelman, in a substantial analysis of male bonding in Shakespeare's comedies, finds that 'We do not move directly from family bonds to marriage without an intervening period in which our friendships with same-sex friends help us to establish our identities.'[10] To heterosexually identified readers this might not seem an exceptional thought, but for the gay man it is a slap in the face of a very familiar kind. 'You can have these passions,' it says, 'but they are not sufficient, they should be a stage on the way to something else. So don't push it.'

To be sure, Kahn points out that 'it takes a strong, shrewd woman like Portia to combat the continuing appeal of such ties between men'.[11] And Adelman remarks the tendency towards casuistical 'magical restitutions' and the persistence of 'tensions that comedy cannot resolve'.[12] So hetero-patriarchy is not secured without difficulty or loss. None the less, when Adelman writes 'We do not move directly ... to marriage', the gay man may ask, 'Who are "We"?' And when Kahn says 'men first seek to mirror themselves in a homoerotic attachment', the gay man may wonder whether he is being positioned as not-man, or just forgotten altogether. If Antonio is excluded from the good life at the end of the *Merchant*, so the gay man is excluded from the play's address. The fault does not lie with Kahn and Adelman (though in the light of recent work in lesbian and gay studies they might want to formulate their thoughts rather differently). They have picked up well enough the mood and tendency of the play, as most readers and audiences would agree. It is the Shakespearean text that is reconfirming the marginalisation of an already marginalised group.

II PROPERTY AND SODOMY

The reader may be forgiven for thinking that, for a commentator who has claimed to be excluded from the *Merchant*, this gay man has already found quite a lot to say. Perhaps the love that dared not speak its name is becoming the love that won't shut up. In practice, there are (at least) two routes through the *Merchant* for out-groups. One involves pointing out the mechanisms of exclusion in our cultures – how the circulation of Shakespearean texts may reinforce the privilege of some groups and the subordination of others. I have just been trying to do this. Another involves exploring the ideological structures in the playtexts – of class, race, ethnicity, gender and sexuality – that facilitate these exclusions. These structures will not be the same as the ones we experience today, but they may throw light upon our circumstances and stimulate critical awareness of how our life-possibilities are constructed.[13]

In *The Merchant*, the emphasis on the idea of being bound displays quite openly the way ideological structures work. Through an intricate network of enticements, obligations and interdictions – in terms of wealth, family, gender, patronage and law – this culture sorts out who is to control property and other human relations. Portia, Jessica and Launcelot are bound as daughters and sons; Morocco and Arragon as suitors; Antonio and Bassanio as friends, Gratiano as friend or dependant, Nerissa as dependant or servant, and Launcelot as servant; Antonio, Shylock and even the Duke are bound by the law; and the Venetians, Shylock rather effectively remarks, have no intention of freeing their slaves (IV.i.90–8).

Within limits, these bonds may be negotiable: the Duke may commission a doctor to devise a way round the law, friendships may be redefined, servants may get new masters, women and men may contract marriages, Jessica can even get away from her father, though only because he is very unpopular and Lorenzo has very powerful friends; they 'seal love's bonds newmade' (II.iv.6). Otherwise, trying to move very far out of your place is severely punished, as Shylock finds. It is so obvious that this framework of ideology and coercion is operating to the advantage of the rich over the poor, the established over the impotent, men over women, and insiders over outsiders, that directors have been able to slant productions of the *Merchant* against the dominant reading, making Bassanio cynical, Portia manipulative and the Venetians arrogant and racist.

The roles of same-sex passion in this framework should not be taken for granted (I use the terms 'same-sex' and 'cross-sex' to evade anachronistic modern concepts). For us today, Eve Sedgwick shows this in her book *Between Men*, homosexuality polices the entire boundaries of gender and social organisation. Above all, it exerts 'leverage over the channels of bonding between all pairs of men'. Male–male relations, and hence male–female relations, are held in place by fear of homosexuality – by fear of crossing that 'invisible, carefully blurred, always-already-crossed line' between being 'a man's man' and being 'interested in men'.[14] We do not know what the limits of our sexual potential are, but we do believe that they are likely to be disturbing and disruptive; that is how our cultures position sexuality. Fear even of thinking homosexually serves to hold it all in place. So one thing footballers must *not* be when they embrace is sexually excited; the other thing they mustn't be is in love. But you can never be quite sure; hence the virulence of homophobia.

If this analysis makes sense in Western societies today, and I believe it does, we should not assume it for other times and places. As Sedgwick observes, ancient Greek cultures were different.[15] In our societies whether you are gay or not has become crucial – the more so since lesbians and gay men have been asserting themselves. An intriguing thought, therefore, is that in early modern England same-sex relations *were not terribly important*. In *As You Like It* and *Twelfth Night*, homoeroticism is part of the fun of the wooing ('Ganymede', the name taken by Rosalind, was standard for a male same-sex love-object); but it wouldn't be fun if such scenarios were freighted with the anxieties that people experience today. In Ben Jonson's play *Poetaster*, Ovid Senior expostulates: 'What! Shall I have my son a stager now? An engle for players? A gull, a rook, a shot-clog to make suppers, and be laughed at?'[16] It is taken for granted that boys are sexual partners (engles) for players; it is only one of the demeaning futures that await young Ovid if he takes to the stage. Moralists who complained about theatre and sexual licence took it for granted that boys are sexually attractive.

'Sodomy' was the term which most nearly approaches what is now in England called 'gross indecency'; it was condemned almost universally in legal and religious discourses, and the penalty upon conviction was death. Perhaps because of this extreme situation, very few cases are recorded. Today, staking out a gay cruising space is a sure-fire way for a police force to improve its rate of convictions. But in the Home Counties through the reigns of Elizabeth I and James I – sixty-eight years – only six men are recorded as having been indicted for sodomy. Only one was convicted, and that was for an offence involving a five-year-old boy.[17]

In his book *Homosexual Desire in Shakespeare's England*, Bruce R. Smith shows that while legal and religious edicts against sodomy were plain, paintings and fictive texts sometimes indicate a more positive attitude. This derived mainly from the huge prestige, in artistic and intellectual discourses, of ancient Greek and Roman culture where same-sex passion is taken for granted.[18] Smith locates six 'cultural scenarios': heroic friendship, men and boys (mainly in pastoral and educational contexts), playful androgyny (mainly in romances and festivals), transvestism (mainly in satirical contexts), master–servant relations, and an emergent homosexual subjectivity (in Shakespeare's sonnets). Within those scenarios, it seems, men did not necessarily connect their practices with the monstrous crime of sodomy – partly, perhaps, because that was so unthinkable. As Jonathan Goldberg emphasises, the goal of analysis is 'to see what the category [sodomy] enabled and disenabled, and to negotiate the complex terrains, the mutual implications of prohibition and production'.[19] The point is hardly who did what with whom, but the contexts in which anxieties about sodomy might be activated. So whether the friendships of men such as Antonio and Bassanio should be regarded as involving a homoerotic element is not just a matter of what people did in private hundreds of years ago; it is a matter of definition within a sex-gender system that we only partly comprehend.

Stephen Orgel asks: 'why were women more upsetting than boys to the English?' That is, given the complaints that boy-actors incite lascivious thoughts in men and women spectators, why were not women performers employed – as they were in Spain and Italy? Orgel's answer is that boys were used because they were less dangerous; they were erotic, but that was less threatening than the eroticism of women. So this culture 'did not display a morbid fear of homosexuality. Anxiety about the fidelity of women, on the other hand, does seem to have been strikingly prevalent'.[20] Leontes and Polixenes lived guiltlessly together, we are told in *The Winter's Tale*, until they met the women who were to be their wives (I.ii.69–74). The main faultlines ran through cross-sex relations.

Because women may bear children, relations between women and men affected the regulation of lineage, alliance and property, and hence offered profound potential disruptions to the social order and the male psyche. Same-sex passion was dangerous if, as in the instance of Christopher Marlowe's *Edward II*, it was allowed to interfere with other responsibilities. Otherwise, it was thought compatible with marriage and perhaps preferable to cross-sex infidelity. The preoccupation, in writing of this period, is with women disturbing the system – resisting arranged marriages, running off with the wrong man, not bearing (male) children, committing adultery, producing illegitimate offspring, becoming widows and exercising the power of that position. In comedies things turn out happily, in tragedies sadly. But, one way or the other, Shakespearean plays, as much as the rest of the culture, are obsessively concerned with dangers that derive from women.

'We'll play with them the first boy for a thousand ducats', Gratiano exclaims, betting on whether Nerissa or Portia will bear the first boy-child (III.ii.213–14). As Orgel remarks, patriarchy does not oppress only women; a patriarch is not just a man, he is the head of a family or tribe who rules by paternal right.[21] To be sure, women are exchanged in the interest of property relations in Shakespearean plays, as in the society that produced them. But the lives of young, lower-class and outsider men are determined as well. In *The Merchant*, as everywhere in the period, we see a traffic in boys who, because they are less significant, are moved around the employment-patronage system more fluently than women. Class exploitation was almost unchallenged; everyone – men as much as women – had someone to defer to, usually in the household where they had to live. The most likely supposition is that, just as cross-sex relations took place all the time – Launcelot is accused, in passing, of getting a woman with child (III.v.35–6) – same-sex passion also was widely indulged.[22]

Traffic in boys occurs quite casually in *The Merchant*. Launcelot is a likely lad. He manages to square it with his conscience to leave his master Shylock, but it is unclear where he will go (II.ii.1–30). He runs into his father, who indentured Launcelot to Shylock and is bringing a present for the master to strengthen the bond. Launcelot persuades him to divert the gift to Bassanio, who is providing 'rare new liveries', for the expedition to Belmont (II.ii.104–5). The father attempts to interest Bassanio in the boy, but it transpires that Shylock has already traded him: 'Shylock thy master spoke with me this day, / And hath preferr'd thee' (II.ii.138–9). Nor is Launcelot the only young man Bassanio picks up in this scene: Gratiano presents his own suit and gets a ticket to Belmont conditional upon good behaviour. And when Jessica assumes the guise of a boy, the appearance is of another privileged young man, Lorenzo, taking a boy into his service and giving him new livery: 'Descend, for you must be my torch-bearer. ... Even in the lovely garnish of a boy' (II.vi.40,45). When the young doctor claims Portia's ring from Bassanio for services rendered, therefore, a pattern is confirmed.

My point is not that the dreadful truth of the *Merchant* is here uncovered: it is really about traffic in boys. Rather, that such traffic is casual, ubiquitous and hardly remarkable. It becomes significant in its resonances for the relationship between Antonio and Bassanio because Portia, subject to her father's will, has reason to feel insecure about the affection of her stranger-husband.

III FRIENDLY RELATIONS

Heroic friendship is one of Smith's six 'cultural scenarios' for same-sex relations.[23] In Shakespeare, besides the sonnets, it is represented most vividly in the bond between Coriolanus and Aufidius in *Coriolanus*:

> Know thou first,
> I lov'd the maid I married; never man
> Sigh'd truer breath; but that I see thee here,
> Thou noble thing, more dances my rapt heart
> Than when I first my wedded mistress saw
> Bestride my threshold.
>
> (IV.v.114–19)[24]

Unlike Portia, Aufidius's wife is not there to resent him finding his warrior-comrade more exciting that she.

In his essay 'Homosexuality and the Signs of Male Friendship in Elizabethan England', Alan Bray explores the scope of the 'friend'.[25] Even as marriage was involved in alliances of property and influence, male friendship informed, through complex obligations, networks of extended family, companions, clients, suitors and those influential in high places. Claudio in *Measure for Measure* explains why he and Juliet have not made public their marriage vows:

> This we came not to
> Only for propagation of a dower
> Remaining in the coffer of her friends,
> From whom we thought it meet to hide our love
> Till time had made them for us.
>
> (I.ii.138–42)

On the one hand, it is from friends that one anticipates a dowry; on the other hand, they must be handled sensitively. Compare the combination of love and instrumentality in the relationship between Bassanio and Antonio: the early modern sense of 'friend' covered a broad spectrum.

While the entirely respectable concept of the friend was supposed to have nothing to do with the officially abhorred concept of the sodomite, in practice they tended to overlap.[26] Friends shared beds, they embraced and kissed; such intimacies reinforced the network of obligations and their public performance would often be part of the effect. So the proper signs of friendship could be the same as those of same-sex passion. In instances where accusations of sodomy were aroused, very likely it was because of some hostility towards one or both parties, rather than because their behaviour was altogether different from that of others who were not so accused.

The fact that the text of the *Merchant* gives no plain indication that the love between Antonio and Bassanio is informed by erotic passion does not mean that such passion was inconceivable, then; it may well mean that it didn't require particular presentation as a significant category. What is notable, though, is that Portia has no hesitation in envisaging a sexual relationship between Bassanio and the young doctor: 'I'll have that doctor for my bedfellow', she declares, recognising an equivalence (V.i.33). She develops the idea:

> Let not that doctor e'er come near my house –
> Since he hath got the jewel that I loved,
> And that which you did swear to keep for me,
>
> (V.i.223–5)

The marriage of Bassanio and Portia is unconsummated and 'jewel' is often genital in Shakespearean writing: the young doctor has had the sexual attentions which were promised to Portia. 'Ring', of course, has a similar range, as when Gratiano says he will 'fear no other thing / So sore, as keeping safe Nerissa's ring' (V.i.306–7).[27] Portia's response to Bassanio (allegedly) sleeping with the young doctor is that she will do the same:

> I will become as liberal as you,
> I'll not deny him anything I have,
> Not, not my body nor my husband's bed.
> (V.i.226–8)

Notice also that Portia does not express disgust, or even surprise, that her husband might have shared his bed with a young doctor. Her point is that Bassanio has given to another something that he had pledged to her. Nor does she disparage Antonio (as she does Morocco). Shylock, for the social cohesion of Venice, has to be killed, beggared, expelled, converted or any combination of those penalties. Same-sex passion doesn't matter nearly so much; Antonio has only to be relegated to a subordinate position.

Bray attributes the instability in friendly relations to a decline in the open-handed 'housekeeping' of the great house. Maintaining retinues such as those Bassanio recruits – young men who look promising and relatives who have a claim – was becoming anachronistic. So the social and economic form of service and friendship decayed, but it remained as a cultural form, as a way of speaking. The consequent unevenness, Bray suggests, allowed the line between the intimacies of friendship and sodomy to become blurred.[28] Don Wayne, in his study of Ben Jonson's poem 'To Penshurst' and the country-house genre, relates the decline of the great house to the emergence of a more purposeful aristocracy of 'new men' who 'constituted an agrarian capitalist class with strong links to the trading community'; and to the emergence, also, of 'an ideology in which the nuclear, conjugal family is represented as the institutional foundation of morality and social order'. We associate that development with the later consolidation of 'bourgeois ideology', but 'images and values we tend to identify as middle class had already begun to appear in the transformation of the aristocracy's own self-image'.[29]

The Merchant of Venice makes excellent sense within such a framework. Portia's lavish estate at Belmont is presented as a fairy-tale place; in Venetian reality Bassanio, an aristocrat who already cultivates friends among the merchant class, has to raise money in the market in order to put up a decent show. At the same time, Portia's centring of the matrimonial couple and concomitant hostility towards male friendship manifests an attitude that was to be located as 'bourgeois'. This faultline was not to be resolved rapidly; Portia is ahead of her time. Through the second half of the seventeenth century, Alan Bray and Randolph Trumbach show, the aggressively manly, aristocratic rake, though reproved by the churches and emergent middle-class morality and in violation of the law, would feel able to indulge himself with a woman, a young man or both.[30]

If I have begun to map the ideological field in which same-sex passion occurred in early modern England and some of its points of intersection in *The Merchant*, I am not trying to 'reduce' Shakespeare to an effect of history and structure. I do not suppose that he thought the same as everyone else – or, indeed, that *anyone* thought the same as everyone else. First, diverse paths may be discerned in the period through the relations between sexual and 'platonic', and same-sex and cross-sex passions. These matters were uncertain, unresolved, contested – that is why they made good topics for plays, satires, sermons and so on. Second, playtexts do not have to be clear-cut. As I have argued elsewhere, we should envisage them as working across an ideological terrain, opening out unresolved faultlines, inviting spectators to explore imaginatively the different possibilities. Anyway, readers and audiences do not have to respect closures; they are at liberty to credit and dwell upon the adventurous middle part of a text, as against a tidy conclusion.[31] As Valerie Traub remarks, whether these early comedies are found to instantiate dissidence or containment is a matter of 'crediting *either* the expense of dramatic energy *or* comedic closure'.[32]

Generally, though, there is a pattern: the erotic potential of same-sex love is allowed a certain scope, but has to be set aside. The young men in *Love's Labour Lost* try to maintain a fraternity but the women draw them away. In *Romeo and Juliet* Mercutio has to die to clear the ground for Romeo and Juliet's grand passion. In *Much Ado About Nothing* Benedick has to agree to kill Claudio at his fiancée's demand. *As You Like It* fantasises a harmonious male community in the forest and intensifies it in the wooing of Orlando and Ganymede, but finally Rosalind takes everyone but Jacques back into the old system. Yet there are ambiguities as well. In the epilogue to *As You Like It* the Rosalind/Ganymede boy-actor reopens the flirting: 'If I were a woman, I would kiss as many of you as had beards that pleased me, complexions that liked me, and breaths that I defied not' (V.iv.214–17).[33] And Orsino in *Twelfth Night* leaves the stage with Viola still dressed as Cesario because, he says, her female attire has not yet been located. Even Bassanio can fantasise: 'Sweet doctor', he says to Portia when she has revealed all, 'you shall be my bedfellow, – / When I am absent then lie with my wife' (V.i.284–5).

And why not? Was it necessary to choose? Although the old, open-handed housekeeping was in decline, the upper-class household was not focused on the marital couple in the manner of today. Portia welcomes diverse people to Belmont; Gratiano and Nerissa for instance, whose mimic-marriage reflects the power of the household. *The Two Gentlemen of Verona* starts with the disruption of friendship by love for a woman, but ends with a magical reunion in which they will all live together: 'our day of marriage shall be yours, / One feast, one house, one mutual happiness' (V.iv.170–1). In a discussion of *Twelfth Night* elsewhere, I have suggested that Sebastian's marriage to a stranger heiress need not significantly affect Antonio's relationship with him.[34] They might all live together in Olivia's house (as Sir Toby does); she may well prefer to spend her time with Maria and Viola (who will surely tire of Orsino) rather than with the naïve, swashbuckling husband whom she has mistakenly married. So Antonio need not appear at the end of *Twelfth Night* as the defeated and melancholy outsider that critics have supposed; a director might show him delighted with his boyfriend's lucky break.

This kind of ending might be made to work in the *Merchant*. R. F. Hill suggests it, and Auden reports a 1905 production which had Antonio and Bassanio enter the house together.[35] However, Portia plays a harder game than Rosalind and Viola. She doesn't disguise herself, as they do, to evade hetero-patriarchal pressures, but to test and limit her husband. When disguised as a boy she does not, Geary observes, play androgynous games with other characters or the audience.[36] Antonio is invited into the house only on her terms.

Overall in these plays, Traub concludes, the fear 'is not of homo-eroticism *per se*; homoerotic pleasure is explored and sustained *until* it collapses into fear of erotic exclusivity and its corollary: non-reproductive sexuality' – a theme, of course, of the sonnets.[37] The role of marriage and child-(son-)bearing in the transmission of property and authority is made to take priority. If (like me) you are inclined to regard this as a failure of nerve, it is interesting that the *Merchant*, itself, offers a comment on boldness and timidity. 'Who chooseth me, must give and hazard all he hath' – that is the motto

on the lead casket (II.ix.21). Bassanio picks the right casket and
Portia endorses the choice but, as Auden points out, it is Shylock
and Antonio who commit themselves entirely and risk everything;
and in the world of this play there are penalties for doing that.[38]

IV SUBCULTURES AND SHAKESPEARE

Traub notes a reading of *Twelfth Night* that assumes Olivia to be
punished 'comically but unmistakably' for her same-sex passion for
Viola. But 'to whom is desire between women funny?' Traub asks.[39]
This was my initial topic: must Shakespeare, for out-groups such as
Jews, feminists, lesbians, gays and Blacks, be a way of re-experi-
encing their marginalisation? I have been trying to exemplify elements in a critical practice for dissident readers. Mainstream
commentators on the *Merchant* (whether they intend to or not)
tend to confirm the marginalisation of same-sex passion. Lesbians
and gay men may use the play (1) to think about alternative
economies of sex-gender; (2) to think about problematic aspects of
our own subcultures. But (the question is always put): Is it
Shakespeare? Well, he is said to speak to all sorts and conditions, so
if gay men say 'OK, this is how he speaks to us' – that, surely, is
our business.

With regard to the first of these uses, the *Merchant* allows us to
explore a social arrangement in which the place of same-sex passion
was different from that we are used to. Despite and because of the
formal legal situation, I have shown, it appears not to have attracted very much attention; it was partly compatible with marriage, and was partly supported by legitimate institutions of
friendship, patronage and service. It is not that Shakespeare was a
sexual radical, therefore. Rather, the early modern organisation of
sex and gender boundaries was different from ours, and the ordinary currency of that culture is replete with erotic interactions that
strike strange chords today. Shakespeare may speak with distinct
force to gay men and lesbians, simply because he didn't think he
had to sort out sexuality in modern terms. For approximately the
same reasons, these plays may stimulate radical ideas about race,
nation, gender and class.

As for using *The Merchant* as a way of addressing problems in
gay subculture, the bonds of class, age, gender and race exhibited in
the play have distinct resonances for us. The traffic in boys may

help us to think about power structures in our class and generational interactions. And while an obvious perspective on the play is
resentment at Portia's manipulation of Antonio and Bassanio, we
may bear in mind that Portia too is oppressed in hetero-patriarchy,
and try to work towards a sex-gender regime in which women and
men would not be bound to compete.[40] Above all, plainly, Antonio
is the character most hostile to Shylock. It is he who has spat on
him, spurned him and called him dog, and he means to do it again
(I.iii.121–6). At the trial it is he who imposes the most offensive
requirement – that Shylock convert to Christianity (V.i.382–3).
Seymour Kleinberg connects Antonio's racism to his sexuality.

> Antonio hates Shylock not because he is a more fervent Christian
> than others, but because he recognises his own alter ego in this de-
> spised Jew who, because he is a heretic, can never belong to the state.
> . . . He hates himself in Shylock: the homosexual self that Antonio
> has come to identify symbolically as the Jew.[41]

Gay people today are no more immune to racism than other people,
and transferring our stigma onto others is one of the modes of self-
oppression that tempts any subordinated group. And what if one
were Jewish, and/or Black, as well as gay? One text through which
these issues circulate in our culture is *The Merchant of Venice*, and
it is one place where we may address them.

From *Alternative Shakespeares*, vol. 2, ed. Terence Hawkes
(London: Routledge, 1996), pp. 122–39.

NOTES

[Written in a personal, committed, critical voice, Alan Sinfield's essay
exposes the illusion of objectivity in literary criticism that has done so
much to sustain conservative interpretations and uses of Shakespeare. In its
emphasis on the intricate intertwining of class, race, ethnicity, gender and
sexuality, the essay seeks to avoid ranking such categories in a hierarchy of
oppressions, though one term may be more analytically central. In this
case, Sinfield's focus is on sexuality. The centrality to his argument of institutionalised heterosexism, rather than homosexuality understood as a category of individual identity, forcefully lays bare the connections between
sexuality and gender. In asking how 'readers not situated squarely in the
mainstream of Western culture today may relate to such a powerful cultural icon as Shakespeare', the essay poses one of the crucial questions that,

in their different ways, most of the scholars whose work is included in this volume are trying to address.   Ed.)

1. David Lister, 'Shylock: Unacceptable Face of Shakespeare', *Independent on Sunday*, 17 April 1994, p. 3. See Alan Sinfield, *Cultural Politics – Queer Reading* (Philadelphia, PA, 1994), pp. 1–8, 19–20.

2. Christopher Booker, 'A Modern Tragedy of Errors', *Daily Telegraph*, 23 April 1992.

3. Kathleen McLuskie, 'The Patriarchal Bard: Feminist Criticism and Shakespeare', in Jonathan Dollimore and Alan Sinfield (eds), *Political Shakespeare: New Essays in Cultural Materialism* (Manchester, 1985), p. 97. For a reply to her critics by McLuskie, see her *Renaissance Dramatists* (Hemel Hempstead, 1989), pp. 224–9, and for further comment see Jonathan Dollimore, 'Shakespeare, Cultural Materialism, Feminism and Marxist Humanism', *New Literary History*, 21 (1990), 471–93.

4. W. H. Auden, 'Brothers and Others', in *The Dyer's Hand* (London, 1963); see also Graham Midgley, '*The Merchant of Venice*: a Reconsideration', *Essays in Criticism*, 10 (1960), 119–33.

5. W. H. Auden, *Collected Shorter Poems, 1927–1957* (London, 1969), p. 282.

6. Keith Geary, 'The Nature of Portia's Victory: Turning to Men in *The Merchant of Venice*', *Shakespeare Survey*, 37 (1984), 63–4.

7. Lawrence W. Hyman, 'The Rival Loves in *The Merchant of Venice*', *Shakespeare Quarterly*, 21 (1970), 112.

8. Harry Berger, 'Marriage and Mercifixion in *The Merchant of Venice*: the Casket Scene Revisited', *Shakespeare Quarterly*, 32 (1981), 161–2; see also Hyman, 'Rival Lovers' and Geary, 'Portia's Victory'.

9. Coppélia Kahn, 'The Cuckoo's Note: Male Friendship and Cuckoldry in *The Merchant of Venice*', in Peter Erickson and Coppélia Kahn (eds), *Shakespeare's 'Rough Magic'* (Newark, DE, 1985), p. 106.

10. Janet Adelman, 'Male Bonding in Shakespeare's Comedies', in Erickson and Kahn, *Shakespeare's 'Rough Magic'*, p. 75.

11. Kahn, 'The Cuckoo's Note', p. 107.

12. Adelman, 'Male Bonding', p. 80.

13. Another way is blatantly reworking the authoritative text so that it is forced to yield, against the grain, explicitly oppositional kinds of understanding; see Alan Sinfield, *Faultlines* (Berkeley and Oxford, 1992), pp. 16–24, 290–302.

14. Eve Kosofsky Sedgwick, *Between Men* (Columbia, OH, 1985), pp. 88–9; see also Jonathan Dollimore, *Sexual Dissidence: Augustine to Wilde, Freud to Foucault* (Oxford, 1992), Chs 17–18.

15. Sedgwick, *Between Men*, p. 4.

16. Ben Jonson, *Poetaster*, ed. Tom Cain (Manchester, 1995), I.ii.15–17; see also III.iv.277–8 and V.iii.580–1. On boys in theatre, see Lisa Jardine, *Still Harping on Daughters: Women and Drama in the Age of Shakespeare* (Brighton, 1983), Ch. 1.

17. See Alan Bray, *Homosexuality in Renaissance England* (London, 1982), pp. 38–42, 70–80; Bruce R. Smith, *Homosexual Desire in Shakespeare's England: A Cultural Poetics* (Chicago, IL, 1991), pp. 47–52.

18. Cf. Smith, ibid., pp. 13–14, 74–6 *et passim*.

19. Jonathan Goldberg, *Sodometries: Renaissance Texts, Modern Sexualities* (Stanford, CA, 1992), p. 20; see also Bray, *Homosexuality*, p. 79.

20. Stephen Orgel, 'Nobody's Perfect: or Why Did the English Stage Take Boys for Women?' *South Atlantic Quarterly*, 88 (1989), 8, 18.

21. Ibid., p 10.

22. See Lisa Jardine, 'Twins and Travesties: Gender, Dependency and Sexual Availability in *Twelfth Night*'; and Susan Zimmerman, 'Disruptive Desire: Artifice and Indeterminacy in Jacobean Comedy', both in Susan Zimmerman (ed.), *Erotic Politics: Desire on the Renaissance Stage* (New York and London, 1992).

23. Smith, *Homosexual Desire*, pp. 35–41, 67–72, 96–9, 139–43.

24. See Alan Sinfield, *The Wilde Century* (London and New York, 1994), pp. 25–37; and Sinfield, *Faultlines*, pp. 127–42 (this is an extension of the discussion of *Henry V* published first in John Drakakis [ed.], *Alternative Shakespeares* [London, 1985]), and pp. 237–8 (on *Tamburlaine*).

25. Alan Bray, 'Homosexuality and the Signs of Male Friendship in Elizabethan England', *History Workshop*, 29 (1990), 1–19.

26. Ibid.

27. See Eric Partridge, *Shakespeare's Bawdy* (London, 1955), pp. 135, 179.

28. Bray, 'Homosexuality', 12–13.

29. Don E. Wayne, *Penshurst: The Semiotics of Place and the Poetics of History* (London, 1984), pp. 23–5.

30. See Bray, *Homosexuality*; Randolph Trumbach, 'Sodomitical Sub-cultures, Sodomitical Roles, and the Gender Revolution of the Eighteenth Century: the Recent Historiography', in Robert Purks Maccubin (ed.), *'Tis Nature's Fault* (Cambridge, 1987); Randolph Trumbach, 'Gender and the Homosexual Role in Modern Western Culture: the 18th and 19th Centuries Compared', in Dennis Altman, Carole Vance, Martha Vicinus and Jeffrey Weeks (eds), *Homosexuality, Which Homosexuality?* (London, 1989); Sinfield, *The Wilde Century*, pp. 33–42.

31. Cf. Sinfield, *Faultlines*, pp. 47–51, 99–106.

32. Valerie Traub, *Desire and Anxiety: Circulations of Sexuality in Shakespearean Drama* (London and New York, 1992), p. 120; see also Bruce R. Smith, 'Making a Difference: Male/Male "Desire" in Tragedy, Comedy and Tragic-Comedy', in Zimmerman (ed.), *Erotic Politics*.

33. See Valerie Traub, *Desire and Anxiety*, p. 128.

34. Cf. Sinfield, *Faultlines*, p. 73.

35. R. F. Hill, '*The Merchant of Venice* and the Patterns of Romantic Comedy', *Shakespeare Survey*, 28 (1975), 86: W. H. Auden, 'Brothers and Others', p. 233.

36. Geary, 'Portia's Victory', p. 58.

37. Traub, *Desire and Anxiety*, pp. 123, 138–41.

38. W. H. Auden, 'Brothers and Others', p. 235.

39. Traub, *Desire and Anxiety*, p. 93.

40. See the suggestive remarks in Goldberg, *Sodometries*, pp. 142, 273–4.

41. Seymour Kleinberg, '*The Merchant of Venice*: the Homosexual as Anti-Semite in Nascent Capitalism', in Stuart Kellog (ed.), *Literary Visions of Homosexuality* (New York, 1985), p. 120. Anti-Semitism and homophobia are linked by Leslie Fielder, *The Stranger in Shakespeare* (St Albans, 1974), Ch. 2, and by Hans Mayer, *Outsiders*, trans. Denis M. Sweet (Cambridge, MA, 1982), pp. 278–85.

6

The Homoerotics of
Shakespearean Comedy

VALERIE TRAUB

The following comparative analysis of *As You Like It* and *Twelfth Night* attempts to demonstrate the differential ways homoeroticism is treated: how it is experienced as pleasure and when it elicits anxiety for both male and female characters. These plays are sites of struggle for the signification of homoeroticism: they demonstrate that within the early modern erotic economy the homoerotic relation to desire could be represented as both celebratory and strained. At the same time, the representations of homoeroticism in these comedies are as much cultural fantasies as is the representation of the maternal body in the *Henriad* – both representations are 'fantasmic' interventions in 'real' cultural practices, and as such signal the dialectical relation between the psychic and the social.

The homoeroticism of *As You Like It* is playful in its ability to transcend binary oppositions, to break into a dual mode, a simultaneity, of desire. In so far as Rosalind/Ganymede is a multiply sexual object (simultaneously heterosexual and homoerotic), Orlando's effusion of desire toward her/him prevents the stable reinstitution of heterosexuality, upon which the marriage plot depends. By interrupting the arbitrary binarism of the heterosexual contract, male homoeroticism, even as it affirms particular masculine bonds, transgresses the erotic imperative of the Law of the Father. The proceedings of Hymen that conclude the play, once read in terms of the 'mock' marriage which precedes them, enact only an ambivalent closure. The reinstitution of gender role (and

Rosalind's political subordination under her husband's rule) is incommensurate with a rigidification of sexuality.

The homoeroticism of *Twelfth Night*, on the other hand, is anxious and strained. This text explores a diversity of desire, proceeding with erotic plurality as far as it can; then, in the face of anxiety generated by this exploration, it fixes the homoerotic interest onto a marginalised figure. The homoerotic energies of Viola, Olivia and Orsino are displaced onto Antonio, whose relation to Sebastian is finally sacrificed for the maintenance of institutionalised heterosexuality and generational continuity.[1] In other words, *Twelfth Night* closes down the possibility of homoerotic play initiated by the material presence of the transvestised boy actors. The fear expressed, however, is not of homoeroticism *per se*; homoerotic pleasure is explored and sustained *until* it collapses into fear of erotic exclusivity and its corollary: non-reproductive sexuality. The result is a more rigid dedication to the ideology of binarism, wherein gender and status inequalities are all the more forcefully reinscribed.

Much virtue in If
Touchstone, *As You Like It*

In '"The Place of a Brother" in *As You Like It*: Social Process and Comic Form', Louis Adrian Montrose began the pathbreaking work of placing women's subordination in Shakespearean drama within the context of male homosocial bonds.[2] In a historicisation and politicisation of C. L. Barber's analysis of Rosalind in *Shakespeare's Festive Comedy*, Montrose argued that

> Rosalind's exhilarating mastery of herself and others has been a compensatory 'holiday humor', a temporary, inversionary rite of misrule, whose context is a transfer of authority, property and title from the Duke to his prospective male heir.[3]

More recently, Jean Howard continues within the Barber–Montrose lineage:

> The representation of Rosalind's holiday humor has the primary effect, I think, of confirming the gender system and perfecting rather than dismantling it by making a space for mutuality within relations of dominance.[4]

However, she complicates the analysis of Rosalind's subordination through reference to the French feminist analytic of female 'masquerade':

> the figure of Rosalind dressed as a boy engages in playful masquerade as, in playing Rosalind for Orlando, she acts out the parts scripted for women by her culture. Doing so does not release Rosalind from patriarchy but reveals the constructed nature of patriarchy's representation of the feminine and shows a woman manipulating those representations in her own interest, theatricalising for her own purposes what is assumed to be innate, teaching her future mate how to get beyond certain ideologies of gender to more enabling ones.[5]

The distance traversed in the progression from Barber to Montrose to Howard indicates a corresponding movement from an essentialist view of gender, to an emphasis on social structure as determining gender, to an assertion of the limited possibilities of subversive manipulation within dominant cultural codes. The subjective if constrained agency conferred by Howard upon Rosalind as a woman can be extended as well to Rosalind as erotic subject. In excess of the dominant ideology of monogamous heterosexuality, to which Rosalind is symbolically wed at the end of the play, exist desires unsanctioned by institutional favour. By means of her male improvisation, Rosalind leads the play into a mode of desire neither heterosexual nor homoerotic, but both heterosexual *and* homoerotic. As much as she displays her desire for Orlando, she also enjoys her position as male object of Phebe's desire and, more importantly, of Orlando's. S/he thus instigates a deconstruction of the binary system by which desire in subsequent centuries came to be organised, regulated and disciplined.

That homoerotic significations will play a part in *As You Like It* is first intimated by Rosalind's adoption of the name Ganymede when she imagines donning doublet and hose. Of all the male names available to her, she chooses that of the young lover of Zeus, familiar to educated Britons through Greek and Latin literature and European painting, and to less privileged persons as a colloquial term used to describe the male object of male love. As James Saslow, who traces the artistic representation of Ganymede in Western culture from the fifteenth to the seventeenth centuries, argues, 'the very word *ganymede* was used from medieval times well into the seventeenth century to mean an object of homosexual desire'.[6] Saslow's argument is seconded by Orgel: 'the name Ganymede [could not] be used in the Renaissance without this connotation'.[7]

That Rosalind-cum-Ganymede becomes the object of another woman's desire is obvious. Consciously, of course, Phebe believes Ganymede to be a man, and is thus merely following the dominant heterosexual course. And yet, what attracts Phebe to Ganymede are precisely those qualities that could be termed 'feminine'. Notice the progression of the following speech:

> It is a pretty youth – not very pretty. . . .
> He'll make a proper man. The best thing in him
> Is his complexion. . . .
> He is not very tall; yet for his years he's tall.
> His leg is but so so; and yet 'tis well.
> There was a pretty redness in his lip,
> A little riper and more lusty red
> Than that mix'd in his cheek; 'twas just the difference
> Betwixt the constant red and mingled damask.
> (III.v.113–23)

During the first half of her recollection, as she measures Ganymede against the standard of common male attributes – height, leg – Phebe fights her attraction, syntactically oscillating between affirmation and denial: he is; he is not. In the last four lines, as she 'feminises' Ganymede's lip and cheek, she capitulates to her desire altogether.

Many critics acknowledge the underlying homoeroticism of Phebe's attraction; however, they tend to undermine its thematic importance by relegating it to the status of a temporary psychosexual stage. C. L. Barber, for instance, remarks: 'She has, in effect, a girlish crush on the femininity which shows through Rosalind's disguise; the aberrant affection is happily got over when Rosalind reveals her identity and makes it manifest that Phebe has been loving a woman.'[8] When Barber says that Phebe's 'aberrant' affection is 'happily got over' he reveals the extent to which homophobic anxiety structures the developmental logic of his response. But if a 'girlish crush' is outgrown or overcome, what are we to make of Rosalind's desire to 'prove a busy actor' in the 'pageant truly play'd' of Phebe and Silvius? (III.iv.50–8). Although her ostensible motivation is her belief that 'the sight of lovers feedeth those in love' (56), s/he soon interjects in order to correct the literal-minded-

ness that feeds Phebe's 'proud disdain' (III.iv.52). And yet the pleasure Rosalind/Ganymede takes in this task seems in excess of her
putative function. Significantly, it is s/he who first mentions the possibility of Phebe's attraction, interpreting and then glorying in
Phebe's changed demeanor:

> Why, what means this? Why do you look on me?
> I see no more in you than in the ordinary
> Of nature's sale-work. 'Od's my little life
> I think she means to tangle my eyes too!
> (III.v.41–4)

Is there not a sense in which Rosalind/Ganymede *elicits* Phebe's
desire, constructing it even as she refuses it? Indeed, in these lines
the conflict between discourses of gender and of sexuality are in-
tensely manifested: at the level of gender, Rosalind restates compulsory heterosexuality; at the level of sexuality, Ganymede elicits a
desire for that which falls outside (or on the cusp) of the binarism
of gender. At any rate, s/he is represented as delighting in her role
of the rejecting male:

> Down on your knees,
> And thank heaven, fasting, for a good man's love;
> For I must tell you friendly in your ear,
> Sell when you can, you are not for all markets.
> (III.v.57–60)

And why does s/he put Silvius through the exquisite torment of
hearing Phebe's love letter to Ganymede read aloud, if not to ag-
grandise her own victorious position as male rival? (IV.iii.14–64).
Indeed, as a male, her sense of power is so complete that s/he pre-
sumes to tell Silvius to tell Phebe, 'that if she love *me*, I charge her
to love *thee*' (IV.iii.71–2, my emphasis).

Homoerotic desire in *As You Like It* thus circulates from
Phebe's desire for the 'feminine' in Rosalind/Ganymede to
Rosalind/Ganymede's desire to be the 'masculine' object of
Phebe's desire. Even more suggestive of the text's investment in
homoerotic pleasure is Orlando's willingness to engage in love-
play with a young shepherd. Throughout his 'courtship' of
Ganymede (who is now impersonating Rosalind), Orlando
accepts and treats Ganymede as his beloved. To do so requires
less his willing suspension of disbelief than the ability to hold in

suspension a dual sexuality that feels no compulsion to make arbitrary distinction between kinds of objects. That Rosalind-cum-Ganymede takes the lead in their courtship has been noted by countless critics; that there is a certain homoerotic irony in that fact has yet to be noted. As a 'ganymede', Rosalind would be expected to play the part of a younger, more receptive partner in an erotic exchange. S/he thus not only inverts gender roles; s/he disrupts alleged homoerotic roles as well.

What began as a game culminates in the 'mock' marriage, when Orlando takes for his wife the boy he believes to be fictionalising as Rosalind. It is Celia, not Orlando, who hesitates in playing her part in the ceremony – 'I cannot say the words', she responds to Orlando's request that she play the priest (IV.i.121) – in part because those words possess a ritualistic power to *enact* what is spoken. In so far as ritual was still popularly believed to be imbued with sacred or magical power, the fact that Orlando does not hesitate, but eagerly responds in the precise form of the Anglican marriage ceremony – 'I take thee, Rosalind, for wife' (IV.i.129) – suggests the degree to which the play legitimises the multiple desires it represents. The point is not that Orlando and Ganymede formalise a homosexual marriage, but rather that as the distance between Rosalind and Ganymede collapses, distinctions between homoerotic and heterosexual collapse as well. As the woman and the shepherd boy merge, Orlando's words resound with the conviction that, for the moment, he (as much as Rosalind and the audience) is engaged in the ceremony as if it were real. As both a performative speech act and a theatricalisation of desire, the marriage is both true and fictional at once. The subversiveness of this dramatic gesture lies in the dual motion of first, appropriating the meaning of matrimony for deviant desires; and second, exposing the heterosexual imperative of matrimony as a reduction of the plurality of desire into the singularity of monogamy. The 'mock' marriage is not a desecration but a deconstruction – a displacement and subversion of the terms by which desire is encoded – of the ritual by which two are made one.

When Hymen in Act V symbolically reintroduces the logic of heterosexual marriage, the text's devotion to simultaneity would appear to be negated. The terms in which Hymen performs the quartet of marriages make the ideological function of the ritual clear: 'Peace, ho! I bar confusion. / 'Tis I must make conclusion / Of these most strange events' (V.iv.124–6). 'Hymen's bands'

(V.iv.128) are called forth to 'make conclusion' not only of erotic 'confusion' but of the play. And yet the play does not end with Hymen's bars and bands, but with a renewed attack on the pretensions of erotic certitude. In a repetition of her previous gender and erotic mobility, Rosalind-cum-boy actor, still wearing female attire, leaps the frame of the play in order to address the audience in a distinctly erotic manner: 'If I were a woman I would kiss as many of you as had beards that pleas'd me, complexions that lik'd me, and breaths that I defied not' (Epilogue 16–19). As Orgel, Howard, Phyllis Rackin and Catherine Belsey all intimate, the effect of this statement is to highlight the constructedness of gender and the flexibility of erotic attraction at precisely the point when the formal impulse of comedy would be to essentialise and fix both gender and eroticism.

Throughout the play, what makes erotic contingency possible is a simple conjunction: 'if'. Indeed, Touchstone's discourse on the virtues of 'if' can serve as an index of the play's entire erotic strategy: 'If you said so, then I said so' (V.iv.99–100). The dependence on the conditional structures the possibility of erotic exploration without necessitating a commitment to it. Orlando can woo and even wed Ganymede as '*if* thou wert indeed my Rosalind' and as *if* the marriage were real (IV.i.189–90, my emphasis). Through the magic of 'if', the boy actor playing Rosalind can offer and elicit erotic attraction to and from each gender in the audience. 'If' not only creates multiple erotic possibilities and positions, it also conditionally resolves the dramatic confusion that the play cannot sustain. As Rosalind says to Silvius, Phebe and Orlando, respectively: 'I would love you, if I could'; 'I will marry you, if ever I marry a woman, and I'll be married tomorrow'; and 'I will satisfy you, if ever I satisfied man, and you shall be married tomorrow' (V.ii.108–12). Even Hymen's mandate is qualified; 'Here's eight that must take hands / To join in Hymen's bands / *If* truth hold true contents' (V.iv.127–9, my emphasis).

My own reliance on 'if' should make it clear that I am not arguing that Rosalind or Orlando or Phebe 'is' 'a' 'homosexual'. Rather, at various moments in the play, these characters temporarily inhabit a homoerotic position of desire. To insist on a mode of desire as a position taken up also differs from formulating these characters as 'bisexual': as Phyllis Rackin reminds us, bisexuality implicitly defines the desiring subject as divided in order to maintain the ideologically motivated categories of homo- and hetero- as inviolate.[9] The entire logic of *As You Like It* works against such categorisation, against fixing upon and reifying any one mode of desire.

Simultaneity and flexibility, however, are not without their costs. In so far as the text circulates homoerotic desire, it displaces the anxieties so generated in the following tableau described by Oliver, Orlando's brother.

> A wretched ragged man, o'ergrown with hair,
> Lay sleeping on his back. About his neck
> A green and gilded snake had wreath'd itself,
> Who with her head nimble in threats approach'd
> The opening of his mouth. . . .
> A lioness, with udders all drawn dry,
> Lay couching, head on ground, with catlike watch,
> When that the sleeping man should stir. . . .
>   (IV.iii.107–17)

The dual dangers to which the sleeping Oliver is susceptible are, on the face of it, female: the lioness an aged maternal figure ('with udders all drawn dry'), the female snake seductively encircling Oliver's neck. Let us first give this passage a conventional psycho-analytic reading: the virile and virtuous Orlando banishes the snake and battles with the lion while his evil 'emasculated' brother, un-conscious of his position as damsel in distress, sleeps on – their sibling rivalry displaced onto and mediated by gender conflict. Yet at the same time as the snake encircles her prey, she approaches and almost penetrates the vulnerable opening of Oliver's mouth. Rather than posit the snake, in this aspect, as a representation of the 'phallic mother', I want to argue that in the snake's figure are concentrated the anxieties generated by the text's simultaneous commitment to homoeroticism and heterosexuality. If Oliver is en-dangered by the snake's 'feminine' sexual powers, he is equally threatened by her phallic ones. He becomes both the feminised object of male aggression and the *eff*eminised object of female desire. The snake thus represents the erotic other of the text, the reservoir of the fears elicited by homoerotic exchanges – fears, I want to insist, that are not inherent in the experience of homoerotic desire, but that are produced by those ideologies that position ho-moeroticism as unnatural, criminal and heretical.

Indeed the relations represented in this tableau suggest that no desire, male or female, heterosexual or homoerotic, is free of anxiety. As Touchstone says in a lighter vein, 'as all is mortal in nature, so is all nature in love mortal in folly' (II.iv.52–3). But what is most interesting is that in this play sexual danger is encoded as feminising to the object persistently figured as male. Consistently, the text seems less interested in the threat of a particular mode of desire (hetero/homo) than in the dangers desire *as such* poses to men. It is, in this sense, thoroughly patriarchal, positing man as the centre of, and vulnerable to, desire. That the text marginalises this expression of vulnerability by not dramatising it on stage but reporting it only in retrospect suggests the extent to which the anxiety is repressed in the interests of achieving comic, heterosexual closure, however partially or problematically.

My highlighting of the affirmative possibilities of multiple pleasures is not meant to imply that As You Like It represents a paradisiacal erotic economy, a utopian return to a polymorphously perverse body unmediated by cultural restraints. As the penultimate gesture toward the institution of marriage clearly indicates, endless erotic mobility is difficult to sustain. But just as clearly, *As You Like It* registers its lack of commitment to the binary logic that dominates the organisation of desire. If *As You Like It* suggests that 'folly' of desire, part of that folly is the discipline to which it is subject.

My desire / More sharp than filed steel
Antonio, *Twelfth Night*

The sexual economy of *Twelfth Night* is saturated with multiple erotic investments: Viola/Cesario's dual desire of Olivia and Orsino; Orsino's ambivalent interest in Viola/Cesario; Sebastian's responses to Olivia and Antonio; and finally, Antonio's exclusive erotic wish for Sebastian. Although Viola's initial impulse for adopting male disguise is to serve the duke as a eunuch (I.ii.56), her status as sexually neutral dissipates as she quickly becomes both erotic object and subject. Critics often mention Viola's passivity, her inclination to commit 'What else may hap to time' (I.ii.60), but they fail to recognise that as Cesario she woos Olivia with a fervour that exceeds her 'text' (I.v.227). S/he asks, with no apparent mandate, to see Olivia's face; and upon viewing the 'picture' (I.v.228), responds, 'if you were the devil, you are fair' (I.v.246).

Critics also point to Viola/Cesario's anxiety over the predicament caused by the disguise:

> I am the man. If it be so, as 'tis,
> Poor lady, she were better love a dream.
> Disguise, I see, thou art a wickedness
> Wherein the pregnant enemy does much. . . .
> How will this fadge? My master loves her dearly;
> And I, poor monster, fond as much on him;
> And she, mistaken, seems to dote on me.
> What will become of this? As I am man,
> My state is desperate for my master's love;
> As I am woman – now alas the day! –
> What thriftless sighs shall poor Olivia breathe!
> O time, thou must untangle this, not I;
> It is too hard a knot for me t'untie.
>
> (II.ii.25–41)

The image by which Viola/Cesario expresses her plight is far more resonant than many critics have noted. The implied double negative of a *knot* that *cannot* be untied is precisely the figuration of her complex erotic investments: s/he 'fonds' on her master, while simultaneously finding erotic intrigue and excitement as the object of Olivia's desire. The flip side of her anxiety about Olivia's desire is her own desire to be the *object* of Olivia's desire. This desire s/he can *(k)not* untie because of its status as negation. Why this desire is negated in this play I will take up in a moment. For now, what is important is that the play sets up Viola/Cesario's dual erotic investment, not so much to resolve it as to sustain its dramatic possibilities and to elicit the similarly polymorphous desires of the audience, whose spectator pleasure would be at least in part derived from a transgressive glimpse of multiple erotic possibilities.

To substantiate the play's investment in erotic duality, one can compare the language used in Viola/Cesario's two avowals of love: the first as Orsino's wooer of Olivia, and the second as s/he attempts to communicate love to Orsino. In both avowals, Viola/Cesario theatricalises desire, using a similar language of conditionals towards both erotic objects. Compare the syntactical and semantic structure of Viola/Cesario's comment to Olivia, 'If I did love you in my master's flame, / With such a suff'ring, such a deadly life, / In your denial I would find no sense; / I would not understand it' (I.v.259–62) to her comment to Orsino: 'My father had a daughter lov'd a man, / As it might be, perhaps, were I a woman, / I should your lordship' (II.iv.107–9). What predisposes us to credit the second comment as truth but the first as false, a suspect performance, is, I suggest, largely our assumption of universal heterosexuality. Both speeches are equally theatricalisations of desire. As such, both work to undermine the dichotomy between truth and falsehood, fiction and reality, heterosexuality and homoeroticism.

This is not to suggest that Viola/Cesario's position in relation to homoerotic desire is celebrated in the text: unlike Rosalind, her erotic predicament threatens her with destruction – or at least so s/he believes – at the hands of Sir Andrew, who is manipulated by Sir Toby to challenge his rival to a duel. The weapon of choice is not incidental, as the whole point of the threatened battle is for Viola/Cesario to demonstrate the 'little thing' that 'would make me tell them how much I lack of a man' (III.iv.302–3). As Toby says: 'Therefore, on, or strip your sword stark naked; for meddle you must, that's certain, or forswear to wear iron about you' (III.iv.252–4). At this (phallic) point, Viola/Cesario's 'lack' is upheld as the signifier of gender difference. And yet, to the extent that masculinity is embodied in the sword, it depends upon a particular kind of performance rather than any biological equipment. This theatrical moment simultaneously reinscribes a binary code of gender into the action, *and* suggests the extent to which gender is prosthetic.[10] It seems telling that at precisely this point of pressure on the meaning of gender, the play of erotic difference is abandoned. Or, more accurately, deflected, for who should enter to defend Viola/Cesario but Antonio, the figure who is positioned most firmly in a homoerotic relation to desire.

The entire first scene between Antonio and Sebastian is focused on Sebastian's denial of the sailor's help, and Antonio's irrepressible desire not only to protect but accompany the man with whom, we later learn, he has spent 'three months . . . / No int'rim, not a minute's vacancy, / Both day and night' (V.i.90–2). Antonio singlemindedly pursues Sebastian through the (to him) dangerous streets of Illyria: 'But come what may, I do adore thee so / That danger shall seem sport, and I will go' (II.i.44–5). It is not fortuitous that this scene (II.i) intervenes between Viola/Cesario's wooing of Olivia, when s/he exceeds her 'text' (I.v), and her contemplation of the danger inherent in this action: 'It is too hard a knot for me t'untie' (II.ii). For Antonio's words allude to the perils in early modern culture of an exclusively homoerotic passion: in order to remain in the presence of one's beloved, 'danger' must be figuratively, if not literally, transformed into 'sport'. That the danger is not limited to the threat of Orsino's men (the force of law) is revealed in Antonio's plea to Sebastian, 'If you will not murder me for my love, let me be your servant' (II.ii.33–4). The love Antonio extends is somehow capable of inciting the beloved to murder.

An even greater danger is intimated in this scene, which will ultimately have severe repercussions on the fate of Antonio's desire. Sebastian explains to Antonio that his father 'left behind him myself and a sister, both born in an hour. If the heavens had been pleas'd, would we had so ended! But you, sir, alter'd that, for some hour before you took me from the breach of the sea was my sister drown'd' (II.i.17–22). Sebastian's life is saved when he is pulled from the 'breach of the sea', an image of the surf that invokes the rebirthing we expect from Shakespearean shipwrecks. But this rebirth is coincident with the supposed death of Sebastian's sister; she is 'drown'd already ... with salt water' and drowned again in Sebastian's tearful 'remembrance' (II.i.29–30). In other words, Sebastian's rebirth into Antonio's love is implicated in the destruction of the only woman Sebastian has loved: Viola.

As mentioned, Viola/Cesario *is* threatened with destruction. Crucially, it is Antonio who saves her/him, thinking that he is defending his beloved. His entrance at this moment enacts the central displacement of the text: when the ramifications of a simultaneous homoeroticism and heterosexuality become too anxiety-ridden, the homoerotic energy of Viola/Cesario is displaced onto Antonio – the one figure, as Laurie Osborne notes, whose passion for another does not arise from deception or require a woman for its expression.[11]

Just before the swordfight Antonio finds Sebastian, and greets him with these words;

> I could not stay behind you. My desire,
> More sharp than filed steel, did spur me forth;
> And not all love to see you, though so much
> As might have drawn one to a longer voyage,
> But jealousy what might befall your travel,
> Being skilless in these parts. . . . My willing love,
> The rather by these arguments of fear,
> Set forth in your pursuit.
>
> (III.iii.4–12)

Why do editors gloss 'jealousy' as anxiety, when both words were available to Shakespeare, and both scan equally well?[12] Antonio is clearly both anxious about the dangers that might 'befall' his beloved, and jealous of the attractions that might entice him. And not without reason: Sebastian falls rather easily to the 'relish' of Olivia's charms (IV.i.59).

Antonio's discourse partakes of what I will call a 'rhetoric of penetration'. Male desire in Shakespearean drama is almost always figured in phallic images – which may seem tautological until one remembers the commonly accepted notion that Shakespeare's fops are not only 'effeminate' but 'homosexual'. On the contrary, *Twelfth Night* represents male homoerotic desire as phallic in the most active sense: erect, hard, penetrating. Antonio describes his desire in terms of sharp, filed steel which spurs him on to pursuit, 'spur' working simultaneously to 'prick' him (as object) and urge him on (as subject). To the extent that heterosexual desire in Shakespearean drama is often associated with detumescence (the triumph of Venus over Mars, the pervasive puns on dying), and homoerotic desire is figured as permanently erect, it is the desire of man for man that is coded as the more 'masculine'.[13]

Many critics have noted in addition that in the early modern period excessive heterosexual lust seems to engender in men fears of 'effeminacy'. Romeo, for instance, complains that desire for Juliet 'hath made me effeminate, / And in my temper soft'ned valor's steel!' Similarly, the Romans maintain that Antony's lust for Cleopatra has so compromised his gender identity that he 'is not more manlike / Than Cleopatra, nor the queen of Ptolemy / More womanly than he.' In contrast, extreme virility, manifested in Spartan self-denial and military exploits, is not only depicted as consistent with erotic desire for other men; it also is expressed in it, as when Aufidius says to Coriolanus, 'Let me twine / Mine arms about that body whereagainst / My grained ash an hundred times hath broke', and goes on to compare the joy he feels at seeing Coriolanus as being greater than that which he felt 'when I first my wedded mistress saw / Bestride my threshold'.[14]

Fops, on the other hand, while commonly perceived as having a 'passive' interest in male homoerotic encounters, are almost always involved in pursuing (if unsuccessfully) a heterosexual alliance.[15] Sir Andrew, for instance, hopes to marry Olivia, if only for her status and money. True, he is manipulated by Sir Toby, and he may therefore be seen to partake of a homoerotic triangular relation, whereby he woos his ostensible object (Olivia) in order to concretise ties with his real object (Toby).[16] However, Sir Andrew seems more accurately represented as void of erotic desire, merely attempting to fulfil the social requirements of heterosexuality. Indeed, he seems a vessel into which desires are poured, especially Sir Toby's triangular manipulation for wealth, ease and power through the exchange of the body of his niece. Rather than being homosexual, fops are figured as always already effeminated by their heterosexual relation to desire.

Orsino, whose languid action and hyper-courtly language situate him as foppish, appears to be more in love with love than with any particular object. As Jean Howard points out, Orsino

> initially poses a threat to the Renaissance sex–gender system by languidly abnegating his active role as masculine wooer and drowning in narcissistic self-love. . . . His narcissism and potential effeminacy are displaced, respectively, onto Malvolio and Andrew Aguecheek, who suffer fairly severe humiliations for their follies.[17]

Orsino is narcissistic and 'effeminate', but I would argue that neither his narcissism nor his 'effeminacy' is indicative of desire for males *per se*. Orsino's 'effeminacy', a gender characteristic, accompanies both his heterosexual desire for Olivia and his homoerotic desire for Cesario. What is most interesting, however, is the extent to which Orsino's desire is anxious, or in our modern parlance, homo*phobic*. In contrast to Orsino's homosocial ease with Cesario – their intimacy is established in three days (I.iv.3) – the possibility of a homo*erotic* basis to his affection for his servant creates tension: he defers accepting Viola as his betrothed until she has adopted her 'maiden weeds' (V.i.252). Indeed, he refuses to really 'see' her as a woman, continuing to refer to her as Cesario, 'For so you shall be, while you are a man; / But when in other habits you are seen, / Orsino's mistress and his fancy's queen' (V.i.383–5). To the extent that his anxiety *is* desire, Orsino figures as the repressed homoerotic analogue to Antonio.

Throughout his canon, Shakespeare associates 'effeminacy' in men with the fawning superciliousness of the perfumed courtier, and with the 'womanish' tears of men no longer in control. Both Hotspur and Hamlet, for example, rail against the 'effeminacy' of courtiers; Laertes and Lear describe their tears as 'womanish'. Hamlet is as disgusted by Osric and Guildenstern as he is by Ophelia and Gertrude; it is this fear of 'effeminacy' that stimulates the homophobic disgust in his charge, 'Sblood, do you think I am easier to be play'd on than a pipe?'[18]

There is little in the canon to suggest that Shakespeare linked 'ef-feminacy' to homoeroticism, unless we look to the feminine quali-ties of Cesario that ambivalently attract Orsino to his page. Historically, the charge of 'effeminacy' seems to have been limited to such 'boys' as Cesario, or to those adult men who were 'uxori-ously' obsessed with women. The unfailing correspondence of adult homoeroticism and 'effeminacy' is a later cultural development, and is imported into Shakespeare's texts by critics responding to a dif-ferent cultural milieu.[19] In *Twelfth Night*, both Antonio and Sebastian pointedly use their phallic swords, and are implicitly con-trasted to Sir Andrew, whom even Viola/Cesario one-ups, despite the little thing that would make [her] tell them how much [she] lack[s] as a man'. 'Appropriate' male desire is phallic, whether ho-moerotic or heterosexual; without that phallic force, men in Shakespearean drama are usually rendered either asexual or nomi-nally heterosexual.

Despite the attractions of homoeroticism, the pleasure *Twelfth Night* takes in it is not sustained. Not only are Viola/Cesario and Sebastian betrothed respectively to Orsino and Olivia, but Antonio is marginalised – in part because he publicly speaks his desire, in part because his desire is exclusive of other bonds. Like *The Merchant of Venice*'s Antonio, this Antonio gives his beloved his 'purse'; shortly thereafter he is seized by the duke's men. As he struggles with the officers, Antonio states to 'Sebastian':

> This comes with seeking you.
> But there's no remedy; I shall answer it.
> What will you do, now my necessity
> Makes me to ask you for my purse? It grieves me
> Much more for what I cannot do for you
> Than what befalls myself.
> (III.iv.333–8)

After Viola/Cesario offers money but denies not only their acquain-tance, but knowledge of Antonio's 'purse', the officers attempt to take Antonio away; but he resists:

> Let me speak a little. This youth that you see here
> I snatch'd one half out of the jaws of death,
> Reliev'd him with such sanctity of love,
> And to his image, which methought did promise
> Most venerable worth, did I devotion.
> (III.iv.360–4)

'What's that to us?' reply the officers, and Antonio is compelled to curse:

> But O how vile an idol proves this god!
> Thou hast, Sebastian, done good feature shame.
> In nature there's no blemish but the mind;
> None can be call'd deform'd but the unkind.
>
> (III.iv.366–9)

To which the officers conclude: 'The man grows mad. Away with him!' (III.iv.372)

Antonio is labelled mad by the law not only because of the linguistic and class impropriety of his speech, but because his vocalisation of desire is caught uncomfortably between the only two discourses available to him: platonic friendship and sodomy. There are literally no early modern terms by which Antonio's desire can be understood.

Antonio's imprisonment, we conventionally expect, will be revoked when Viola/Cesario's problems are resolved. With the entrance of Sebastian not only do brother and sister rediscover each other, but 'nature to her bias', according to most critics, draws Olivia to Sebastian and Orsino to Viola (V.i.257). This appeal to 'nature' can be seen to dissolve the previous dramatic energy expended in portraying socially illegitimate alliances, the conventional betrothals displacing the fantasy embodied by Viola/Cesario of holding in tension simultaneous objects of desire. Many feminist and psychoanalytic critics read this conclusion as a celebration of psychic androgyny in which Viola/Cesario is fantastically split, 'An apple cleft in two' into Viola and Sebastian (V.i.221). However pertinent such a reading may be to the gender politics of the play (and I think that it bypasses rather than resolves the question of gender identity posed by transvestism), it ignores the erotic politics. Antonio's final query, 'Which is Sebastian?' is answered by the 'identification' of Sebastian and Viola and the quick, symmetrical pairings. Or is it? Is the Sebastian whose words to Antonio are: 'Antonio, O my dear Antonio! / How have the hours rack'd and torture'd me, / Since I have lost thee!' (V.i.215–17) the same Sebastian who has just sanctified his love to Olivia? Despite his miraculous betrothal, Sebastian's own desire seems more complicated than the assumption of 'natural' heterosexuality would suggest. In fact, Sebastian's desire, like Viola/Cesario's, seems to obliterate the distinction between homoerotic and heterosexual – at least until the institution of marriage comes into (the) play. As a re-assertion of the essential heterosexuality of desire, Sebastian's allu-sion to 'nature's bias' seems a bit suspect.

Joseph Pequigney offers an alternative interpretation of 'nature to her bias' which not only reopens the question of the meaning of 'bias', but inverts its relation to 'nature'. He notes that 'bias' derives from

> the game of bowls played with a bowl or ball designed to run obliquely, and 'bias' denotes either the form of the bowl that causes it to swerve or, as in the metaphor, the curved course it takes. Nature then chose an oblique or curved rather than a straight way of operat-ing. . . . This homoerotic swerving or lesbian [*sic*] deviation from the heterosexual straight and narrow is not unnatural, but, to the con-trary, a modus operandi of Nature.[20]

Despite its closure, then, *Twelfth Night*'s conclusion seems only ambivalently invested in the natural heterosexuality it imposes.

Comparison of the treatment of homoeroticism in *As You Like It* and *Twelfth Night* suggests that when homoeroticism is not a mutual investment it becomes problematic. This may seem distress-ingly self-evident, but to say it underscores the point that the anxiety exposed in Shakespearean drama is not so much about a particular mode of desire, as about the psychic exposure entailed by a lack of mutuality. Heterosexual desire is equally troubling when unrequited. Despite *Twelfth Night*'s nod to heterosexual impera-tives in the ambiguous allusion to 'nature to her bias', and despite both texts' ultimate movement toward heterosexuality, homoeroti-cism is constructed throughout as merely one more mode of desire. As Antonio puts it, in the closest thing we have to an anti-homophobic statement in an early modern text: 'In nature there's no blemish but the mind; / None can be call'd deform'd but the unkind' (*Twelfth Night*, III.iv.368–9). Both modes of desire are re-sponsive to social and institutional pressures; both are variously at-tributed to 'noble' and 'irrational' impulses. In other words, Shakespearean drama measures homoerotic and heterosexual im-pulses on the same scale of moral and philosophical value.

Secondly, the relative ease or dis-ease with homoerotic desire seems to depend on the extent to which such desire is recuperable within a simultaneous homoeroticism and heterosexuality that will ensure generational reproduction. Specifically, in these plays the dramatised fantasy of eliding women in erotic exchanges seems to initiate anxiety. When homoerotic exchanges threaten to replace heterosexual bonds, when eroticism is collapsed into anxiety about reproduction, then homoeroticism is exorcised at the same time as the female gender is resecured into the patriarchal order.

The specific anxiety about reproduction I hypothesise as a *structuring* principle for the movement of these comedies is not explicitly voiced in either play. It is, however, a dominant theme in the sonnets, beginning with the first line of the first poem to the young man: 'From fairest creatures we desire increase / That thereby beauty's rose might never die'.[21] As the poet exhorts his beloved to 'Look in thy glass, and tell the face thou viewest / Now is the time that face should form another' – that if he should 'Die single ... thine image dies with thee' (Sonnet 3) – the failure to reproduce is figured in narcissistic, even masturbatory, terms: 'For having traffic with thyself alone / Thou of thyself thy sweet self dost deceive' (Sonnet 4). The sonnets' psychic strategy is founded on a paradox: the narcissism of taking the self as masturbatory object can only be countered and mastered by the narcissism of reproducing oneself in one's heirs.

That the failure to reproduce signified by this masturbatory fantasy is a veritable death knell is evidenced by Sonnet 3: 'who is he so fond will be the tomb / Of his self-love, to stop posterity?' Indeed, if one notes that the final couplet of six out of the first seven sonnets explicitly offers death as the sole alternative to reproduction, the anxiety animating the exhortation to reproduce becomes quite clear. The sheer repetition of the sentiment (twelve sonnets out of the first sixteen) attests to the presence of a repetition compulsion, indicating unresolved psychic distress.[22] Such distress obviously structures the reproductive madness of Sonnet 6:

> Then let not winter's ragged hand deface
> In thee thy summer, ere thou be distill'd.
> Make sweet some vial; treasure thou some place
> With beauty's treasure, ere it be self-kill'd.
> That use is not forbidden usury
> Which happies those that pay the willing loan;
> That's for thyself to breed another thee,
> Or ten times happier, be it ten for one;
> Ten times thyself were happier than thou art,
> If ten of thine ten times refigur'd thee.

That ten is ten times better than one is self-evidently true only if the one is not the one who carries, labours and delivers those ten offspring. The misogynistic pun on vial, referring both to the vessel of the womb and its supposedly vile character indicates a structuring ambivalence. The logic of the sequence implies that homoerotic love can only be justified through a heterosexual reproductivity that is always already degraded by its contact with female genitalia – the underlying fantasy being the wish for reproduction magically untainted by the female body.

'Make thee another self, *for love of me*' (Sonnet 10, my emphasis). Surely it is not fortuitous that the homoerotic investment of the sonnets elicits such a strong investment in reproduction. This investment is finally mediated, and the anxiety regarding women's necessary role in reproduction is displaced, as the poet appropriates for himself reproductive powers. From Sonnet 15, in which the poet claims to 'engraft' his beloved 'new', through the subsequent four poems, heterosexual reproduction slowly but surely gives way to the aesthetic immortality 'engrafted' on the beloved by the poet's skill. The power to create life is transformed into the exclusively male power of the poet's invocation to an exclusively male audience: 'So long as men can breathe or eyes can see, / So long lives this and this gives life to thee' (Sonnet 18).

The historical reasons for the reproductive anxiety explicitly rendered in the sonnets, and implied by the structure of the comedies, are obviously complex. In order to unpack them, it may be useful to reinsert gender provisionally as a relevant analytic category, to examine the relation of homoerotic desire to the gender system. Eve Sedgwick argues that male homoeroticism was not perceived as threatening in early modern culture because it was not defined in opposition or as an impediment to heterosexuality; Trumbach and Saslow emphasise that the general pattern of male homoeroticism was 'bisexual'. *Exclusive* male homoeroticism however (homoeroticism that did not admit the need for women) would disrupt important early modern economic and social imperatives: inheritance of name, entitlement and property. Each of these imperatives, crucial to the social hierarchies of early modern England, was predominantly conferred through heterosexual marriage. I am suggesting, then, that the salient concern may be less the threat posed by homoerotic desire *per se* than that posed by non-monogamy and non-reproduction.

In addition, despite patriarchal control of female sexuality through the ideology of chastity and laws regulating marriage and illegitimacy, there seems to have been a high cultural investment in female erotic pleasure – not because women's pleasure was perceived as healthy or intrinsically desirable, but because it was thought necessary for successful conception to occur. According to Thomas Laqueur, early modern medical texts (including those of midwives) judged both male and female erotic pleasure as essential to generation.[23] Viewed as structurally inverted men, women were thought to ejaculate 'seed' at the height of their sexual pleasure; conception supposedly began at the meeting of male and female seed. Because they were perceived as naturally cooler than men, women were thought to achieve orgasm only after the proper 'heating' of their genitalia. In light of this social investment, it seems possible that an exclusive male homoeroticism could be seen as leaving female reproductive organs out, as it were, in the cold.

In so far as As You Like It gestures outward toward an eroticism characterised by a diffuse and fluid simultaneity, it does so because the text never feels compelled to fix, to identify, or to name the desires it expresses. In contrast, Twelfth Night closes down erotic possibility precisely to the degree it complies with the social imperative to name desire, to fix it within definitive boundaries, and to identify it with specific characters. The 'unmooring of desire, the generalizing of the libidinal' that Greenblatt sees as 'the special pleasure of Shakespearean fiction' is, when one gets down to it, more comfortably evidenced in As You Like It than in Twelfth Night.[24] In the tensions exposed between the two plays, it may be that we start to move from what we are beginning to discern as Renaissance homoeroticism to what we know as modern homosexuality, from an inventive potentiality inherent in each subject to the social identity of a discrete order of being.[25]

It is of more than passing interest that in so far as each play enacts a 'textual body', only Twelfth Night depends on a phallic representation of male homoeroticism. Much recent feminist and film criticism has implicated a phallic mode of representation within the visual economy of the 'gaze', wherein value is ascribed according to what one sees (or fails to see): hence, the psychoanalytic verities of female 'castration' and 'penis envy'. In those modes of representation governed by phallocentric prerogatives, argue many feminist film theorists, only two positions seem possible: the subject and the object of the gaze.[26] Although many theorists are now complicating this binary picture, arguing that women, in particular, negotiate as subjects and not merely as objects of the gaze, it might be helpful to distinguish the erotic economies of Twelfth Night and As You Like It along the following lines: Twelfth Night is predominantly phallic and visual;

not only is Antonio's desire figured in phallic metaphors, but Orsino's desire waits upon the ocular proof of Viola/Cesario's 'femininity'. The final value is one of boundary setting, of marginalising others along lines of exclusion. The erotics of *As You Like It*, on the other hand, are diffuse, non-localised, and inclusive, extending to the audience an invitation to 'come play' – as does Rosalind-cum-boy-actor in the Epilogue.[27] Bypassing a purely scopic economy, *As You Like It* possesses provocative affinities with the tactile, contiguous, plural erotics envisioned by Luce Irigaray as more descriptive of female experience. We don't return to such a polymorphous textual body until the cross-gendered erotic play of *Antony and Cleopatra*.

This introduction of a diffuse, fluid erotics, and my analysis of the reproductive anxieties engendered by male homoeroticism, provoke the broader question of the relation of male homoeroticism to feminist politics. Contrary to the beliefs of those feminists who conflate male homosociality with homoeroticism, male homoeroticism has no unitary relationship to the structures and ideologies of male dominance. Patriarchal power is homosocial; but it also has been, at various times including the present, homophobic. As Sedgwick has demonstrated, 'while male homosexuality does not correlate in a transhistorical way with political attitudes toward women, homophobia directed at men by men almost always travels with a retinue of gynephobia and antifeminism'.[28] Male homoeroticism can be manipulated to reinforce and justify misogyny, or it can offer itself up as the means to deconstruct the binary structures upon which the subordination of women depends.

The logic of the sonnet sequence is, I believe, thoroughly misogynistic, and its homoerotics seem utterly entwined with that misogyny: a debased female reproduction is excised, and its creative powers appropriated, by the male lover-poet who thereby celebrates and immortalises his male beloved. Conversely, the circulation of male homoerotic desire in *As You Like It* and *Twelfth Night* does not seem to depend upon an aversion to women or an ideology of male dominance as its *raison d'être*. The homoeroticism of *As You Like It* is not particularly continuous with the homosociality of the Duke's court (the homoerotic exchanges occur primarily between those excluded from it), nor are Antonio's, Viola/Cesario's, Orsino's or Olivia's homoerotic interests particularly supportive of the patriarchal impulses of *Twelfth Night*. Indeed, whether the homoeroticism is embodied as male or female does not seem to have much impact on its subversive potential.

Viola/Cesario's desire for a dual mode of eroticism is more threatening within the play than is Orlando's similar desire, but it is less dangerous than the exclusivity posed by Antonio.

In fact, the male and female homoeroticism of both plays interrupts the ideology of a 'natural' love based on complementary yet oppositional genders. In so doing, the deviations from the dominant discourse of desire circulating throughout these texts transgress the Law of the Father, the injunction that sexuality will follow gender in lining up according to a 'natural' binary code. By refusing such arbitrary divisions of desire, homoeroticism in *As You Like It* and *Twelfth Night* disrupts the cultural code that keeps both men and women in line, subverting patriarchy from within.

This is not to suggest that Shakespeare's plays do not demonstrate countless commitments to misogyny. Why homoeroticism would be so thoroughly supportive of the misogyny of the sonnets, and so seemingly independent of misogyny in these plays is an important question raised by my analysis. To what extent does genre influence the expression of erotic desire and anxiety? To begin to answer that question, and to substantiate those claims I have made, the treatment of homoeroticism in Shakespeare's predecessors, contemporaries and followers must be analysed. Obvious sites of inquiry would be a comparison of Shakespearean homoeroticism with that of Marlowe, and a study of the use of transvestism in Lyly, Sidney, Spenser, Jonson, Middleton and Dekker.[29] What is crucial at this point is that the relation between gender and eroticism be carefully teased out, that eroticism be posed as a problematic in its own right – both intimately connected to and rigorously differentiated from gender.

The danger of pursuing this kind of inquiry at this moment is in ignoring gender differentials altogether, in an energetic pursuit of 'sexuality'. But if we remember that the analyses of both gender and eroticism are only part of a larger project of theorising about and from the multiple subject positions we all live, and if we reflect on the complexity of our own erotic practices, perhaps we can trace the play of our differences without reifying either them or ourselves. Erotic choice is, as Robert Stoller remarks, 'a matter of opinions, taste, aesthetics'; it is also a matter of political theatre, in which we all, even now, play a part.[30]

From *Desire and Anxiety: Circulations of Sexuality in Shakespearean Drama* (London: Routledge, 1992), pp. 122–44.

NOTES

[Taken with 'Desire and the Differences it Makes', the chapter that precedes it in her book, Valerie Traub's essay is a ground-breaking effort to produce a lesbian reading of Shakespeare. Rather than trying to identify elements of lesbian characterisation, or locate latent lesbian desire in the plays, Traub explores the dramatic circulation of erotic energies. Disentangling questions of gender difference, sexual difference and desire through meta-theoretical/critical engagement with previous scholarship, she takes up important questions about the relationship between theory and history. In the omitted first section of the chapter, she uses the boy-actor as a way into seeing Shakespearean comedies as dramatic events where 'a complex subjectivity always already imbricated by gender and erotic pressures' is both constructed and dissolved (p. 112). She resists 'fixing erotic identity onto specific characters', arguing instead 'that the texts themselves display a homoerotic circulation of desire' (p. 114).

I am grateful to Professor Traub for allowing me to make some cuts to this essay, as indicated.   Ed.]

1. Antonio's marginalisation parallels that of Antonio in *The Merchant of Venice*, whose bond to Bassanio is initially honored and redeemed by Portia, but later displaced by her manipulations of the ring plot which, paradoxically, foster her subordination in a patriarchal heterosexual economy.

2. Louis Adrian Montrose, '"The Place of a Brother" in *As You Like It*: Social Process and Comic Form', *Shakespeare Quarterly*, 32:1 (1981), 28–54.

3. Ibid., 51.

4. Jean Howard, 'Crossdressing, the Theatre and Gender Struggle in Early Modern England', *Shakespeare Quarterly*, 39:4 (1988), 434.

5. Ibid., 435. Terms can be confusing here, in part due to translation. In Luce Irigaray's formulation, *la mascarade* is 'An alienated or false version of femininity arising from the woman's awareness of the man's desire for her to be his other, the masquerade permits woman to experience desire not in her own right but as the man's desire situates her.' Masquerade is the role (playing) required by 'femininity'. Thus, Rosalind's improvisation is really closer to *mimétisme* (mimicry) which, in Irigaray's terms, is 'An interim strategy for dealing with the realm of discourse (where the speaking subject is posited as masculine), in which the woman deliberately assumes the feminine style and posture assigned to her within this discourse in order to uncover the mechanisms by which it exploits her' (*This Sex which is not One*, trans. Catherine Porter [Ithaca, NY: Cornell University Press, 1985], p. 220).

6. James Saslow, *Ganymede in the Renaissance: Homosexuality in Art and Society* (New Haven, CT: Yale University Press, 1986), p. 2.

7. Stephen Orgel, 'Nobody's Perfect: Or, Why did the English Stage take Boys for Women?', *South Atlantic Quarterly*, 88 (1989), 7–29 (p. 22).

8. C. L. Barber, *Shakespeare's Festive Comedy: A Study of Dramatic Form and its Relation to Social Custom* (New York: Princeton University Press, 1963), p. 231. See also W. Thomas MacCary, *Friends and Lovers: The Phenomenology of Desire in Shakespearean Comedy* (New York: Columbia University Press, 1985).

9. Phyllis Rackin, 'Historical Difference/Sexual Difference', in *Privileging Gender in Early Modern England*, ed. Jean R. Brink (Kirksville: 16th Century Journal Publisher, 1992).

10. Peter Stallybrass helped me with this formulation.

11. Laurie Osborne, 'The Texts of *Twelfth Night*', *ELH* (Spring, 1990), 37–61. Osborne's excellent analysis of the manipulation of the placement of the Antonio scenes in eighteenth- and nineteenth-century performance editions suggests that the playtexts themselves indicate changing significations of homoeroticism.

12. The *Oxford English Dictionary*'s first entry for 'anxiety' as in 'The quality or state of being anxious; uneasiness or trouble of mind about some uncertain event; solicitude, concern', is 1525. The first entry for 'jealous', as in 'Vehement in feeling, as in wrath, desire, or devotion' is 1382: for 'Ardently amorous; covetous of the love of another, fond, lustful' is 1430; and for 'Zealous or solicitous for the preservation or well-being of something possessed or esteemed; vigilant or careful in guarding; suspiciously careful or watchful' is 1387.

13. I am indebted to Peter Stallybrass for reminding me of the difference between heterosexual and homoerotic phallic imagery.

14. *Romeo and Juliet*, III.i.113–25; *Antony and Cleopatra*, I.iv.5–7; and *Coriolanus*, IV.v.111–23. I am indebted to Phyllis Rackin for reminding me of some of these instances, and her further amplification in her talk 'Historical Difference/Sexual Difference'.

15. Randolph Trumbach's historical analysis bears this out; see 'The Birth of the Queen: Sodomy and the Emergence of Gender Equality in Modern Culture, 1660–1750', *Hidden from History: Reclaiming the Gay and Lesbian Past*, ed. Martin Duberman *et al.* (New York: New American Library, 1989), p. 133.

16. For an analysis of triangular desire, see René Girard, *Deceit, Desire, and the Novel: Self and Other in Literary Structure*, trans. Yvonne Freccero (Baltimore, MD: Johns Hopkins University Press, 1965).

17. Howard, 'Crossdressing', p. 432.

18. *Henry IV, Part 1*, I.iii.29–69; *Hamlet*, V.ii.82–193 and III.ii.368–9; *King Lear*, II.iv.271–8.

19. Randolph Trumbach, 'The Birth of the Queen', in *Hidden from History*, ed. Martin Duberman *et al.* (New York, 1989), pp. 129–40, p. 134.

20. Joseph Pequigney, 'The Two Antonios and Same-Sex Love in *Twelfth Night* and *The Merchant of Venice*', unpublished manuscript presented to the Shakespeare Association of America (1989), p. 11.

21. I am following David Bevington's numbering of the sonnets; he follows Thomas Thorpe, the original publisher of the sequence. In 'Making Love Out of Nothing At All: the Issue of Story in Shakespeare's Procreation Sonnets', *Shakespeare Quarterly*, 41, 4 (Winter 1990), 470–88, Robert Crosman takes up the issue of homoeroticism from a sympathetic if rather uninformed historical perspective. Whereas Pequigney argues that the first seventeen 'procreation' sonnets record a gradual evolution of the poet's feelings for the young man, Crosman argues that Shakespeare first pretended to fall in love with his patron as a strategy of flattery, and then discovered he was no longer pretending.

22. For an explanation of the repetition compulsion, see Sigmund Freud, *Beyond the Pleasure Principle*, trans. James Strachey (New York: Norton, 1961).

23. Thomas Laqueur, *Making Sex: Body and Gender from the Greeks to Freud* (Cambridge, MA: Harvard University Press, 1990).

24. Stephen Greenblatt, 'Fiction and Friction', in *Shakespearean Negotiations: The Circulation of Social Energy in Renaissance England* (Oxford: Clarendon Press, 1988), p. 89.

25. Saslow makes a similar point about Michelangelo's status as a transitional figure; see 'Homosexuality in the Renaissance: Behaviour, Identity, and Artistic Expression', in *Hidden from History: Reclaiming the Gay and Lesbian Past*, ed. Martin Duberman, Martha Vicinus and George Chauncey Jr (New York: New American Library, 1989), pp. 90–105.

26. See, for instance, Laura Mulvey, 'Visual Pleasure and Narrative Cinema', and 'Afterthoughts on "Visual Pleasure and Narrative Cinema" inspired by *Duel in the Sun*', *Feminism and Film Theory*, ed. Constance Penley (London: Routledge, 1988), pp. 57–79; Janet Bergstrom and Mary Ann Doane, 'The Female Spectator: Contexts and Directions', *Camera Obscura: A Journal of Feminism and Film Theory*, 20/21 (May/Sept. 1989), pp. 5–27; and Irigaray, *This Sex which is not One*, pp. 23–33.

27. Jean Howard alerted me to the fact that class differences are implicated in these erotic differences: as nostalgic pastoral, *As You Like It*'s

class hierarchy is diffused and inclusive; *Twelfth Night*, on the other hand, is thoroughly aristocratic and, with the exception of Maria, marginalises those figures below the rank of 'gentleman'.

28. Eve Sedgwick, *Between Men: English Literature and Male Homosocial Desire* (New York: Columbia University Press, 1985), p. 216.

29. Phyllis Rackin has initiated such a comparative analysis of transvestism in 'Androgyny, Mimesis, and the Marriage of the Boy Heroine on the English Renaissance Stage', *PMLA*, 102 (1987), 29–41.

30. Robert Stoller, *Observing the Erotic Imagination* (New Haven, CT: Yale University Press, 1985), p. 15.

7

Mourning and Misogyny: *Hamlet* and the Final Progress of Elizabeth I

STEVEN MULLANEY

I

In 1597, André Hurault, Sieur de Maisse and Ambassador Extraordinary from Henri IV, noted that although the English people still professed love for their aging queen, the sentiments of the nobility were such that 'the English would never again submit to the rule of a woman'.[1] There may have been more coincidence between high and low opinion than de Maisse thought. On the evening of Elizabeth's death six years later, the streets of London were lit by festive bonfires and punctuated by cries of 'We have a king!'[2] The advent of an orderly and Protestant succession does not in itself account for such a celebratory spirit; in fact, it was a significant transformation in the body politic, a reincorporation and regendering of monarchy, that was being heralded. Rather than a seamless transition of power reminding all the populace that the corporate body of the monarch was immortal, unchanging, and un-altered by the demise of a particular sovereign, the death of Elizabeth marked a breach in the body politic as much as a continu-ation of it, and one that could be figured, at least by some, as a welcome discontinuity. The queen is dead – long live the king.

There were extensive and sincere eulogies, to be sure, heartfelt expressions of grief over the passing of Elizabeth, but during the last years of her reign the 'political misogynism of the early years' (Haigh, p. 166) had also resurfaced strongly throughout her court and beyond its confines. It would not take many years of Jacobean rule to complicate the desire for a male sovereign, of course. As Christopher Haigh has noted, an idealised portrait of Elizabeth as a shrewd ruler and capable strategist emerged gradually over the first decade of James's reign, oftentimes in the form of a 'coded commentary' on the defects of that reign (Haigh, p. 167). But the recuperation and even reinvention of such a queen – Gloriana, the Virgin Queen, who had reigned for a remarkable span of forty-five years – seems a more complicated cultural process than Haigh's pragmatic account suggests. It is this process of accommodation and revision, marked as it is by an uncertain economy between mourning and misogyny, that I wish to examine here; I am interested not only in Elizabeth herself but also in the complex and ambivalent affective process that her death allows us to glimpse – a process that might be called mourning under the sign of patriarchy. Indeed, the possibility I wish to entertain is that, for the Renaissance, (male) mourning is sometimes difficult to dissociate from misogyny: that misogyny may in fact be an integral part of the mourning process when the lost object or ideal being processed is a woman, especially but not exclusively when that woman is a queen of England, too.

. . . .

In this context, both mourning and misogyny pose interpretive challenges specific to late-sixteenth-century English culture. Misogyny presents an interpretive embarrassment of riches: it is everywhere, unabashed in its articulation and so overdetermined in its cultural roots that individual instances sometimes seem emotionally underdetermined, rote and uninflected expressions of what would go without saying if it weren't said so often.[3] By contrast, articulated expressions of grief are far less common. Private personal diaries, in which one would expect to find subjective emotional responses recorded, are themselves rare in the period; the expressions of individual grief which do exist can easily strike the modern reader as remote and unfeeling, leading even so astute a student of the past as Lawrence Stone to confuse historical and cultural difference with absence and to declare that major bereavements were not felt as such in the period, since 'in the sixteenth and seventeenth centuries interpersonal relations were at best cold and at worst hostile'.[4] For any inquiry into the entanglement or interaction of such forms of affect, Elizabeth clearly provides a salutary and strategic methodological focus, as a woman who so fully commanded the political life of the nation and for such an extensive period that she also inscribed herself deeply in the cultural imagination of Renaissance England. The final progress of Elizabeth – the cultural processing of her age, in both senses of that term – was completed long after her funeral procession took place but begun some years before it, when her aging body first announced the proximity of her last days; it was enacted not in the streets of London or in the provinces but in the political unconscious, and to catch a glimpse of it we have to broaden our field of inquiry beyond the traditional resources of political history – journals and letters written before and after the queen's death, or the histories of Greville and Camden – and turn, among other places, to the Elizabethan and Jacobean stage. It has often been remarked that the resurgent political misogyny of Elizabeth's court in the 1590s coincided with a dramatic increase, as it were, of misogyny onstage; in the years after her death, as recent studies have also begun to detail, the popular stage manifested an acute and complex investment in the imaginary reworking and resolution of Elizabeth's reign.[5] But my own recourse to the popular theatre is not solely motivated by such topical resonances. For anyone concerned, as I am here, with the cultural construction of emotions and other forms of affect, the popular stage represents a unique historical resource, and one whose significance in its own time cannot be limited to the passive role of merely recording or reflecting early modern structures of feeling.

The symbolic economy of English culture (by which I refer not just to official efforts to manage and maintain dominant systems of belief but to the entire repertoire of cultural representations and practices, official and unofficial, that shaped the political, social and psychological subject and defined his or her place in the cultural hierarchy) underwent a significant and radical transformation in the sixteenth century. The English Reformation itself was hardly a tidy affair, marked as it was by the succession of no less than five official state religions, each claiming the status of unrivalled and absolute truth, and all within the space of a single generation; one of the results was to displace and destabilises the very notion of the orthodox or the absolute, producing a sceptical if not cynical relativism evident, in court records, even among the lower classes. During the same period, individuals commanded an increasingly greater access to heterodox ideas and ideologies, aided as they were by the rapid expansion of print culture and by what we think was a slow yet steady rise in literacy. But contemporary fears of an increasingly informed and hence more autonomous subject were focused not only on those who could read, and with good reason; as Tessa Watt has recently reminded us, the boundary between oral and literate cultures in the period was highly permeable, such that ideas and ideologies were disseminated not only by direct and unmediated access to a printed text but also by diverse processes of re-presentation and representation, in official and unofficial forums ranging from the pulpit to the tavern.[6] In the case of sixteenth-century London, however, what the debate over literacy obscures is a much more explosive expansion of the symbolic economy – the one produced by the fiercely contested emergence and rapid institutionalisation of the popular stage.

The controversy provoked by the popular theatre was largely ideological and political rather than aesthetic, and the reasons for this are relatively clear. Public drama was not customarily graced with the status of literature or, less anachronistically, of poesy. More important, in an age when the domain in which knowledge was produced and circulated was still a relatively contained system, any significant expansion of that domain, any significant difference in the degree to which ideas and attitudes could be disseminated, threatened to become a difference in kind as well – to alter the structure of knowledge by redefining its boundaries, to force a transition from a relatively limited and closed symbolic system to a more radically open economy of knowledge and representation. That the emerging institution in question was, at best, quasi-illicit only exacerbated the dilemma of its emergence. Combatted throughout its history by the city, licensed but hardly controlled by the court, the Elizabethan public theatre emerged from and appropriated a place within the fissures and contradictions of the cultural landscape; although it rapidly became, in Jean Howard's words, 'one of the chief ideological apparatuses of Elizabethan society',[7] it was neither the product nor the organ of the state but rather the result of a historically determined collusion between artisanal entrepreneurs and a socially diverse and astoundingly large audience. And unlike other expansions of the discursive domain in the period, literacy was not the price of admission to the theatre, a fact which gave the stage a currency and accessibility rivalled only by the pulpit, which it threatened to eclipse.

Unlike the pulpit, of course, the stage was an affective rather than a didactic forum; the ideas and ideologies, stories and histories real (whatever that might mean) and imaginary that it made available, and hence appropriable, for a significant portion of the population were also dramatically embodied, and by modes of theatrical representation that were themselves significant departures from English dramatic tradition.[8] The shift away from the morality tradition and its abstract personification of states-of-being and toward the particular, discursive and theatrical embodiment of affective characters demanded and produced new powers of identification, projection and apprehension in audiences, altering the threshold not only of dramatic representation but also of self-representation, not only of the fictional construction of character but also of the social construction of the self.[9] As a forum for the representation, solicitation, shaping and enacting of affect in various forms, for both the reflection and, I would argue, the reformation of emotions and their economies, the popular stage of early modern England was a unique contemporaneous force. It may well have participated in what many before me, from Weber and Elias to Foucault, have posited as a fundamental reshaping of the political, social and psychological subject during this period; it certainly served as a prominent affective arena in which significant cultural traumas and highly ambivalent events, such as the death of Elizabeth, could be directly or indirectly addressed, symbolically enacted and brought to partial and imaginary resolution.

As I noted above, misogyny is generally on the rise in the drama of late Elizabethan and early Jacobean years, but it intersects with mourning in certain plays and genres more fully and forcefully than in others. Revenge tragedy has long been recognised, on the one hand, for the speed with which it becomes virtually synonymous with stage misogyny and, on the other, for its generic and sometimes profound investment in recognisably Renaissance processes of mourning – revenge, after all, is the private response to socially unaccommodated grief – but typically mourning and misogyny have been considered in isolation from one another, in separate studies and only in so far as they duplicate Renaissance habits of thought articulated elsewhere, in medical or philosophical discourse. Yet it is in late Elizabethan and early Jacobean revenge tragedy that the aging and posthumous body of Elizabeth is most fully engaged and problematised, in an apprehensive interplay of mourning and misogyny, revisionary desire and aggression, idealisation and travesty.

. . . .

II

In 1600 the Virgin Queen was sixty-eight years old, and contemporaneous accounts of her appearance detail the degree to which she was showing her age. In that same year, however, the Rainbow Portrait was issued, placing in circulation a new image of an unaging and youthful Gloriana. Yet the contradiction between the age inscribed on the queen's body and the highly sexualised aura generated by the cult of Elizabeth over the years and reinvoked in such late portraits was more complexly wrought than any distinction between reality and image can encompass; presenting or representing her body – 'showing her age', to recall my own colloquial expression in a fuller register – necessitated a full and overdetermined embodiment of this sovereign contradiction. Although prospects of childbearing and marriage were long past and a Protestant successor was waiting in the wings, the aging of Elizabeth during the last decade of her reign was still a highly fraught political, physical and symbolic issue, as she herself well knew.

'I think not to die so soon,' Elizabeth told the French ambassador in 1597, '... and am not so old as they think' (De Maisse, p. 82). De Maisse had already recorded, in journal entries from previous audiences, some of Elizabeth's efforts to counter what 'they think', to embody in her age an alluring and captivating appeal:

> She was strangely attired in a dress of silver cloth, white and crimson. . . . She kept the front of her dress open, and one could see the whole of her bosom [gorge], and passing low, and often she would open the front of this robe with her hands as if she was too hot. . . . Her bosom [or throat; gorge][10] is somewhat wrinkled as well as [one can see for] the collar that she wears round her neck [col], but lower down her flesh is exceeding white and delicate, so far as one could see.
>
> As for her face, it is and appears to be very aged. It is long and thin, and her teeth are very yellow and unequal, compared with what they were formerly. . . . Many of them are missing so that one cannot understand her easily when she speaks quickly. Her figure is fair and tall and graceful in whatever she does. (De Maisse, pp. 25–6)

The queen's behaviour was apparently not exceptional; in an entry that records a subsequent audience de Maisse tells us

> [S]he was clad in a dress of black taffeta. . . . She had a petticoat of white damask, girdled, and open in front, as was also her chemise, in such a manner that she often opened this dress and one could see all her belly, and even to her navel. . . . When she raises her head she has a trick of putting both hands on her gown and opening it insomuch that all her belly can be seen. (De Maisse, pp. 36–7)

As Louis Montrose has noted in detail, Elizabeth's display of her bosom was a complex register of cultural and sumptuary symbolism, signifying her status as a maiden and as a nurturing and bountiful mother, a 'virgin-mother – part Madonna, part Ephesian Diana', whose 'conspicuous self-displays were also a kind of erotic provocation'.[11] In private the signs of age in the queen's face were apparently left unobscured by cosmetics, heightening the incongruity between advanced age ('her face … is … very aged … long and thin') and the exposed bosom of a maiden ('lower down her flesh is exceeding white and delicate'). In the public domain this incongruity was lessened and mystified to a certain degree by the circulation of painted images of the unaging sovereign body, but even here the line between image and reality, idealised portrait and the physical lineaments of age, is difficult to draw. Anthony Rivers, a Jesuit priest, reported that at Christmas celebrations in 1600, Elizabeth was painted 'in some places near half an inch thick'.[12] The queen was painted on canvases more than one; she was herself one of those canvases, a painted image no less than the Rainbow Portrait was.

Of course few outside the court saw either the Rainbow Portrait or the queen's holiday face, but it would be a mistake to conclude from this that Elizabeth's erotic displays and painted selves were either inconsequential or mere vanity, given all that was at stake in the sovereign aura. They were efforts to imbue the aging natural body of the monarch with the ageless aura of the body politic, which, as Marie Axton notes, 'was supposed to be contained within the natural body of the Queen'.[13] Elizabeth's attempt to reinvest her final years with the erotic dynamics of courtship and desire – with the dynamics of Petrarchan romance that had so fully informed her earlier reign[14] – was an effort to close the gap or internal fissure that was, in the 1590s, increasingly apparent between the queen's two bodies. It was an ambivalent enterprise at best, especially where cosmetic portraiture or face-painting was concerned, as Thomas Tuke's 'Treatise against Painting' makes clear. According to Tuke, the painted woman, like the monarch, has two bodies; but the painted woman is an idolatrous and even curiously transvestite parody of the incorporated monarchical body, one that violates categories of gender and grammar as well as prerogatives of divine creation:

> She is a creature that has need to be twice defined. . . . [T]hough she be the creature of God, as she is a woman, yet is she her own creatress, as a picture. Indeed a plain woman is but half a painted woman, who is both a substantive and an adjective, and yet not of the neuter gender: but a feminine as well consorting with a masculine, as ivy with an ash.[15]

Tuke and other commentators also describe the poisonous effects of the mercury-based cosmetics used in the period; as Laurie A. Finke has noted, such descriptions serve as both medical warnings and ideologically potent metaphorical images, vividly registering 'all the horrors, both visual and olfactory, of [a] putrefying corpse'.[16] In such treatises a cosmetically enhanced visage figures as a sign not of sexual allure but of the skull beneath the skin – or rather, sexual allure and the skull are combined in a conundrum that *is* the aging female body, for in a period that linguistically coded sexual climax as a form of death, 'dying' the face introduces a third register to the common Renaissance pun. The painted lady does not disguise death or obscure the skull beneath her painted flesh; she is a *memento mori* herself, without need of demystification.

Even aside from the necessity to paint 'near half an inch thick', however, the erotic dynamics of Elizabethan rule had always entailed a certain ambivalence and danger, involving as they did the construction of an ambiguous desire for the queen, not as monarch but as woman. An incident in 1600 documents Elizabeth's continuing success, even in her later years, in thus constructing her subjects' desires, and illustrates some of the danger involved as well. On 3 June of that year, Elizabeth's secretary, William Waad, wrote to Cecil concerning the antic disposition of one Abraham Edwardes, a 'Kentish man born, and ... a mariner', who first came to Waad's attention when he sent 'so passionate a letter to her Majesty' and was subsequently arrested and imprisoned 'for drawing his dagger in the presence chamber'. Rather than charging Edwardes with attempted regicide, Waad counselled his removal to

Bedlam Hospital, noting that 'the fellow is greatly distracted, and seems rather to be transported with a humour of love, than any purpose to attempt anything against her Majesty'.[17]

Waad provides a curiously one-dimensional, even proto-Freudian interpretation of the scene. Edwardes's display of love in the form of a drawn dagger seems at least to combine sexual and other potential forms of physical aggression and violence; whatever the case, his act was in itself a violation of the queen's presence, and one that is tempting to relate to Hamlet's audience with another queen, when he needs to remind himself to use verbal rather than physical violence in Gertrude's chamber: 'I will speak daggers to her, but use none' (III.ii.387). It is relatively certain that some version of *Hamlet* was being presented onstage by 1600, and the play may have made its first appearance as early as 1598 or 1599, so topical allusion in the usual sense of the phrase is not at issue. Juxtaposed with Hamlet's royal audience, however, Edwardes's 'humour of love' does allow us to see the queen – Elizabeth or Gertrude – through period eyes, shifting critical focus from the long-romanticised melancholy of the Dane to the aging yet erotic body of the queen, and in a manner that supplements recent suggestions that *Hamlet* is a play keenly aware of its *late* Elizabethan status, in which the impending transfer of power 'from one monarch to another had to be rethought in view of the aging body of the queen'.[18]

III

Cecil seems to have adhered to Waad's advice: Abraham Edwardes was not prosecuted as an attempted regicide, despite appearances and the ease with which a case against him could have been made, but was instead confined as an antic lover, overly receptive to the queen's graces. *Hamlet* may serve to condition our surprise at such peculiar and lenient treatment. In the play Hamlet's own role as an antic lover is debunked rather than confirmed by the crown, but regicide is similarly displaced from his and our attention by the eroticised and aging figure of the queen. Mourning for a dead king, even revenge, is displaced or at least overlaid and complicated by misogyny toward a queen who is too vital, whose sexuality transgresses both her age and her brief tenure as widow.

Hamlet's first appearance onstage sets the pattern. Isolated by the mourning clothes he refuses to abandon and more aggressively distanced from the court by his barbed comments and asides (and perhaps by his stage position as well),[19] Hamlet styles his grief as that which 'passes show':

> Seems madam? Nay, it is. I know not 'seems'.
> 'Tis not alone my inky cloak, good mother,
> Nor customary suits of solemn black.
> Nor windy suspiration of forc'd breath.
> No, nor the fruitful river in the eye,
> Nor the dejected haviour of the visage,
> Together with all forms, moods, shapes of grief,
> That can denote me truly. These indeed seem,
> For they are actions that a man might play;
> But I have that within which passes show,
> These but the trappings and the suits of woe.
>   (I.ii.76–86)

What you see is what you get: surface and depth, appearance stage posture and being coincide and cohere fully in a proclamation of sincerity that marks all around him as theatrical dissemblers. When alone onstage, however, Hamlet immediately reveals that all is not as it seems:

> Fie on't, ah fie, 'tis an unweeded garden
> That grows to seed; things rank and gross in nature
> Possess it merely. That it should come to this!
> But two months dead – nay, not so much, not two –
> ...
> Why, she would hang on him
> As if increase of appetite had grown
> By what it fed on; and yet within a month –
> Let me not think on't – Frailty, thy name is woman. . . .
>   (I.ii.135–46)

Grief over his father's death is overlaid and supplanted by obsessive disgust over what has failed to die, here figured as the unweeded garden of Gertrude's sexual appetite, the incestuous 'dexterity' of the queen (l. 157) which indeed occupies the core of Hamlet's being and 'denote[s him] truly', as a generalised sign of the bestial inconstancy of all womankind. Like son, like father: at the first mention of his 'seeming-virtuous queen', the Ghost forgets his purpose and digresses upon Gertrude's lust and lewdness, her taste for 'garbage';

and it is only the morning air that reminds him that his time is short, and that he has yet to inform Hamlet of the details of Claudius's crime. The vengeful charge of the Ghost itself focuses not on the past crime of regicide but on the ongoing sexual transgression: 'Let not the royal bed of Denmark be / A couch for luxury and damned incest' (I.v.82–3). Even in the later Mousetrap scene, Claudius is hardly the observed of all observers; throughout the Player Queen and King's prologue, Hamlet's attention is for Gertrude alone, this part of the Mousetrap functioning clearly to catch the conscience not of the king but of the queen.

This obsessive concern with Gertrude is hardly news; a long history of oedipal readings begins here, typically effacing the sovereign cast of Hamlet's obsessive misogyny – Gertrude as queen – by an exclusive focus on the domestic scene, viewing the play as one more family romance – Gertrude as mother – only incidentally staged in terms of state hierarchies and monarchical sexuality. Performances governed by this critical tradition often portray Gertrude as a young queen, sometimes played by an actress, who is, if anything, younger than the actor playing Hamlet. Quite recently, however, critics have suggested that the aging widowed queen of the play resonates strongly with the aging virgin queen on the throne. As Peter Erickson has remarked, 'Gertrude represents the convergence of three issues – sexuality, aging ... , and succession – that produced a sense of contradiction, even breakdown, in the cult of Elizabeth in the final years of her reign. . . . The latent cultural fantasy in *Hamlet* is that Queen Gertrude functions as a degraded figure of Queen Elizabeth.'[20] What I earlier called the conundrum of the aging female body, with its overdetermined registers of sexuality and death, unites the two monarchs. Aspects of the two that might seem to distinguish them – Gertrude's status, for example, as both widow and mother – also contribute to the association of royal bodies when viewed in a sixteenth-century context. Elizabeth styled herself, of course, as the sovereign mother of her subjects; she also presided over a period in which widows occupied an increasingly anomalous and threatening position, whether they remarried or remained single. As independent yet marriageable women, they recovered the one position of power available to most women in early modern patriarchal society – the social space on the threshold of marital alliance which Elizabeth had occupied so masterfully throughout her reign – but this time without parental strictures and often with enhanced economic power as well, derived from the estates inherited from their husbands. Remarriage might seem to resolve the threat posed by female independence, bringing the woman back into the fold of patriarchal hegemony, but, as Barbara J. Todd has demonstrated, in the later part of the sixteenth century the reverse was true: remarriage raised fears of greater independence, and of a kind where economic and sexual hierarchies are difficult to disentangle. After about 1570, wills began to restrict widows' access to inherited estates if they remarried, and the economic grounds for such restrictions are often overlaid with sexual anxieties. 'The remarriage of any widow,' as Todd puts it, 'confronted every man with the threatening prospect of his own death and the entry of another into his place.'[21]

Gertrude's transgression is not merely against her first husband, however. What distracts Hamlet from his almost blunted purpose is Gertrude's *aging* sexuality, conceived at times as a contradiction in terms, at times as a violation of her own body akin in its unnaturalness to a rebellion in the body politic: hers is a passion that 'canst mutine in a matron's bones' (III.iv.83), at once unimaginable and yet impossible not to imagine and visualise in graphic detail. At her age the queen's sovereignty should extend to and rule over such desires – 'You cannot call it love; for at your age / The heyday in the blood is tame' (ll. 68–9) – and if not, such passion is a mutineer, a traitor, a figure of 'rebellious hell'. The heyday in Gertrude's blood can be denigrated but cannot be exorcised from Hamlet's mind or her matron's bones or her chamber, where she lives 'In the rank sweat of an enseamed bed, / Stew'd in corruption, honeying and making love / Over the nasty sty!' (ll.92–4).

Where modern productions sometimes efface the transgression of aging sexuality, the stage apparatus of the Elizabethan theatre would have necessarily heightened the incongruity and contradiction embodied in Gertrude's figure. Gertrude is verbally inscribed with a sexuality that, according to Hamlet, transgresses the sovereign and aging body of the queen; onstage such a transgression would have been at once refigured and reproduced as a contradiction between the object and means of theatrical representation, the aging but sexually marked discursive body of the queen given its theatrical embodiment not by means of verisimilitude but by means of a homologous, highly sexualised contradiction of a different order.[22] On the Elizabethan stage the skull beneath the painted skin, the mutineer in the matron's bones, would be represented not by an aging actress but by a boy whose sexual register onstage and in the acting company was also ambivalently marked, differently but equally overdetermined, and to a considerable extent indecipherable from our own historical vantage point.[23]

According to Freud, melancholy is produced by an incapacity to acknowledge or properly mourn death; distinguishing between Freud's nearly synonymous use of the terms *incorporation* and *introjection* to describe the mourning process, Nicolas Abraham and Maria Torok have defined incorporation as the sign of this interminable mourning.[24] The temporising process of incorporation intervenes, as Jacques Derrida explains, whenever introjection is blocked or fails for whatever reason:

> Sealing the loss of the object, but also marking the refusal to mourn, such a maneuver is foreign to and actually opposed to the process of introjection. I pretend to keep the dead alive, intact, *safe (save) inside me*, but it is only in order to refuse, in a necessarily equivocal way, to love the dead as a living part of me, dead *save in me*, through the process of introjection, as happens in so-called normal mourning.[25]

Even if we accept such terms as relevant for other times and cultures – and some such distinction between resolved and irresolvable mourning does seem valid whether for a play like *Hamlet* or for even more distant cultural contexts – we must still historicise them. For example, English culture in the last half of the sixteenth century witnessed an intense Protestant campaign against both the expression of grief and the expression of comfort or condolence toward those in mourning. As G. W. Pigman has shown, sixteenth-century treatises on mourning regard grief as a sign of 'irrationality, weakness, inadequate self-control, and impiety'[26] – the latter succinctly registered in Jonson's 'Of Death':

> He that feares death, or mournes it, in the iust,
> Shewes of the resurrection little trust.[27]

Manuals on grief and bereavement counselled angry remonstration against the bereaved rather than sympathy or comfort, producing an ideologically charged cultural climate whose ramifications are difficult to determine with any rigour but which should at least condition modern critical responses to the maimed rites of mourning in a play such as *Hamlet*. The degree to which such strictures affected how people *felt* grief in the period is of course uncertain; for a brief period of time, however, they clearly altered the decorum of bereavement, casting a moralising and religiously charged pall over traditionally available expressions of grief, whether public rites or private rituals and practices. The result for Elizabethan England may well have been a higher ratio of socially induced melancholy, in Abraham and Torok's revised sense of that term, fostering a psychic culture of incorporation rather than introjection.

Hamlet's melancholy, however, is of an entirely different order: produced as much by Gertrude's sexual vitality as by his father's death, it is the result not of an interminable or encrypted mourning but of a 'prevented' mourning in the rhetorical sense of the term – a mourning before the fact, over a vitality that one wants to be or imagines or finally produces as past and dead. It is an all-too-fully proleptic mourning, and misogyny is the sign of this prolepsis: a response to what should be dead but isn't, an aggressive and often counterproductive effort to resolve this dilemma. What is sexually vital in the aging queen becomes variously figured as its opposite, a sign of death. The Player Queen presents one aspect of this sign, and in doing so clarifies the degree to which Gertrude's sexual desire and behaviour do not merely distract Hamlet from his ostensible object of mourning – the former king – but are fully folded into it as an emblem of death to the male order of state and marital hierarchies. 'A second time I kill my husband dead, / When second husband kisses me in bed' (III.ii.179–80). Twice in the play, Hamlet himself configures signs of female sexuality-in-age as *memento mori*, registering not vitality but corruption and death. To Ophelia, whose youth presumably belies the need for cosmetics, he castigates painted women as transgressive and presumptuous usurpers of divine creation ('God hath given you one face and you make yourselves another' [III.i.144–6]); in the graveyard scene Yorick's skull prompts not a reflection on human or even male mortality but a triumphant reading and declaration of *female* mortality: 'Now get you to my lady's chamber and tell her, let her paint an inch thick, to this favor she must come' (V.i.186–9).

Although a commonplace of Renaissance misogyny, Hamlet's move from Yorick's skull to that of the painted lady is also a great deal more. It is the last instance of the pattern I briefly outlined earlier, in which an obsessive misogyny displaces or supplants grief over a male figure, and as such it marks a significant moment in the gynophobia of the play. After this moment Gertrude is no longer vilified and villainised for *her* sexual transgression but is instead represented as the victim of *Claudius's* pandering lust:

He that hath kill'd my king and *whor'd my mother*,
Popp'd in between th'election and my hopes;
Thrown out his angle for my proper life...
                    (V.ii.64–6; my emphasis)

The change is a dramatic one: grammatical object rather than subject, victim rather than sexually transgressive agent, Gertrude no longer precipitates a misogynistic digression: she is no longer the source of obsessive concern that displaces revenge but instead has become one among several motives for revenge. This is not, it should be noted, the only difference in the Hamlet we encounter in Act V; he reveals a new and calm assurance in the working of divine providence as well, a transformation that has sometimes been ascribed to what happens offstage, characterised as a sea-change produced by the fortuitous events onboard the ship bound for England. The muting of misogyny cannot be so ascribed, but may be located in the graveyard scene itself.

Why should the proleptic death of 'my lady', Hamlet's or Shakespeare's painted queen, be figured into a moment of mourning for a court jester? What partial resolution of misogyny is enacted by such a complex and composite figure? In a play where mourning is characteristically prolonged or disrupted by prematurely foreshort-ened or 'maimed' rites, Hamlet's encounter with Yorick's skull pro-vides a subtle if economical glimpse of successful mourning in action, of what Abraham and Torok define as introjection rather than incorporation. Hamlet's caustic and easy cynicism over the levelling effect of death earlier in the scene, when the bones tossed up by the gravedigger are anonymous, ceases when Yorick's skull surfaces and is named. The thing Hamlet holds in his hand recalls and makes present in his mind the living figure, the vital memory from his childhood, even though the two Yoricks register at first as sheer contradiction, and what is alive in memory and imagination seems reduced to this, the decayed skull, in a moment of visceral revulsion:

> Alas, poor Yorick. I knew him, Horatio, a fellow of infinite jest, of most excellent fancy. He hath bore me on his back a thousand times, and now – how abhorred in my imagination it is. My gorge rises at it.   (V.i.178–82)

Successful mourning requires a resolution of the contradiction between what is still vital in the memory and what is dead; rather than deny or avoid the contradiction, Hamlet heightens it by projecting the living memory onto the skull, lips onto the death's head, and exacerbates his revulsion by planting an imaginary (recollected) kiss on the grotesque, composite overlay. He then shifts from commentary to direct address:

> Here hung those lips that I have kissed I know not how oft. Where be your gibes now, your gambols, your songs, your flashes of merriment, that were wont to set the table on a roar? Not one now to mock your own grinning? Quite chop-fallen?   (ll.183–6)

The Yorick in Hamlet's mind would have mocked his own death, even his own death's head; that was, after all, his profession. The Yorick in Hamlet's hand is somber, serious, 'grinning' but 'quite chop-fallen'. The moment of direct address, however, is also the moment of full introjection of that which is vital, making the living memory not only a part of Hamlet but also the part he now plays, literally in the face of death; the memory is made present not only in mind but also in body and behaviour, embodied and given voice and new life onstage, as Hamlet becomes Yorick, the jester mocking his own grinning.

Why such a moment is interrupted by Hamlet's final piece of misogyny, and with such a satisfied and resolute tone, is unclear unless we press the peculiarities of the scene further. The exhumation of Yorick's skull is accompanied by a curious exhumation of the past as well, a precise but perplexing concatenation of dates – not only the odd concurrence of Hamlet's birth, Fortinbras senior's death, and the sexton's entrance into his profession but also the number of years Yorick has lain in the grave – that has drawn critical attention largely because it identifies Hamlet as thirty years of age, and we all want him to be younger than that. But Hamlet's present age is hardly the final equation the scene produces; Yorick's tenure in the grave, twenty-three years, dates instead a specific moment in the past, Hamlet's age when Yorick died, and it is hardly an insignificant number. Seven was not only the canonical age of reason. In the Renaissance it was also the age of transition from childhood to youth, and from a culturally ungendered to a culturally gendered world: it was the breeching age, when the smocks in which children of both sexes were dressed gave way to gender-specific clothing, and boys were passed 'out of the hands of women' and 'into the hands of men'.[28] The reference is highly veiled, to say the least, enough so as to raise suspicions of an overly imaginative critical ingenuity at work – were it not for the fact that, a decade later, *The Winter's Tale* repeats and confirms this aspect of Shakespeare's gestational lexicon:

> Looking on the lines
> Of my boy's face, methoughts I did recoil
> Twenty-three years, and saw myself unbreech'd
> In my green velvet coat, my dagger muzzled,
> Lest it should bite its master, and so prove
> (As [ornament] oft does) too dangerous.
> (I.ii.153–8)[29]

Hamlet is not the only Shakespearean male who, in a moment of sexual and gender crisis, looks back to recall himself unbreeched. Here the speaker is Leontes, already in the throes of his developing jealousy, and he reproduces the chronology exactly: he too recoils exactly twenty-three years to remember an early modern version of a pre-oedipal phase.

If the confrontation with Yorick's skull produces the one clear instance of successful mourning in the play, then more than Yorick's death is being mourned. What Hamlet holds in his hand is no mere *memento mori*; it is also, perhaps pre-eminently, a memento of passage into the world that he, like Leontes, is now dismayed by.[30] Passage into the gendered world of sexuality, the world the aging queen refuses to pass beyond, is also being mourned and perhaps even effaced for the moment, when Hamlet returns to Yorick's time and finds there a world where his own gendered identity has not yet been produced, so that signs of adult sexuality – especially in women – can be misrecognised, transvalued, and even laid to rest. '[L]et her paint an inch thick, to this favour she must come. Make her laugh at that' (V.i.187–9).

Recently Judith Butler has suggested that Freud's account of the formation of gender identity in *The Ego and the Id* needs to be read alongside his comments on melancholy. Freudian gender identity, according to Butler, is itself a melancholic structure formed around a taboo against homosexuality which precedes the heterosexual incest taboo:

> Gender identification is a kind of melancholia in which the sex of the prohibited object is internalized as a prohibition. . . . If the melancholic answer to the loss of the same-sexed object is to incor-

porate and, indeed, *to become* that object through the construction of the ego ideal, then gender identity appears primarily to be the internalization of a prohibition that proves to be formative of identity.[31]

For the Victorian age and its aftermath – the period responsible for the invention of homosexuality and its taboo – Butler's revisionary reading is both apt and brilliant.[32] But we are only beginning to recover some sense of earlier economies of sexual practices and cultural prohibitions, and we know next to nothing about the psychological strictures of early childhood in the Renaissance. Despite the fact that its psychological resonances are lost to us, however, the rite of passage known as the breeching age may well have constituted a significant moment of gender formation, analogous – at least in so far as it marks a transition into a more rigidly gendered world – to Butler's melancholic structure. Historically specific, officially and culturally inscribed, the breeching age would have represented a moment crucial not to the early or primary formation of the psychological subject (whatever that might mean in the early modern period) but to the gendered codification of the cultural and political subject. For boys and girls it meant the adoption of gendered clothing; for boys, unlike girls , it meant passing 'out of the hands of women' and into 'the hands of men': moving out of a period when full dependency upon women was culturally maintained as the norm and into male and patriarchal adulthood.

Historically speaking, the more rigidly hierarchical the system of patriarchy, the more rabid and chronic are its expressions of misogyny. They are of course more fully, explicitly and officially licensed, but the reasons are structural as well. The patriarchal hierarchy of early modern England was grounded in an explicit and officially promulgated ideology of male supremacy and autonomy. As Janet Adelman has recently shown, however, such autonomy was everywhere contradicted by inescapable and everyday signs of male dependency on women;[33] some of the more virulent outbreaks of misogyny in the Renaissance are aggressive expressions of this contradiction, and I would include here the affective conflation of mourning and misogyny I have been tracing. In some respects such a conflation should not surprise us. Rage and anger are common components of grief in many cultures, most often directed toward the deceased when the survivor's dependence on that figure is greatest – and most virulent when such dependency is itself a source of ambivalence. In a rigidly hierarchical patriarchy like Renaissance England, the death of an influential woman (whether proleptically or posthumously mourned) would mark the fullest encounter with such ambivalence, when male autonomy would be exposed, in grief itself, as male dependency – as one of the fundamental contradictions of patriarchal society.

If Hamlet could indeed regress beyond the breeching age he would resolve the contradiction, but only by abandoning the patriarchal mystifications of male autonomy and by embracing full dependency upon women. Other than for a brief moment of imaginary resolution, of course, such a regression is impossible. In the scene that follows his encounter with Yorick's skull, Hamlet does indeed embrace his own dependency in an unprecedented and surprising manner, placing his fate in the hands of a special providence, but the divinity that shapes his end is the Christian god, the ultimate patriarch. Like other Shakespearean males, Hamlet achieves a partial if suicidal resolution of the contradictions of patriarchy by constructing a world that is not so much ungendered as free from gender differentiation – a world that is all male.[34]

From *Shakespeare Quarterly*, 45:2 (Summer 1994), 139–58.

NOTES

[This discussion of *Hamlet* displays with helpful clarity some characteristic moves of recent Shakespeare criticism, setting up a carefully historicised encounter between anthropology and psychoanalysis; using anecdotal material as a way of approaching the Shakespearean text; and privileging court culture as a focus of analysis, here with an emphasis on the special status of Elizabeth, a topic of considerable interest to both new historicist and feminist critics. Central to the argument is the claim that in revenge tragedy the aging and dead body of Elizabeth is engaged in terms of a response which entails both mourning and misogyny. In pursuing his analysis of the cultural construction of emotions and subjectivity, placing both in a dynamic relation with the popular theatre as a key cultural institution, Mullaney draws on psychoanalytic concepts to interpret historically distant texts and documents, and uses history to modify and intervene in psychoanalysis.

In order to maintain the focus on Shakespeare, I have omitted the final section of the essay, which traces the still more misogynist mastering of mourning in *Revenger's Tragedy*. I am grateful to Professor Mullaney for allowing me to make this cut. Some notes have also been modified. Ed.]

1. *A journal of all that was accomplished by Monsieur de Maisse Ambassador in England from King Henri IV to Queen Elizabeth Anno Domini 1597*, trans. and ed. G. B. Harrison and R. A. Jones (London, 1931), p. 12. [All further references are to this edition.   Ed.]

2. Quoted from Christopher Haigh, *Elizabeth I* (London, 1988), p. 162. [All further references are to this edition.   Ed.]

3. In a powerful recent essay, Valerie Wayne analyses Renaissance misogynies as forms of 'residual' ideology: oftentimes embodied in a single character who is criticised or denigrated by others, misogynistic discourse is superficially called into quotation at the same time it is kept alive and put to use by the dominant culture; see 'Historical Differences: Misogyny and *Othello*' in *The Matter of Difference: Materialist Feminist Criticism of Shakespeare*, ed. Valerie Wayne (Ithaca, NY, 1991), pp. 153–80.

4. Lawrence Stone, *The Family, Sex and Marriage in England 1500–1800* (New York, 1977), pp. 99.

5. *On Measure for Measure* as a displacement and regendering of Elizabethan monarchy, see Leonard Tennenhouse, 'Representing Power: *Measure for Measure* in its Time', *Genre* 15 (1982), 139–56; and more generally on the Duke's manipulation of Isabella, see my own *The Place of the Stage: License, Play, and Power in Renaissance England* (Chicago, 1988), pp. 88–115. Figures of female autonomy and power are more radically apprehended in *Macbeth*, violently and systematically eradicated in the play's effort to imagine a male world fully independent of women. For impressive treatments of this aspect of the play, see Harry Berger, Jr, 'The Early Scenes of *Macbeth*: Preface to a New Interpretation', *English Literary History*, 47 (1980), 1–31, and his 'Text against Performance in Shakespeare: the Example of *Macbeth*', *Genre*, 15 (1982), pp. 49–80; and Janet Adelman, '"Born of Woman": Fantasies of Maternal Power in *Macbeth*', in *Cannibals, Witches, and Divorce: Estranging the Renaissance*, ed. Marjorie Garber (Baltimore, MD, 1987), pp. 90–121.

6. Tessa Watt, *Cheap Print and Popular Piety, 1550–1640* (Cambridge, 1991), pp. 7–8.

7. Jean E. Howard, 'Renaissance Antitheatricality and the Politics of Gender and Rank in *Much Ado About Nothing*', *Shakespeare Reproduced: The Text in History and Ideology*, ed. Jean E. Howard and Marion F. O'Connor (New York and London, 1987), pp. 163–87, esp. 164.

8. For an excellent speculation on the significance of this shift, see Louis Adrian Montrose, 'The Purpose of Playing: Reflections on a Shakespearean Anthropology', *Helios*, n.s. 7 (1980), pp. 51–74.

9. On this topic, see my *The Place of the Stage*, pp. 88–115.

10. I agree with Lisa Jardine that, given the immediate context, '"gorge" here surely means "throat" rather than "bosom"'; see her essay '"Why should he call her whore?" Defamation and Desdemona's Case', in *Addressing Frank Kermode: Essays in Criticism and Interpretation*, ed. Margaret Trudeau-Clayton and Martin Warner (Urbana and Chicago, IL, 1991), pp. 124–53, esp. p. 146.

11. Louis Adrian Montrose, '"Shaping Fantasies": Figurations of Gender and Power in Elizabethan Culture', in *Representing the English Renaissance*, ed. Stephen Greenblatt (Berkeley, CA, 1988), pp. 31–64, p. 34.

12. Quoted from Harold Jenkins's Arden edition of *Hamlet* (London, 1982), p. 554.

13. Marie Axton, *The Queen's Two Bodies: Drama and the Elizabethan Succession* (London, 1977), p. 12 (author's emphasis removed).

14. On the cultural dynamics of Elizabeth's reign, including her appropriation of Petrarchan conventions, see Louis Adrian Montrose, '"Eliza, Queene of shepheardes", and the Pastoral of Power', *English Literary Renaissance*, 10 (1989), 153–82; and 'Gifts and Reasons: the Contexts of Peele's *Araygnement of Paris*', *ELH*, 47 (1980), 433-61.

15. Thomas Tuke, 'A Treatise against Painting...' (1616), reprinted in *Blood and Knavery: A Collection of English Renaissance Pamphlets and Ballads of Crime and Sin*, ed. Joseph H. Marshburn and Alan R. Velie (Rutherford, NJ, 1973), pp. 176–93, esp. p. 188.

16. Laurie A. Finke, 'Painting Women: Images of Femininity in Jacobean Tragedy', *Theatre Journal*, 36 (1984), 357–70, esp. p. 364.

17. *Calendar of the Manuscripts of ... The Marquis of Salisbury*, 18 vols (London, 1904), vol. 10, pp. 172–3, quoted from Montrose, 'Shaping Fantasies', 54. Waad refers to previous correspondence with Cecil concerning Edwardes which does not appear in the *Calendar*, and which I have been thus far unable to locate.

18. Leonard Tennenhouse, *Power on Display: The Politics of Shakespeare's Genres* (New York and London, 1986), p. 85.

19. On the significance of stage position, see Robert Weimann, *Shakespeare and the Popular Tradition in the Theater: Studies in the Social Dimension of Dramatic Form and Function*, ed. Robert Schwartz (Baltimore, MD, 1978), pp. 73–84 and 224–36.

20. Peter Erickson, *Rewriting Shakespeare, Rewriting Ourselves* (Berkeley, Los Angeles, and London, 1991), pp. 83 and 86.

21. Barbara J. Todd, 'The Remarrying Widow: a Stereotype Reconsidered', *Women in English Society, 1500–1800*, ed. Mary Prior (London and New York, 1985), pp. 54–92, esp. p. 55. Todd's excellent study also provides a context for Shakespeare's will, with the specific disposition of his 'second-best bed' to his widow, as well as for the Player Queen's remarks on remarriage. In his *Advice to a Son*, Ralegh felt called on to stipulate that 'if [thy wife] love again let her not enjoy her second love in the same bed wherein she loved thee' (quoted ibid., p. 73). Hamlet Jr's emphasis on Gertrude's 'incestuous sheets' and Hamlet Sr's remarks on the 'royal bed of Denmark' suggest that the untimeliness of the king's death was an outrage because it prevented him from setting his estate as well as his soul in order, by drawing up a properly patriarchal will – one that would have deprived Gertrude of the 'royal' and presumably best bed.

22. For a suggestive discussion of the gap between the object and means of theatrical representation, see Robert Weimann, 'Bifold Authority in Shakespeare's Theatre', *Shakespeare Quarterly*, 39 (1988), 401–17.

23. For recent critical assessments of English transvestite companies in relation to Renaissance constructions of sexuality, see in particular Stephen Orgel, 'Nobody's Perfect: Or Why Did the English Stage Take Boys for Women?' *South Atlantic Quarterly*, 88 (1989), 7–29; Laura Levine, 'Men in Women's Clothing: Anti-theatricality and Effeminization from 1579 to 1642', *Criticism*, 28 (1986), 121–43; Jean E. Howard, 'Crossdressing, the Theatre, and Gender Struggle in Early Modern England', *Shakespeare Quarterly*, 39 (1988), 418–40; Stephen Greenblatt, *Shakespearean Negotiations: The Circulation of Social Energy in Renaissance England* (Berkeley and Los Angeles, 1988), pp. 66–93; and Mary Beth Rose, 'Women in Men's Clothing: Apparel and Social Stability in *The Roaring Girl*', *ELR*, 14 (1984), 367–91.

24. For Freud's essay 'Mourning and Melancholia', see *The Standard Edition of the Complete Psychological Works of Sigmund Freud*, trans. and ed. James Strachey, 19 vols (London, 1957), vol. 14, pp. 243–58; for their revision of Freud's discussion of incorporation and introjection, see Nicolas Abraham and Maria Torok, 'Introjection – Incorporation: Mourning or Melancholia', *Psychoanalysis in France*, ed. Serge Lebovici and Daniel Widlöcher (New York, 1980), pp. 3–16, esp. pp. 13–14; and *The Wolf Man's Magic Word: A Cryptonymy*, trans. Nicholas Rand (Minneapolis, MN, 1986), passim.

25. '*Fors*: The Anglish Words of Nicolas Abraham and Maria Torok', trans. Barbara Johnson, foreword to *The Wolf Man's Magic Word*, pp. xi–xlvii, esp. pp. xvi–xvii.

26. G. W. Pigman, *Grief and English Renaissance Elegy* (Cambridge, 1985), p. 2.

27. Quoted from Pigman, p. 1.

28. David Hunt, *Parents and Children in History: The Psychology of Family Life in Early Modern France* (New York and London, 1970), p. 183.

29. Quotations of Shakespeare plays other than *Hamlet* follow the *Riverside Shakespeare*, ed. G. Blakemore Evans (Boston, MA, 1974).

30. Hamlet's anxiety over sexuality is global rather than specific; as Valerie Traub notes, 'for Hamlet ... *all* sex is unnatural'; see her illuminating essay on Shakespearean translations of sexually vital women into dead or static objects, 'Jewels, Statues, and Corpses: Containment of Female Erotic Power in Shakespeare's Plays', *Shakespeare Studies*, 20 (1988), 215–38, esp. 218.

31. Judith Butler, *Gender Trouble: Feminism and the Subversion of Identity* (New York and London, 1990), p. 63.

32. For the nineteenth-century invention of homosexuality, see especially David M. Halperin, *One Hundred Years of Homosexuality: And Other Essays on Greek Love* (New York, 1990). For a recent and subtle revision of Halperin relevant to Renaissance constructions of sexuality, see Jonathan Goldberg, *Sodometries: Renaissance Texts, Modern Sexualities* (Stanford, CA, 1992).

33. Janet Adelman, *Suffocating Mothers: Fantasies of Maternal Origin in Shakespeare's Plays* (New York and London, 1992), pp. 130–46.

34. Ibid., passim.

8

He do Cressida in Different Voices

BARBARA HODGDON

When Trojan Hector visits the Greek camp, *Troilus and Cressida* represents his meeting with Achilles as an exchange of male gazes, powerful speaking looks through which each constructs, or attempts to deconstruct, the identity of the other:

> *Achilles.* Now, Hector, I have fed mine eyes on thee;
>   I have with exact view perused thee, Hector,
>   And quoted joint by joint. . . .
> *Hector.* Stand fair, I prithee; let me look on thee.
> *Achilles.* Behold thy fill.
> *Hector.* Nay, I have done already.
> *Achilles.* Thou art too brief. I will the second time,
>   As I would buy thee, view thee limb by limb.
> *Hector.* O, like a book of sport thou'lt read me o'er;
>   But there's more in me than thou understand'st.
>   Why dost thou so oppress me with thine eye?
>   (IV.v.230–40)[1]

Among many other references to sight and bodily display,[2] this passage stands as an especially blatant instance of how Shakespeare's playtext consistently turns the act of spectatorship into a convention which interrogates, theatrically, propositions of identity and value concerning male – as well as female – bodies. Here, too, Hector voices a question that Cressida never asks. For like Hector, males feed their eyes on her 'with exact view', quote her joint by joint, position her as a marketable commodity, read her 'like a book of sport'. But whereas Achilles' look searches Hector's body for a point of entry – 'whether there, or there, or there' (IV.v.242) – in Cressida's case the 'local wound' already has a name; the passage through which men can 'kill' her (and themselves) is known. In her case, too, the interpretive gap to which Hector alludes between reading o'er and understanding has (always) already been foreclosed.

To be sure, the playtext, like Cressida herself, 'holds off' the final revelation of that foreclosure, a strategy which does indeed demonstrate that, like Hector, there's more in her than either the men who oppress her with their gaze or even she herself understands.[3] Ultimately, however, to read her is to recognise that '"As false as Cressid"' constitutes an almost inescapable constant amidst the generalised slippage of identity and value apparent elsewhere – particularly as that slippage concerns the heroic male image – in what Rosalie Colie terms a 'monumental mock'ry' of language and form which 'attacked literature at its very source'.[4] Moving beyond Colie's argument, Elizabeth Freund observes, 'In no other play does [Shakespeare] take on the redoubtable task of refashioning, decomposing, vulgarising, declassicising precursor texts quite so canonical and powerful, and nowhere does he strip *both* his sources *and* his own text of their "original" substance with such spirited iconoclasm.'[5] True, but not, I think, completely true of Cressida. *Refashioned* she undoubtedly is, but not stripped of her originary substance. Indeed the very process of slippage between prestigious and popular forms which hollows out idealist myth to reveal the social seems to *require* that she retain her 'true' identity, be proved false (by nature), be devalued as (common) property.

The facile answer to this seeming paradox – that further debasing the one character already demonised by literary tradition is somewhat unnecessary – conveniently occludes social process, and within that, the positioning of bodies and voices through which the culture defines gender relations in absolutist (moral) terms.[6] Yet *Troilus and Cressida*, as Jonathan Dollimore, among others, points out, consistently calls such absolutist constructions into question.[7] That is another paradox, and one I want to examine further by focusing especially on the issue of Cressida's authenticity. Like Cressida, who sees herself as divided, my project has a double vision. For I want not only to read Shakespeare's playtext in order to raise questions concerning Renaissance representation and reception, but, more importantly, especially since *Troilus and Cressida*'s performance history is concentrated in the recent past,[8] to look at a number of twentieth century performance texts, specific instances of cultural reproduction which arrange, or rearrange, social meaning as theatrical meaning.[9] And I want to begin, as both the Trojan War and *Troilus and Cressida* do, with the question of Helen.

Troilus and Cressida is historically positioned to dramatise the change in gender relations occurring in the shift from feudal courtly love, which accorded women political as well as erotic power, linking the one with the other, to pre-capitalist social relations and the consequent double subordination of women to their husbands as well as to the prince.[10] Shakespeare's playtext constructs the shift as a binary opposition between idolatry and adultery, a move which foregrounds the cultural contradictions and strains of the social process. For in the case of Helen, *Troilus and Cressida* folds the one into the other, collapsing both into a single term: Helen's position as a Trojan icon derives from her adultery, which gives her value in the public realm of male discourse. But whereas Helen's trajectory (at least as she is theorised by the Trojans[11]) seems to insist that idolatry can contain adultery, Cressida's, which parallels Helen's experientially, suggests just the opposite. Far from containing adultery (or, let's be plain, in Cressida's case, faithlessness), idolatry precisely expresses and focuses it. In this sense, Cressida can be recognised as a transhistorically stable sign of an ideological process in conflict with itself. Indeed, *Troilus and Cressida*, which 'turns' Cressida from idealised to fallen woman, may be viewed as a 'set-up', for she begins by (perhaps) flirtatiously laughing at and with the jokes of a man who, through his mediatory role as a bawd, poses a sexual threat to her, and she ends by being positioned as the object of the gaze of several males who together reconstruct her as a whore. Literally as well as figuratively, she occupies the place that Freud assigned to women in the structure of the obscene joke: the place of the object between several male subjects.[12] In this scheme, which wrests power from the woman, in particular the power accruing to both body and voice, the men (and by association, male spectators) have the last laugh, thereby defusing not only the threat of woman's infidelity but also her potential to subvert patriarchal authority by transgressing its laws. In addition, of course, as an object of exchange within male subjectivity, the woman performs useful (patriarchal) cultural work by ratifying and reinforcing the very homosocial bonds that exclude her.[13]

Such a schematic outline of its gender economy offers an extremely attractive synoptic view of Shakespeare's playtext – attractive, that is, for male spectators. Certainly, as my earlier quotation suggests, *Troilus and Cressida* repeatedly calls attention to male looking relations. Troilus is led by 'eyes and ears' (II.ii.63); Ulysses speaks of how the 'present eye praises the present object' (III.iii.180); men search for their own reflections in each other's eyes (III.iii.99). Obsessed as they are with their own looks and with recognising (or pretending not to recognise) one another, their gazes become commodified as a source of knowledge, most especially so once they are turned on women, who are made accountable to them. As in classical Hollywood cinema, such relentless focus on male surveillance works to endorse similar mechanisms in a male spectator and so privileges the male gaze as well as the male project called the play, offering males particular, and particularly gendered specular competence, or what Laura Mulvey has called 'visual pleasure'.[14] But what of a female spectator? To view a spectacle which neatly accounts for her own position and attempts to frame her as false by nature surely constitutes an exercise in restrictive vision. For her, 'visual pleasure' exists primarily in terms of intellectual mastery – in recognising, to paraphrase Stephen Greenblatt, that there is pleasure, no end of pleasure, only not for a female spectator.[15]

This statement, however, assumes a point of view consistent with that of a late twentieth-century female spectator. And this in turn raises several important questions. Would a female spectator in the Renaissance share a similar outlook? And to what extent is it possible to historicise the gendered gaze? Given only negative or, at best, indeterminate evidence about *Troilus and Cressida*'s early seventeenth-century performance history, especially as to whether it was performed in public as well as private playhouses,[16] addressing the first question points toward the second, and any precise answers concerning audience positions and responses can only be broadly sketched in from existing documents, none of which were written by women.[17] Certainly women made up a definitely recognisable segment of the audiences in the public theatres, but it is difficult to mark any decisive shifts in the composition of audiences in the private theatres around the turn of the century.[18] What can be said, however, is that female spectators, like males, spanned the social hierarchy to include representatives of all classes – apple-wives, fish-wives, citizens' wives, ladies and whores – and that, as Andrew

Gurr cautiously notes, 'their reasons for playgoing were most open to question and most subject to attack', primarily from anti-theatrical Puritan commentators. Home was the proper habitat for a respectable woman who, if she went to the theatre at all, went with a male companion (preferably her husband); if alone, she could be considered, if not treated as, a whore. Indeed, even by appearing at the theatre, a woman risked, with such public display, making a spectacle of herself.[19]

Although the assumption that women attended the theatre for harlotry or adultery (rather than, say, to watch an all-male spectacle) begins to wane about 1600, shortly before *Troilus and Cressida* would have been staged, fresh accusations took its place. As Jonson and his fellow theatre poets began to rail against unlearned spectators who came to the theatre only to see sights, not to listen to and be edified by verse, such complaints were levelled specifically against women's 'ignorant eyes'.[20] Beaumont's *The Knight of the Burning Pestle* (1607) describes, in Nell, the Citizen-Grocer's wife, just such a spectator, one who, as a representative of a steadily growing middle-class audience fast becoming central to the theatre's commercial enterprise, condenses many of the supposed attributes of playgoing women. Somewhat 'virtuous' in that she has been pleading with George for a year to take her to the theatre, her taste runs to romance, particularly to chivalric wandering knights, and particularly when played by Ralph, her husband's apprentice. From her seat on the stage among the gentlemen, a position which mocks her social pretensions, she reads all she sees with perfect comic literalness. Yet, however exaggerated by Beaumont's genial satire against the values of citizens' culture (as opposed to those of aristocratic playgoers) and their desire to see old scenes (primarily those acted in the public theatre) replayed on the Blackfriars' stage, the case of Nell reveals one woman's power to alter the staged representation to suit her pleasures.

Apparently Nell was not alone. In the early decades of the century, the woman playgoer grew increasingly vocal about 'see[ing] her shadow there'[21] in representative stereotypes – the shrew, the lusty widow, the country wench, the Amazon, the chaste wife or virgin, the adulteress, the ambitious female. Invited, on the one hand, to assent in such fictions being inscribed on their bodies, on the other, women were, as Jean Howard argues, 'positioned as consumers, critics, spectators, and spectacles'.[22] As early as 1600, the epilogue of Dekker's *Satiromastix*, by recanting the opinions of women expressed in the playtext, records some anxiety about pleasing female spectators, a trend which continues to accelerate throughout the early decades of the new century.[23] Although it was not until the late 1620s and early 1630s that stage plays show further signs of catering specifically to women's tastes, women spectators may have been partially responsible for the radical change, around 1610, in the drama's misogynistic portrayal of women.[24] If indeed, as Louis Montrose and others have observed,[25] the theatre functioned as an agent of cultural transformation, the women who attended it seem to have played some part in creating new subject positions, perhaps even in remapping the representation of gender relations to redirect, and recirculate, the exchange of (visual) pleasure.

This brief history suggests that *Troilus and Cressida* is ideally suited to bring into sharp focus, for female spectators, the contradictions embodied in these heavily gendered looking relations. For Shakespeare's playtext rather precisely analogises and reproduces in its theatre of spectacle the prevalent male anxieties about their exclusive ownership of women, about woman's value and 'place'. In addition, it also analogises the high visibility of women playgoers who were described, looked upon, 'quoted joint by joint', classified, noted, and demonised by male observers. Even in the absence of women's own accounts of their material conditions, it would seem reasonable to assume that perhaps they saw themselves as owners of a potentially transgressive look and, simultaneously, as subject to the male gaze. It is precisely the relative historicity of these looking relations which I wish to investigate further.

In this regard, I see a useful connection between the models generated by recent feminist film theory, which assign gender to as well as psychoanalyse the relations between spectacle and gaze, and Katherine Maus's provocative conjectures about the relations between an eroticised Renaissance spectacle construed, by anti-theatrical commentators, as a 'whorish female' and the jealous male's scopic project as one figure for the Renaissance spectator 'at his most agonisingly involved and his most scandalously marginalised'.[26] Not only is a double standard of spectatorship that positions the male as perceiving subject and the female as perceived object common to both, but the deeply gendered split in subjectivity which both take as a given makes such modes of analysis entirely appropriate to examining looking relations in *Troilus and Cressida*. Indeed, such notions are peculiarly suited both to reading a playtext which positions women as unable to escape their transhistorical citations[27] and to examining its performance texts, which tend to reproduce, and thus reinscribe, the ideological power of those citations on women's bodies. However, it is equally important to acknowledge at the outset the limitations of both Freudian and Lacanian theory, which, in presupposing the dominance of the male gaze, tend to endow it with a universal, even ahistorical, power. For that reason, I want to pursue a slightly different investigation of spectatorly desire by approaching issues of gender in performance not exclusively through an analysis of the male gaze but, rather, by re-examining the economy of exchange between performer and spectator in performance.[28] In this partial reading, my focus rests on Cressida's gaze, and the spectatorly gazes at her, both on the stage and from the audience, in her last appearance. What I propose constitutes a somewhat subversive project which, by attempting to fix an eye on how Cressida is constructed, not only demystifies her ideological function but (potentially) diminishes the male pleasure of the text. What remains to be seen is whether destabilising, if not dismantling, the hegemony of the male gaze can disclose some alteration in the looking relations – even, perhaps, some fissures along the gendered sightlines – that mark *Troilus and Cressida*'s recent cultural historicity.

. . . .

In Cressida's final scene, the encounter with Diomedes observed by Troilus, Ulysses and Thersites (V.ii), becomes doubly, even triply, specularised, a strategy which stigmatises her worth as well as circumscribes and contains her voice and body. Yet the very heavy-handedness of the frames in which she is set also reveals the considerable anxiety that lies behind such misogyny.

As with Cressida's first view of Troilus, Chaucer positions him as a solitary observer of the meeting with Diomedes. But, by adding Ulysses and Thersites, Shakespeare's playtext not only calls attention to but overdetermines the male gaze. Further, on the two occasions when Cressida whispers to Diomedes (V.ii.7; 34), neither onstage nor offstage spectators can hear what she says. At both points, however, Troilus, Ulysses and Thersites speak her body and read it, in Thersites' words, as 'secretly open' (24). For a female spectator, Cressida's voiceless text, deeply triangulated and elaborately mediated by a series of male gazes, may seem to flood this scene. But all that can literally be heard is the playtext's ability to 'speak the father' in a weave of voices and hooks which liberalises the gap Chaucer's text sets up between narrator and tale in his ambiguously ironic 'men saye'. To watch such a spectacle invites a female spectator to occupy one of two traditionally assigned viewing positions – those Tania Modleski recognises as 'the place of the female masochist, identifying with the woman as victim, or the place of the "transvestite", identifying with the active male hero'.[29] But in this case, even the latter position is somewhat compromised, since the act of looking not only immobilises Troilus in self-doubt ('I will not be myself' [63]) but threatens to destabilise his identity as well as Cressida's. Nowhere else in *Troilus and Cressida* do looking relations so clearly articulate the contradictory status of the female spectator as one who is and is not herself, a situation which not incidentally analogises the fluid gender status of the original boy-actor of Cressida's part. Moreover, any attempt to construct an alternative viewing position, and thus to escape from this highly structured economy of looking relations, also rather precisely analogises the problem faced by feminist theory: that of constructing an Archimedean point from which to speak that is not already interpellated within Freudian or Lacanian discourse. Yet any such attempt creates an additional double bind. For to take up such a position involves refusing the (exclusively male) pleasure of the text[30] which, in staging the construction of 'faithless woman', recuperates and rehearses the priorities of neo-chivalric culture.

These priorities are condensed, even emblematised, in the way the scene handles and dispenses with the threats woman poses to the ideologies sustaining that culture. With Cressida quite literally in the hands of the Greeks, she is ideally positioned to repeat (or revenge) Helen's story; she can become the agent linking Troilus with Menelaus. Also potentially dangerous because of her ability to make Troilus (as he himself claims) 'weaker than a woman's tear' (I.i.9), thus feminising his (naturally?) warlike nature,[31] Cressida becomes a pawn in *Troilus and Cressida*'s curiously contradictory logic of male valuation. For this scene shows Greek and Trojan, once drawn into war by their agreement that Helen is worth fighting for, *united* – not by their attitudes toward one another but by their gaze toward, and eventual demonisation of, Cressida. Appropriately, one central element in this scene is a hand property, Troilus' sleeve, which Cressida herself calls to Diomedes' attention: 'You look upon that sleeve' (69). And it is through the handling – both woman-handling and man-handling – of this property that Shakespeare's playtext signifies Cressida's double transgression and inscribes it on her body.[32] Not only does it become a shorthand representation of the sexual encounter which is not (and cannot) be represented, but it also signifies Cressida's attempt, and ensuing failure, to manipulate correctly an emblem of the male chivalric system. In some sense the un-'virtuous fight' between Cressida and Diomedes for the sleeve constitutes a quarrel over Troilus' ownership: it seems to be the worth of that object rather than the ownership of Cressida (which Diomedes assumes that he has) which attracts him. As one of several shifting signifiers of value, among them Cressida's glove and the armor with the putrified core (V.viii.1–2), the sleeve – passed from one pair of male hands to another through Cressida – functions as an emblem of her exclusion from a system which reduces her worth to that of an object within male exchange. In the earlier wooing scene with Troilus, Cressida saw herself, in Dollimore's phrase, 'not only as subordinate to maleness but also obscurely derivative of it'.[33] Now she becomes the means of authorising maleness as well as of perpetuating male definitions of female faithlessness. Finally, the sleeve is redefined in the public realm as a mark that draws Troilus to Diomedes in the homosocial bonding of battle.

What this scene makes patently clear is that Cressida is read (or misread) as a split text. Her deeply specularised, even fetishised, body speaks against her voice, or for her lack of voice, much as though the several texts war with one another before being recanonised, by the male gaze, to prove that woman's sexuality derives from and depends on its male use. At the last, Cressida herself acknowledges that division in terms of looking relations, and attributes it to a natural, universal flaw in gendered vision. In her soliloquy, Shakespeare's playtext once again takes a peculiarly contradictory turn toward her doubleness. On the one hand, by privileging Cressida's dramatic power, the soliloquy works to heal the split between body and voice; on the other, it erodes that power by confirming the proposition that oppression works best when it forces the oppressed to undermine themselves.

. . . .

The performance texts directed by both Hall-Barton (1960) and Barton-Kyle (1976) a construct a complex frame of looking relations. Each stages the encounter between Cressida and Diomedes as a circling dance, watched in the earlier version by upstage rather than downstage spectators and, in 1976, by a Troilus and Ulysses positioned in a down-right stage balcony while Thersites perches on an up-left stage balcony, a strategy that reproduces and exaggerates the triangulated structure of vision. Yet another choice further complicates these sightlines, for the production's open-platform set includes a seating space for the audience which encircles the entire upstage area. Placed among these additional onstage spectators, Thersites can seem, to audience members seated off the stage, to speak for those he sits among; and with Troilus and Ulysses closer to the offstage audience, the visual economy simulates a carefully arranged debate, its spectators already divided. And because Troilus and Ulysses stand in the same place where Cressida and Pandarus earlier watched the heroes' return, the Barton-Kyle *Troilus and Cressida* draws the two scenes together, calling attention to their rhymed – and regendered – looking relations. As he enters, Diomedes carries a large 'Helen doll', which he puts down midstage. At scene's end he retrieves it and slings it over his shoulder, a secondary, bla-tantly symbolic token, together with the sleeve, of his conquest, his use of women. When Diomedes exits, Troilus descends from the balcony to the main stage, as though he may be about to speak to Cressida, but her soliloquy stops him; he stands aside in the shadows to watch and listen. Her exit, in turn, is delayed until after Thersites' 'Unless she say, "My mind is now turned whore"' (113), which her cackling laugh indicates she may hear and concur with – a strategy that works to pull the sonnet's two voices toward one another, condensing them into a single, foreclosed expression.

As in the 1960 version (as well as the earlier performance texts I describe), the encounter between Cressida and Diomedes echoes and inverts the patterns of Cressida's 'virtuous fight' with herself and with Troilus (III.ii). While the earlier scene signals her 'holding off' in her attempts to break away from Troilus, performances of this scene rewrite her delaying tactics as teasing provocation, in which it is Diomedes who wishes to leave. What is most striking about the Barton-Kyle version, however, is that both the Troilus–Cressida and Cressida–Diomedes wooings are replayed, once again, after Cressida's exit. Just before the 'war' with the sleeve, Troilus puts Cressida's glove on his right hand; as she leaves the stage, his first gesture is to strip it off and throw it down – 'think this not Cressida' (132). Now he, like Cressida, is the object of male gaze; and his 'recordation ... of every syllable' (115–16) also replays, with her glove, the pattern of advance and retreat just witnessed – taking it up, throwing it down, taking it up again and then finally dropping it as he leaves, abruptly, at Aeneas' entrance. When Ulysses descends from the balcony, he picks up the glove and smells it, only to discard it at centre stage, where it remains throughout Thersites' commentary, until he retrieves it and fits it on his own right hand – a token of Cressida as 'whore' and 'commodious drab', its power recommodified as 'intelligence' destined for Patroclus' ears and hand (190–3).

If Barton-Kyle's *Troilus and Cressida* deprivileges as well as devalues Cressida by brutally reducing her to fetishised metonymy with the glove, it also makes explicit what the playtext remains somewhat indecisive about: that this is Troilus' tragedy. Certainly, in that Troilus' play with the glove suggests that Cressida, unlike her glove, cannot be so easily put on and taken off, the performance text reprivileges her meaning *for* him. Also, Ulysses' and Thersites' subsequent handling of the glove effectively protects Troilus to displace her final demonising onto two voyeurs, parcelling her out in a final exchange between the most admired Greek and the most scurrilous Trojan. Such a strategy exempts Troilus to resituate the debate over Cressida's worth in terms of what is done to her in his absence; indeed, this particular instance of man-handling replays her arrival in the Greek camp (IV.v). By exposing her construction through a fetishised property, this performance text offers its (doubled) audience a further opportunity to judge the extent to which value lies in the eyes, or hands, of the beholder.

However cruelly reductive to Cressida, the Barton-Kyle *Troilus and Cressida* also makes a spectacle of the two voyeurs, framing one, Ulysses, through the other's gaze, as though organising male desire into a (descending) hierarchy. Committed to a different mode of disclosure, Terry Hands's performance text allows for no such careful anatomising of the male gaze. By positioning Troilus and Ulysses upstage left and Cressida and Diomedes downstage centre, Hands's staging exploits the playtext's split between sight and sound to differentiate at first between two sets of looking relations. As the tug-of-war over a scarf (rather than the sleeve) develops, an audience hears and sees an angry exchange that, since it ends with Cressida lying on the ground and Diomedes standing over her, reads to the distant upstage figures as seduction and submission. As Cressida stands, brushing herself off, she again lashes out at Diomedes as he starts to leave: 'One cannot speak a word / But it straight starts you'; his biting 'I do not like this fooling' tops her accusation (100–1). Then both laugh, as though recognising each other's 'game', which leads to a final reconciliation and to the promise of tomorrow's assignation. Rather than encompassing the exchange between Cressida and Diomedes within the structuring gazes of onstage spectators, Hands's staging privileges offstage spectators, inviting them to interrogate a double spectacle – those looked at as well as the lookers-on. But although this framing generates two *potentially* contradictory readings, Hands's representational choices ultimately flatten any possible ambiguities. Since offstage spectators see with unmediated clarity, Troilus' later refusal to believe that Cressida is neither 'the real thing' nor herself invites, even enforces, his devaluation together with hers. At this and other moments of performance, Hands's own dis-illusionary eye seems to dominate the playtext's suggestions of multiple overlapping layers of illusion, subsuming and absorbing all gazes into one.

Although Hands's performance text exaggerates its compass, such a powerfully panoptical male gaze certainly derives from, and is tied to, both textual authority and authoritative male interpretive strategies. Such strategies erect a standard against which to measure Davies' *Troilus and Cressida*, particularly its distinctly revisionary moves. Not only does it reauthorise Cressida's history but it also dislocates the hegemony of the male gaze and thus renegotiates the exchange of spectatorly pleasure to accommodate another, less misogynous gaze at the heroine trapped within its visual economy. Certainly, up to the eavesdropping scene, Juliet Stevenson's performance had repeatedly undercut the possibility of defining Cressida as archetypally false by nature. Two scenes in particular contribute to reappropriating her 'truth'. Wary and distrustful of Troilus as well as of herself in the wooing scene, hers was indeed a Cressida whose 'fears have eyes' (III.ii.66) and who, when later forced to leave Troy, seemed to watch her own betrayal from an immense distance (IV.iv). At this point, costume functions as an especially telling sign. With her hair down, and wearing a loose white nightgown, she is suddenly put on view to the eyes of Pandarus, Troilus, Aeneas, Paris, and finally, Diomedes; as Cressida leaves for the Greek camp, Troilus puts a dark grey military greatcoat over her shoulders. On the one hand, his gesture acknowledges and seeks to protect her extreme vulnerability; on the other, the image of Cressida literally bearing a man's enveloping coat on her back precisely registers both her possession and the anxious strategies through which the men attempt to mask their own potentially guilty desires. Later, shaken at first by what amounts to a gang rape of speaking looks in the Greek camp (IV.v),[34] she uses her exchange with Menelaus to buy time, so that when Ulysses desires a kiss, she snaps out, 'Why, beg [then]' (48), and points her finger to the ground, as though commanding a dog to beg for a bone. By turning his desiring look back on himself, subjecting Ulysses to her gaze, she not only undermines his famous condemnation of her body language as the scornful revenge of a publicly humiliated man but also exposes the male hypocrisy which drives literary tradition, Shakespeare's playtext, and its interpretive communities. But, however much Stevenson's performance may offer Cressida (as well as a woman spectator) a satisfying opportunity to work through her anger (an emotion traditionally disallowed and unacceptable for women) and turn to look at those who would oppress her within their gaze, because Cressida's final appearance offers a more limited range of representational options, it constitutes the test case for re-envisioning the economy of looking relations.

Davies's staging positions Troilus and Ulysses downstage right and Thersites downstage left, both in deep shadows – a strategy which surrounds the bodies of Cressida and Diomedes with the onlookers' disembodied voices and so privileges the offstage over the onstage gaze. Diomedes enters up centre, under a staircase-balcony, and lights a cigarette in the gloom. Cressida now has her blonde hair braided to one side and wears a gypsy-ish skirt and blouse, a costume more physically revealing than any she has worn before, and one which marks her as a 'Greekish' possession, captive in a strange land. Their rather strained encounter, in which a briskly impatient Diomedes seems less anxious to own Cressida than to settle a bargain, echoes the earlier wooing of Troilus and Cressida only in that it replays their movements up and down the centrally positioned staircase. But the differences in Cressida's changes of mood and the awkward angle of her body as she bends over Diomedes to stroke his cheek invite spectators to read both language and gesture as 'untrue', actions that a woman might play in order to ensure her own survival. As she takes back the sleeve-wrap she had given to Diomedes, for example, her 'It is no matter' (87) seems designed to downplay its importance to her and to close off the exchange. For Stevenson's Cressida, Diomedes indeed seems to represent simply a 'guardian' who may protect her from the other Greeks; it is that fear which animates her self-absorption and, later, the interior quarrel which structures her soliloquy. When she speaks 'I prithee, come' (105), she shrinks back into the deep shadows of the upstage staircase, calling out 'Troilus' in anguish; after hearing no answer, her 'farewell' marks her quiet resignation (106), splitting gaze and self even before she articulates that separation further. To privilege her desperation and sense of self-loss, the performance text gives her a long exit, from the main stage up the curve of the staircase, 'walking in', this last time, alone.

Although positioning Cressida as the object of the male gaze remains 'true' to Shakespeare's playtext, Davies's representational strategies also work to interrogate its predetermined looking relations and so exchange a visual for a verbal economy. For the (relative) darkness of the scene shifts focus from bodies to voices, with several telling effects, not the least of which emphasises the narrative power of the three male onlookers' voices as well as their ability to control the meaning of the spectacle.[35] Further, just as neither onstage nor offstage spectators hear what Cressida whispers to Diomedes, her appeal to Troilus is met only by silence. Indeed, both Stevenson's performance and Davies's representational choices call attention to Troilus' lack of response and, beyond that, to his (chivalric?) loyalty, not to Cressida but to his fellow males. This strategy invites offstage spectators of either gender to turn their own gaze away from those of the (unseen) onstage spectators and to read in Cressida's final look – and its absent but (unknown to her) present subject, Troilus – a divided subject of their own fashioning. If the playtext's strategy depends on exploiting Cressida as subjected to the male gaze, Davies's de-centring of that spectacle exposes how she is constructed by their looks and offers an alternative viewpoint. Moreover, it reveals Cressida as a special instance of what Dollimore calls 'transgressive reinscription':[36] positioned as marginal to the male system which oppresses her with its gaze, at the last she not only internalises, and so validates, its looking relations but simultaneously demystifies their power to construct and fracture her identity.

From *Shakespearean Criticism Yearbook*, 16 (1990), 70–2, 76–9.

NOTES

[Barbara Hodgdon's essay is an outstanding example of performance criticism, underpinned by meticulously researched stage history and by sophisticated theoretical perspectives drawn from film theory. It is also a study of a play, long relatively marginal, whose handling of sexuality and gender have made it of great interest to feminist critics, and which has recently been reappraised more widely. Hodgdon's essay interrogates masculinity as well as femininity, and scrutinises the theatrical construction of embodied identities in order to historicise heterosexual desire as an aspect of social relations and relate it to larger social and political processes.

The original essay was structured to give detailed analyses of Cressida's first and last appearances; because of limitations of space, I have included only Professor Hodgdon's discussions of the last appearance, and I am grateful to her for allowing me to do this.   Ed.]

1. Quotations are from Kenneth Palmer's Arden edition of *Troilus and Cressida* (London, 1981).

2. Harry Berger, Jr, gives a neat summary in '*Troilus and Cressida*: the Observer as Basilisk', *Comparative Drama*, 2 (1968), 130–1.

3. For Cressida's difficulty in understanding herself, see esp. II.ii.116–49.

4. Rosalie L. Colie, *Shakespeare's Living Art* (Princeton, NJ, 1974), p. 317.

5. Elizabeth Freund, '"Ariachne's broken woof": the Rhetoric of Citation in *Troilus and Cressida*', in *Shakespeare and the Question of Theory*, ed. Patricia Parker and Geoffrey Hartman (New York, 1985), p. 35. See also Linda Charnes, '"So Unsecret to Ourselves": Notorious Identity and the Material Subject in Shakespeare's *Troilus and Cressida*', *Shakespeare Quarterly*, 40:4 (Winter 1989), 413–40.

6. Palmer, e.g., consistently reads the social as the moral (Arden edition, pp. 38–93). See also, among others, Douglas Cole, 'Myth and Anti-Myth: the Case of *Troilus and Cressida*', *Shakespeare Quarterly*, 30 (1980), 76–84. Even apologist readings such as Gayle Greene's position Cressida as an inevitable product of a morally degenerate world ('Shakespeare's Cressida: "A Kind of Self"', in *The Woman's Part: Feminist Criticism of Shakespeare*, ed. Carolyn R. S. Lenz *et al.* [Urbana, Il., 1980], pp. 133–49). In 'The Patriarchal Bard: Feminist Criticism and Shakespeare: *King Lear* and *Measure for Measure*', Kathleen McLuskie outlines an alternative project: 'Feminist criticism need not restrict itself to privileging the woman's part or to special pleading on behalf of female characters. It can be equally well served by making a text reveal the conditions in which a particular ideology of femininity functions and by both revealing and subverting the hold which such an ideology has for readers both female and male' (in *Political Shakespeare: New Essays in Cultural Materalism*, ed. Jonathan Dollimore and Alan Sinfield [Manchester, 1985], p. 106). [Reprinted in this volume – see p. 44.   Ed.]

7. Jonathan Dollimore, *Radical Tragedy: Religion, Ideology and Power in the Drama of Shakespeare and his Contemporaries* (Brighton, 1984), esp. pp. 44–7.

8. For a capsule stage history, see Kenneth Muir, *Troilus and Cressida* (Oxford, 1982), pp. 9–12.

9. For an argument legitimating theatrical and performances as texts, see my *The End Crowns All: Closure and Contradiction in Shakespeare's History* (Princeton, NJ, 1990). For the relation between social and theatrical meaning, see McLuskie, 'The Patriarchal Bard', p. 95; and Elin Diamond, 'Brechtian Theory/Feminist Theory', *Drama Review*: 32 (1988), 82–94.

10. See Joan Kelly, 'Did Women have a Renaissance?' in *Women, History and Theory* (Chicago, Il, 1984), esp. pp. 30–47.

11. In II.ii, the Trojan council scene. See also, however, the exchange between Paris and Diomedes concerning who 'deserves fair Helen best' (IV.i.52–79).

12. I draw here on Tania Modleski, 'Rape vs. Mans/laughter: *Blackmail*', in *The Women Who Knows Too Much: Hitchcock and Feminist Theory* (London, 1988), esp. pp. 19–28.

13. For important distinctions between the homosocial and the homo-erotic as well as a pertinent discussion of triangulated relationships, see Eve Kosofsky Sedgwick, *Between Men: English Literature and Male Homosocial Desire* (New York, 1985), esp. pp. 1–27.

14. Laura Mulvey, 'Visual Pleasure and Narrative Cinema' (1975); rpt. in *Feminism and Feminist Film Theory*, ed. Constance Penley (New York, 1988), p. 62. For the notion of the play as a male project, with women as its stagehands, see Naomi Scheman, 'Missing Mothers/Desiring Daughters: Framing the Sight of Women', *Critical Inquiry*, 15 (1988), 87.

15. Stephen Greenblatt's phrase, which concludes his 'Invisible Bullets', is 'There is subversion, no end of subversion, only not for us.' See his *Shakespearean Negotiations: The Circulation of Social Energy in Renaissance England* (Berkeley, 1988), p. 65.

16. For a summary of Peter Alexander's theory concerning Inns of Court performance, see Palmer, Arden edition, pp. 307–10. See also E. A. J. Honigmann, 'The Date and Revision of *Troilus and Cressida*', in *Textual Criticism and Interpretation*, ed. Jerome McGann (Chicago, 1985), pp. 38–54; and Gary Taylor, '*Troilus and Cressida*: Bibliography, Performance, and Interpretation', *Shakespeare Studies*, 15 (1982), 99–136.

17. Andrew Gurr reports that very few women – and those few were among the aristocratic and upper classes – were literate; even in London, few women could write their names. See his *Playgoing in Shakespeare's London* (Cambridge, 1987), p. 55.

18. Ibid., pp. 57–8, 79.

19. Ibid., pp. 57–8; I reproduce Gurr's index listing under 'women' in the alphabetical order he uses, primarily because it nicely mixes class hierarchies. See also Jean Howard, 'Crossdressing, the Theatre, and Gender Struggle in Early Modern England', *Shakespeare Quarterly*, 39 (1988), 440.

20. Gurr, *Playgoing*, pp. 92–4.

21. Thomas Randolph, *The Muses' Looking Glass* (1638), epilogue; reproduced in Gurr, *Playgoing*, p. 238.

22. Howard, 'Crossdressing', p. 440.

23. Dekker's epilogue is reproduced in Gurr, *Playgoing*, p. 214. See also Linda Woodbridge, *Women and the English Renaissance: Literature and the Nature of Womankind, 1540–1620* (Urbana, Il., 1984), pp. 250–1; and Richard Levin, 'Women in the Renaissance Theatre Audience', *Shakespeare Quarterly*, 40: 2 (Summer 1989), 165–74.

24. Woodbridge, *Women*, pp. 250–1; Gurr, *Playgoing*, pp. 102–4.

25. Louis Adrian Montrose, 'The Purpose of Playing: Reflections on a Shakespearean Anthropology', *Helios*, n.s. 7 (1980), 51–74; and Howard, 'Crossdressing', esp. pp. 437–40.

26. Katherine Eisaman Maus, 'Horns of Dilemma: Jealousy, Gender, and Spectatorship in English Renaissance Drama', *ELH*, 54 (1987), 578. For the initial theoretical work on the gendered gaze, see Mulvey's 'Visual Pleasure'. Further studies respond to, extend and/or qualify her formulations. See Teresa de Lauretis, *Alice Doesn't: Feminism, Semiotics, Cinema* (Bloomington, IN, 1984); Mary Ann Doane, *The Desire to Desire: The Women's Film of the 1940s* (Bloomington, IN, 1987); and Modleski, *Women Who Knew Too Much*. See also my 'Kiss Me Deadly; or The Des/Demonized Spectacle', in *Othello: New Perspectives*, ed. Virginia M. Vaughan and Kent Cartwright (Cranbury, NJ, 1990).

27. For the notion of citation, see Freud, '"Ariachne's broken woof"', p. 24.

28. I draw here on Peggy Phelan, 'Feminist Theory, Post-structuralism, and Performance', *Drama Review*, 32 (1988), 111.

29. Modleski, *Women Who Knew Too Much*, p. 25.

30. Cf. McLuskie, 'The Patriarchal Bard', who in turn refers to Jonathan Culler's discussion of 'Reading as a Woman' in *Theory and Criticism after Structuralism* (Ithaca, NY, 1982), pp. 43–63, where he implies that positioning the reader as a woman is not only a matter of free choice but a coherent position that determines clear-cut readings.

31. Coppélia Kahn notes this feminising tendency in *Man's Estate: Masculine Identity in Shakespeare* (Berkeley, CA, 1981), pp. 131–2.

32. Only one other property, Desdemona's handkerchief, is so liberally handled, and so gendered and regendered with contradictory signs. See Lynda E. Boose, 'Othello's Handkerchief: The Recognizance and Pledge of Love', *English Literary Renaissance*, 9 (1975), 360–74; and Karen Newman, '"And wash the Ethiop white": Femininity and the Monstrous in *Othello*', in *Shakespeare Reproduced: The Text in History and Ideology*, ed. Jean E. Howard and Marion F. O'Connor (New York, 1987), pp. 143–62.

33. Dollimore, *Radical Tragedy*, p. 48.

34. David Burke, who played Hector, put it this way: 'I'm not saying we could get Cressida down on the floor and rape her – that would be violating the text – but you can see brutal acts of lechery in the eye, in the manner. A look between two men can tell you as much if not more than a hand stuck up a dress' (quoted in a programme note).

35. For this function of the voice-over in film, see Kaja Silverman, *The Acoustic Mirror: The Female Voice in Psychoanalysis and Cinema* (Bloomington, IN, 1988), pp. 48–9; 130–3; 136–40. Admittedly, cinema intensifies the effect of such vocal control over and above that of theatrical representation.

36. Jonathan Dollimore, 'Subjectivity, Sexuality and Transgression: the Jacobean Connection', *Renaissance Drama*, n.s. 17 (1986), 57.

9

Revolutions, Petty Tyranny and the Murderous Husband

FRANCES DOLAN

The commonplace analogy of household and Commonwealth suggests that representations of domestic authority and obedience would change in the mid and late seventeenth century in tandem with reconceptualisation of the relation of citizen to government and of the subject's right to civil disobedience. Indeed, they did. Although murderous husbands remained two to three times more common than murderous wives throughout the century, popular representations shift their attention from the murderous wife to the murderous husband only in the second half of the century. While before 1650 representations of murderous wives outnumber those of murderous husbands, after 1650 the opposite is true. For instance, I have examined thirty-two accounts of wives who murder their husbands, only four of which were published after 1650. In contrast, I have examined twenty accounts of husbands who murder their wives, only two of which were published before 1650.[1]

Just as popular accounts construct a wife's murder of her husband as petty treason, they construct a husband's murder of his wife as petty tyranny. Yet petty tyranny was not a legal category, nor did the law distinguish wife murder from other kinds of murder. Even when pamphlets or ballads present husbandly excesses as irresponsible and analogous to tyranny, they do not represent this petty tyranny as threatening social order in the same ways that petty treason did. Certainly early modern culture did not encourage men to kill their wives, or dismiss the significance of such crimes: men who were convicted of murdering their dependents paid for this crime with their lives, and pamphlets and ballads increasingly disseminated their stories as the century waned. However, neither the legal nor the literary representations of such crimes emphasise their significance outside of the home or beyond the lives of those involved. In contrast to the petty traitor, who overturns the hierarchy that is supposed to govern domestic relations, the domestic tyrant grotesquely caricatures his role, expanding the parameters of the patriarch's authority rather than openly challenging domestic hierarchy.

. . . .

Performed in 1604, *Othello* anticipates the post-1650 pattern in part because the protagonist's race prepared its original audience to question his authority.[2] On the one hand, Othello is the victim of a plotting subordinate (Iago), a 'cursèd slave' (V.ii.300) who 'poisons' him with the fiction of another subordinate's plot (his wife's adultery).[3] On the other hand, Othello is a domestic tyrant who murders his wife on spurious grounds.[4]

If in *Othello*, as in so many representations of domestic conflict, danger lies in the familiar, Othello stands both as the victim of those dangerous familiars and as one himself – in the state, as well as the household. Like Caliban, Othello is the 'outsider-within', 'more familiar than strange', as Emily Bartels argues.[5] Because, as 'both monster and *hero*', he has more power and dignity than Caliban, he poses more of a threat to those who employ him and to his own dependents and intimates.[6] He is 'an extravagant and wheeling stranger, / of here and everywhere' (I.i.139–40), who was yet loved and oft invited by Brabantio (I.iii.130). A 'bond slave' (I.ii.101) to his 'masters' (I.iii.79) in the signiory, he is also a valued general whom the senate 'cannot with safety cast' (I.i.153); he is depended on yet distrusted in a way characteristic of servants.[7] Critics have long noted Othello's ambiguous social positioning: because of his racial difference from the Venetians, Othello does not hold his authority securely and confidently, especially at home; because he is a successful, trusted general, he is not really a servant. Like Caliban, Othello internalises the racist assessments of his worth, ultimately accepting the role that grants him the least amount of dignity and authority, in this case, that of cuckold.

Despite what G. K. Hunter calls the play's 'claustrophobic intensity', *Othello* does not fit neatly into 'the critical category domestic tragedy', as Karen Newman points out when she urges us to 'reread *Othello* from another perspective, also admittedly historically bound, that seeks to displace conventional interpretations by exposing the extraordinary fascination with and fear of racial sexual difference which characterises Elizabethan and Jacobean culture'.[8] My interest is in the complex interrelations between discourses of domesticity and those of difference, between the familiar and the strange in the play. It is not only that, as Emily Bartels argues, discourses of racial difference themselves targeted 'not the outsider but the insider, the population that threatens by being too close to home, too powerful, too successful, or merely too present';[9] it is also that, in focusing on a black hero, *Othello* draws on several distinct, even competing, cultural constructions of domestic threat, of the difference that can undermine domesticity from within. A crucible of cultural fears and anxieties, the play anticipates later cultural obsessions as well as confronting its audience with the full range of contemporary fears: the racial other; the traitor who schemes against the nation from within; the witch; the plotting subordinate; the abusive authority figure. Granting Othello the prestige and sympathy of protagonist status, the play yet allies him with each of these spectres of disorder.

Although the most discussed domestic conflict in the play is that between Othello and Desdemona, the play begins as Iago describes a conflict between himself and Othello that is both professional and domestic; Iago first presents himself as a *servant* and Othello as his *master*. Iago's malignity seems more motivated and comprehensible in the context of other representations of scheming subordinates, which similarly criminalise subordinates' ambition. Iago 'attends on himself' by fostering Othello's suspicions and 'engender[ing]' a plot against his master that exploits both Othello's distrust of his wife and his trust in his ensign (I.i.153; I.iii.404). In the first scene of the play, Iago complains about arbitrary preferment as 'the curse of service' and he also proposes a solution to that curse.

> I follow him [Othello] to serve my turn upon him;
> We cannot all be masters, nor all masters
> Cannot be truly followed.
>
> (I.i.36, 44–6)

By this strategy, Iago cunningly transforms obedience into self-promotion and pursues his master's interests only to the extent that they overlap with his own: 'In following him, I follow but myself' (I.i.60). As opposed to 'duteous and knee-crooking' servants, Iago links himself with those who 'have some soul' (ll.47, 56); that soul is found in the scandalous separation between the servant's interest and the master's interest.

> others there are,
> Who, trimmed in forms and visages of duty,
> Keep yet their hearts attending on themselves.
> (I.i.51–3)

In Iago's view, presented as villainous, 'outward action' and 'the native act, and figure of my heart' cannot correspond for a servant (ll.63–4). While self-interest is too dangerous a livery to wear, the master's livery should also not shape the servant too much, because, in Iago's view, a servant's 'soul' exists only in resistance. Iago makes service bearable by so redefining the verbs 'serve', 'follow', and 'attend' that they are no longer recognisable.

Iago's reinvention of service decisively defeats Desdemona's attempt to reinvent marriage to allow both spouses to be subjects and heroes.[10] In contrast to the prevalent representations of conspiring wives and servants, here the treacherous servant works *against* the wife. As critics have noted, Desdemona dwindles when the play abandons the romantic comic structure of the first acts; she is lost without the roles of romantic heroine and loving wife that the play's first generic movement affords her.[11] By act IV, her diminishment accrues greater significance when we see that the play oscillates between competing plots of domestic violence, neither of which offers Desdemona an acceptable role. In both plots, husband and wife are antagonists; each offers her a role that violates what Mary Beth Rose calls her 'visionary construction of marriage'. She can be either an adulterous wife or a murdered wife. If, as Rose argues, Desdemona aspires to be a heroine of marriage, embarking on a shared adventure,[12] Iago defeats her by drawing on the deeply entrenched, reactionary cultural interest in insubordinate wives, which associates female self-assertion with betrayal, adultery and violence. First, Iago manipulates Brabantio's fears by interpreting Desdemona's elopement as 'a gross revolt' (I.i.137). Then Brabantio and Iago use this 'revolt' to warn Othello to anticipate duplicity and to construe Desdemona's self-determination as criminal: 'She has deceived her father, and may do thee' (I.iii.296; cf. III.iii.211). Othello's doubts about his own worth and the depth of his love for Desdemona prepare him to experience her infidelity as a fatal assault. By seeing how Iago deploys the fiction of the traitorous wife, and remembering how pervasive that fiction was, we gain one more perspective on the endlessly interesting question of why Othello so readily distrusts Desdemona.

While the play begins as a romantic comedy, it also has affinities to darker, crueller comic traditions, such as the cuckold joke and charivari. In this, it resembles *Arden of Faversham*, with the additional twist that Othello's rare helps to position him as the butt of a mean joke.[13] Like Arden, he is, in his subordinate's view, 'the impediment most profitably removed' (II.i.279–80), trapped into being what he most fears, 'a fixed figure for the time of scorn / To point his slow and moving finger at' (IV.ii.56–7). Iago and Emilia offer a farcical perspective on adultery, trivialising what Othello experiences as the most intimate and fatal of betrayals as a 'small vice', not even 'peculiar' to him (IV.iii.72f; IV.i.68–70). Also in the tradition of cuckold jokes and shaming rituals, Iago casts Desdemona as the woman on top: 'Our general's wife is now the general' (II.iii.308–9); 'She may make, unmake, do what she list' (l.340).[14] If Iago successfully deploys the structures of inversion and exaggeration to humiliate and punish those who challenge domestic norms, the play's central action follows him. As Michael Bristol argues, playwright and audience are both implicated: 'The play as a whole is organized around the abjection and violent punishment of its central figures'[15] Even Thomas Rymer, outraged at the absurdity of a black hero and fully complicit in the trivialisation of Othello, censures the playwright's cruelty toward his characters. In fact, Rymer depicts Shakespeare as himself a tyrant, who 'in a barbarous arbitrary way, executes and makes havock of his subjects, *Hab-nab*, as they come to hand.'[16]

Several of Shakespeare's doomed subjects themselves to respond 'in a barbarous arbitrary way' to their subordinates' self-assertions ('revolts'): Barbantio fears that Desdemona's 'escape would teach [him] tyranny' if he had another child (I.iii.200); suspicion turns Othello's love to 'tyrannous hate' (III.iii.464). When Othello acts on these feelings, he anticipates the popular representations of violent, murderous husbands. After Othello publicly slaps and insults his wife, Lodovico assumes that he has lost his mind: 'Are his wits safe? Is he not light of brain?' (IV.i.274). Othello justifies his murder of Desdemona by casting himself not as a jealous, vengeful husband but as a domestic governor who 'proceed[s] upon just grounds' (V.ii.143). In this role, he collects the evidence, forms a judgement, and carries out the punishment best suited to the crime, strangling Desdemona in the very 'bed she hath contaminated'; 'Good, good! The justice of it pleases. Very good' (IV.i.208; cf. V.i.37).[17] Although as Mary Beth Rose argues, Othello 'constructs his murder of Desdemona as an execution of justice and revenge undertaken (dispassionately) as a public service',[18] he finally murders Desdemona, as Richard S. Ide observes, '*in propria persona*: as a base, selfish, passionately jealous husband'.[19] Othello himself comes to see his action as unjust and unjustified, the act of an absurd master and an abusive husband, too weak and foolish to overmaster his ensign and his own fears, yet so brutal and tyrannical that he would murder his own wife on a rumour.

As Iago joins the two plots, Emilia disentangles them. Choosing her role as loyal servant over her role as wife, she identifies Iago as a petty traitor, Othello as a domestic tyrant, and Desdemona as the victim of them both. Proclaiming that 'the Moor hath killed my mistress!' (V.ii.17), not that 'Othello has killed his wife', she privileges her own relation to Desdemona as that least compromised by betrayal and violence. While Emilia bravely chooses among competing alliances, identifies conspiracies, and places blame, the two distinct plots – of petty treason and domestic tyranny – remain in tension. Iago plotted against Othello, but Othello murdered Desdemona.

A comparison to Elizabeth Cary's *The Tragedie of Mariam* (1613) can elucidate how both the structure of *Othello* and the characterisation of the hero remain persistently dual even in the last act. Like *Othello*, *Mariam* anticipates later interest in domestic tyranny by demonising and racialising the tyrannous husband as a dark 'other'. Further, as a play written by a woman, with an outspoken female protagonist, *The Tragedie of Mariam* is particularly well positioned to question not only the limits on a husband's authority but the possibility of a wife's resistance. Compared to *Othello*, *Mariam* more obviously structures the action around antagonistic plots of a wife's treason and a husband's tyranny, linking the two with a false accusation. In *Mariam*, Herod, the tyrannous king and husband, has his wife executed on the false charges that she committed adultery and plotted to poison him, the two wifely transgressions so conventionally linked. It is easier to recognise and separate the two distinct 'plots' of spousal conflict in *Mariam* than in *Othello*. When we first meet Mariam, ruminating on the (false) news of Herod's death, she confides how 'oft' she has 'wished his Carkas dead to see'.[20] Mariam, Doris (Herod's bitter ex-wife) and Salome (his sister, whose hand is 'ever readie lifted ... to aime destruction at a husbands throat') dominate the first three acts of the play until Herod returns (II.iv.884–5). With Herod's arrival, the play shifts its focus from angry, rebellious and murderous wives to an angry, repressive and vengeful tyrant.

In contrast to Desdemona, Mariam is implicated in the false charges brought against her: she has wished her husband dead; she has resisted him and his authority; she has participated in a kind of adultery, simply by displacing his first wife and children. Until the fifth act, when Mariam is safely dead, the play dramatises Mariam's conflicts ambivalently, exploring her justifications for resistance, yet presenting that resistance as 'a subversive political act that defies Herod's authority as King, as well as husband'.[21] Since the play is Mariam's tragedy rather than Herod's, it concludes with a relatively unambiguous indictment of the tyrannous husband. Herod censures himself as a tyrant who deserves his subjects' rebellion: 'Why graspe not each of you a sword in hand, / To ayme at me your cruell Soveraignes head' (V.i.2115–16). The concluding Chorus also condemns him as one who 'hath his power so much betraide' and who 'lunatickly rave[s]' (V.i.2228, 2230).

The characterisation of Herod is less sympathetic and nuanced than that of othello, but he, too, is *racialised*, his tyrannical behaviour presented as that of a man against a woman who 'was so white': 'If she had bene like an *Egiptian* blacke, / And not so faire, she had bene longer livde' (V.i.2092; 2181–2).[22] Herod, like Othello, 'transgresses the norms associated with the idea of a husband' while he reveals the potential for tyranny inherent in those norms.[23] By emphasising the 'fairness' of the murdered wives, most lovable when silent, pallid and dead, and presenting the murderous husbands as foreign, duped and dark, both *Mariam* and *Othello*, like the later depictions of murderous husbands, avoid holding the available conceptions of marriage and spousal roles accountable for the tragic outcome. Each play deflects much of the blame for domestic tyranny onto racialised difference between the husband and wife, which undermines the husband's authority, and onto malevolent schemers like Iago and Salome.

Seeing *Othello* as a palimpsest, like Emilia's plain speaking, does not resolve all conflicts: the representation of Iago's schemes is indebted to depictions of traitorous servants, but he is a military subordinate, not a domestic servant;[24] Iago fatally casts Desdemona as an adulterous wife, but he accuses her falsely; Othello is simultaneously more and less powerful than his white, Venetian ensign, a master and a servant of the state, insider and outsider, the victim of conspiracy, and a man who murders his wife. Connecting *Othello* to these two narratives of domestic conflict, each of which locates the threat so differently, offers additional evidence of the play's complexity, particularly of the ways in which it casts each of its central characters in conflicting roles. In its last act, *The Tragedie of Mariam* excludes 'the slaughtered Mariam' from view and leaves both Herod and Salome unpunished for Mariam's death; it closes with an uncluttered, less ambivalent emphasis on the tyrant's arbitrary and unchecked power as the cause of the tragedy. In contrast, *Othello* concludes with the unseemly image of the bloody, crowded conjugal bed. Like other representations of wife murder, this image shockingly conjoins marital sex and violence; yet it is also grotesquely adulterous and comic. Piling one body on top of another, forcing spectators to look at all the casualties at once, the play's final act also piles one plot on top of another, refusing to disentangle them even at the end. Focusing on the play's palimpsestic structure also reveals that Othello's race crucially informs the play's form and its relation to other popular materials. By making his protagonist black, Shakespeare prepared his original audience to question Othello's authority, to suspect that he might misuse it groundlessly, and to explore the interrelations of different and domestic, dangerous and familiar.

Comparing *Othello* and *Mariam* suggests that early seventeenth-century drama could anticipate later inquiries into domestic tyranny only under unusual conditions: when a playwright racialises the differences between spouses and thus somewhat distances them from the conflict in most English marriages, or when a female playwright focuses on a wife's subjectivity. Furthermore, in these two plays the analogies between the household and the Commonwealth have a particular force, since both focus on the actions of public men – a general and a king – in domestic situations. Indeed, both men conflate 'state affairs' and 'house affairs' with disastrous results, approaching 'private and domestic quarrels' with all of the violence and dispatch required to defeat the Turks in bloody battle or murder one's way to the throne (*Othello*, I.iii.193; I.iii.149; II.iii.209). Blurring the distinction between Othello's and Herod's acts as husbands and as public authority figures, the two plays cast them as dangerous familiars – untrustworthy 'others' undermining order from within – in both spheres. The analogy between household and Commonwealth thus operates in these plays to dissociate tyranny from English patriarchal authority, political and domestic.

Although our culture focuses much of its anxiety about domestic order on the threat of abusive authority, British culture prior to the Civil War focused its anxieties on the threat of the insubordinate or murderous dependent. Before 1650, and a collective act of treason, the domestic ramifications of that anxiety were explored through representations of the murderous wife. After 1650, however, while the murderous wife remained a focus of anxiety, the murderous husband attracted increasing attention. Interest shifted from the treacherous subordinate to the irresponsible, even lunatic, authority figure. Husbands and masters may have been reluctant to draw parallels between their rebellion as citizens and their wives' and dependents' frustrations, but they found the story of abused authority – of tyranny – on domestic and political levels increasingly compelling as they justified and instantiated their rebellions. After the 1688 Revolution, when representations of murderous husbands are especially numerous, the limits on and responsibilities of power were once again of particular concern.

By telling the stories of household governors who fail to fulfil the responsibilities accompanying their authority, representations of domestic tyranny suggest the dangers of trusting husbands not to abuse their power. Francis Barker contends that a new form of masculine subjectivity, the self-regulating 'private and judicious individual', emerged in the second half of the seventeenth century. This individual, the propertied male head of household, enjoyed considerable power over others, power that was ambiguously defined and beyond official regulation except in the most extreme instances. Representations of those extremes explore the dangers for dependents and for the social order when the household governor is not self-regulating but arbitrary, not private but inscrutable, not judicious but a brutal lunatic, not individual but estranged from and irresponsible toward his dependents.[25] Yet by dwelling on murder – the most extreme abuse of authority – and demonising it as the work of tyrants, lunatics and Moors, the representations of wife-killing avoid implying that marriage is arbitrary, tyrannous and exploitative, or that wives' rebellion might be justified.

From *Dangerous Familiars: Representations of Domestic Crime in England, 1550–1700* (Ithaca, NY: Cornell University Press, 1994), pp. 89–91, 110–20.

NOTES

[By connecting dramatic representations of marital conflict and wife-murder to popular discourses about petty treason and domestic tyranny, Frances Dolan shows that the relation between historical factors and theatrical representation may be oblique, complicated and resistant to being mapped in any obvious, straightforward way. She examines how the intersection of Othello's blackness with other anxiety-provoking categories operates dramatically, and further enriches her discussion of the hugely influential representation of racial difference in Shakespeare's play by comparing it with the racialisation of identities in Elizabeth Cary's less familiar *Tragedy of Mariam* (1613). The essay concludes by laying out the complex political implications of these connections between racialised and gendered identities, and between public and private categories of behaviour.

I am grateful to Professor Dolan for allowing me to omit a passage which places her discussion of these plays in the context of long-term processes of social change.   Ed.]

1. In Chapter 1, I cite eleven pamphlets, two ballads and one play about actual cases in which wives murder their husbands. In addition, I have consulted two ballads, one play, and three tracts. The pamphlets have the following dates: 1583, 1591, 1592, 1604, 1609, 1635, 1641, [1675], 1678, [1687], 1688. The ballads date from 1616, 1628 (2), and 1629. The plays date from 1592 and 1599. There are also five prose accounts and a ballad about the Arden of Faversham case and five prose accounts and a ballad on the Sanders case, dramatised as *A Warning for Fair Women*. In contrast, I have found thirteen popular narratives about husbands who kill their wives, many of which are brief – broadsides rather than pamphlets – and seven ballads. Accounts of murderous husbands appear in fewer genres, are less detailed, and, most significantly, proliferate only in the second half of the century. The dates for the pamphlets I have consulted are: 1598, 1607, 1653 (2), 1655, 1677, 1679, 1680 (3), 1682, 1684, 1690. The ballads date from: 1685, 1690, 1695, 1697 (3), and *circa* late seventeenth century. Only two of the twenty accounts occur before 1650, while seven occur between 1680 and 1690 alone. In contrast, I have found twenty-eight

plays, ballads and pamphlets about wives killing their husbands written before 1650. I am not interested in attempting a statistical survey of these materials; the arbitrary survival of such ephemera would qualify any conclusions that could be drawn. Nevertheless, I want to convey a sense of what I have found.

In her own work on popular representations of spouse killing, Joy Wiltenburg sees the same trend. See her *Disorderly Women and Female Power in the Street Literature of Early Modern England and Germany* (Charlottesville: University of Virginia Press, 1992), ch. 9, esp. pp. 214, 221. By the eighteenth century, shaming rituals had similarly shifted their attention from disorderly women to wife-beaters. See Elizabeth Pleck, *Domestic Tyranny: The Making of Social Policy against Family Violence from Colonial Times to the Present* (New York: Oxford University Press, 1987), p. 233, n. 37, and chs 1 and 2; and David Underdown, 'The Taming of the Scold: the Enforcement of Patriarchal Authority in Early Modern England', in *Order and Disorder in Early Modern England*, ed. Anthony Fletcher and John Stevenson (Cambridge: Cambridge University Press, 1985), pp. 116–36, esp. p. 121.

2. On Othello's race, and its crucial significance, see Michael D. Bristol, 'Charivari and the Comedy of Abjection in *Othello*', *Renaissance Drama*, n.s. 21 (1990), 3–21; Ruth Cowhig, 'Blacks in English Renaissance Drama and the Role of Shakespeare's Othello', in *The Black Presence in English Literature*, ed. David Dabydeen (Manchester: Manchester University Press, 1985), pp. 1–25; G. K. Hunter, '*Othello* and Colour Prejudice', *Proceedings of the British Academy*, 53 (1967), 139-63; Arthur Kirsch, *Shakespeare and the Experience of Love* (Cambridge: Cambridge University Press, 1981), ch. 2; Ania Loomba, *Gender, Race, and Renaissance Drama* (Manchester: Manchester University Press, 1989), ch. 2; Karen Newman, '"And wash the Ethiop white": Femininity and the Monstrous in *Othello*', in *Shakespeare Reproduced: The Text in History and Ideology*, ed. Jean E. Howard and Marion F. O'Connor (New York: Methuen, 1987), pp. 143–62, also found in Newman's recent book, *Fashioning Femininity and English Renaissance Drama* (Chicago, IL: University of Chicago Press, 1991); and Valerie Traub, *Desire and Anxiety: Circulations of Sexuality in Shakespearean Drama* (London: Routledge, 1992), pp. 33–41. See also Anthony Gerard Barthelemy, *Black Face, Maligned Race: The Representation of Blacks in English Drama from Shakespeare to Southerne* (Baton Rouge, LA: Louisiana State University Press, 1987), pp. 150–62; and Jack D'Amico, *The Moor in English Renaissance Drama* (Tampa, FL: University of South Florida Press, 1991), pp. 177–96.

3. In the tradition of petty traitors, Iago 'poisons' his master's 'delight' (I.i.70): 'I'll pour this pestilence into his ear' (II.iii.350); 'Dangerous conceits are in their natures poisons' (III.iii.342). All citations of

Othello are from *William Shakespeare: The Complete Works*, ed. David Bevington, 4th edn (New York: Harper Collins, 1992).

4. Peter Stallybrass argues that sometimes Othello can be seen as 'the master of an insubordinate servant' ('Patriarchal Territories: the Body Enclosed', in *Rewriting the Renaissance: The Discourses of Sexual Difference in Early Modern Europe*, ed. Margaret W. Ferguson, Maureen Quilligan and Nancy J. Vickers [Chicago, IL: University of Chicago Press, 1986], pp. 123–42, esp. p. 140); Emily Bartels argues that Brabantio casts Desdemona as 'a traitor' ('Making More of the Moor', *Shakespeare Quarterly*, 41: 4 (1990), 433–54, p. 450). But no one I know of has connected the play to the popular discourses about domestic tyranny and petty treason. Also, although many scholars have connected the play to discourses about marriage and sexuality, they have not explored its relation to those about master–servant relations. Patricia Parker's analysis of 'structures of "following" and their "preposterous" inverse' identifies what I would call a rhetorical analogue to petty treason ('Preposterous Events', *Shakespeare Quarterly*, 43:2 [1992] 186–213, esp. p. 187).

5. Bartels, 'Making More of the Moor', p. 435.

6. This is Karen Newman's phrase, emphasis added ('"And wash the Ethiop white"', p. 150).

7. On Othello's multiple, contradictory positions, see Bartels, 'Making More of the Moor', pp. 433, 435, 451, and passim; Loomba, *Gender, Race*, pp. 41, 48–9, 54; Michael Neill, 'Unproper Beds', *Shakespeare Quarterly*, 40:4 (1989), 433–54, p. 412; Newman,'"And wash the Ethiop white"', pp. 150, 153; Mary Beth Rose, *The Expense of Spirit* (Ithaca, NY: Cornell University Press, 1988), p. 132; and Stallybrass, 'Patriarchal Territories', p. 140.

8. Hunter, '*Othello* and Colour Prejudice', p. 161; Newman, '"And wash the Ethiop white"', pp. 156–7.

9. Bartels, 'Making More of the Moor', p. 433.

10. On the 'heroics of marriage' in *Othello*, see Rose, *Expense of Spirit*, pp. 131–55. See also the discussions of marital eroticism in Kirsch, *Shakespeare and the Experience of Love*, passim; and Stephen Greenblatt, *Renaissance Self-Fashioning from More to Shakespeare* (Chicago, IL: University of Chicago Press, 1980), ch. 6.

11. On Desdemona's fracturing and diminution, see Loomba, *Gender, Race*, pp. 57–9; Rose, *Expense of Spirit*, pp. 151–4; and Stallybrass, 'Patriarchal Territories', p. 141.

12. Rose, *Expense of Spirit*, esp. p. 138.

13. See Bristol's provocative argument ('Charivari').

14. On the play's affinities to comedy, see Bristol, 'Charivari'; Greenblatt, *Renaissance Self-Fashioning*, p. 234; Neill, 'Unproper Beds'; and Susan Snyder, '*Othello* and the Conventions of Romantic Comedy', *Renaissance Drama*, n.s. 5 (1972), 123–41.

15. Bristol, 'Charivari', p. 3.

16. Thomas Rymer, 'A Short View of Tragedy' (1692) in *The Critical Works of Thomas Rymer*, ed. Curt A. Zimansky (New Haven, CT: Yale University Press, 1956), pp. 162–3.

17. On Othello's murder/execution of Desdemona, see Greenblatt. *Renaissance Self-Fashioning*, p. 250; Rose, *Expense of Spirit*, p. 142; and Rymer, 'Short View', pp. 134, 160, 162–3.

18. Rose, *Expense of Spirit*, p. 142.

19. Richard S. Ide, *Possessed with Greatness: The Heroic Tragedies of Chapman and Shakespeare* (Chapel Hill, NC: University of North Carolina Press, 1980), p. 69.

20. Elizabeth Cary, *The Tragedies Of Mariam*, ed. A. C. Dunstan (The Malone Society Reprints; Oxford: Oxford University Press, 1914), 1.1.20; subsequent references to this edition are located in the text. Recent analyses of the play's ambivalences and contradictions include: Elaine Beilin, *Redeeming Eve: Women Writers of the English Renaissance* (Princeton, NJ: Princeton University Press, 1987), ch. 6; Sandra K. Fischer, 'Elizabeth Cary and Tyranny, Domestic and Religious', in *Silent But for the Word: Tudor Women as Patrons, Translators, and Writers of Religious Works*, ed. Margaret P. Hannay (Kent, OH: Kent State University Press, 1985), pp. 225–37; and Betty S. Travitsky, 'The *Feme Covert* in Elizabeth Cary's *Mariam*', in *Ambiguous Realities: Women in the Middle Ages and Renaissance*, ed. Carole Levin and Jeanie Watson (Detroit, IL: Wayne State University Press, 1987), pp. 184–96. Margaret W. Ferguson suggests that 'an overdetermined topical allegory in *Mariam*' draws parallels between Henry VIII and Herod as tyrants ('Running on with Almost Public Voice: the Case of "E. C"', in *Tradition and the Talents of Women*, ed. Florence Howe [Urbana, IL: University of Illinois Press, 1991], pp. 37–67, esp. p. 66, n. 48).

21. Nancy Gutierrez, 'Valuing *Mariam*: Genre Study and Feminist Analysis', *Tulsa Studies in Women's Literature*, 10 (1991), 233–51, esp. p. 245.

22. I depend here on Dympna Callaghan's illuminating analysis of the significance of race in the play: 'Re-reading *The Tragedie of Mariam, Faire Queen of Jewry*', in *Women, 'Race', and Writing in the Early Modern Period*, ed. Margo Hendricks and Patricia Parker (London: Routledge, 1994).

23. Bristol, 'Charivari', p. 9, see also p. 15; see also Rose, *Expense of Spirit*, p. 131 and passim.

24. On the significance of the fact that Iago is an ensign who covets a lieutenancy and how lieutenancy 'collapses military and domestic structures', see Julia Genster, 'Lieutenancy, Standing In, and *Othello*', *ELH*, 57 (1990), 785–809, esp. p. 786.

25. Francis Barker, *The Tremulous Private Body: Essays on Subjection* (London: Methuen, 1984), p. 55 and passim.

10

Macbeth and the All-singing, All-dancing Plays of the Jacobean Witch-vogue

DIANE PURKISS

> *Dostoyevsky's devils tell us: I'm nothing but an obsession. And then:*
> *I am the nothing that manifests itself as obsession. I am your obses-*
> *sion. I am your nothing.*
>
> Octavio Paz, *On Poets and Others*

A protocol has been established: one must always begin on witchcraft and drama with James I, the king who argued for the reality of witches' compacts with the devil, and believed that he had himself been the target of witches' machinations. James was personally involved in prosecuting the witches who had tried to sink his ship, showing miraculous knowledge of what he and his bride said on their wedding night. Taking place in Scotland in 1591, this trial showed the influence of Continental theories of diabolic pacts and sexual transgression, unlike most English trials. Torture was used to extract confessions, including the Scottish practice of thrawing (or wrenching) the neck with a rope. Taken together with the prosecution's reliance on evidence from the accused, torture rendered the giving of evidence a matter of bodily and vocal articulation: that is, bodies were turned into texts, were made to speak, were read, and the results displayed.[1]

However, James was inspired to go beyond the normative the-atricality of a witch-trial. Despite his anxiety about the power of witches, James showed signs of seeing the accused witches as a show staged for his benefit. The king's interest was caught by the evidence given by Agnes Tompson. Tompson deposed that

> upon the night of All Hallows Eve last, she was accompanied as well with the persons aforesaid as also with a great many other witches to the number of two hundred, and that all they together went by sea, each one in a riddle or sieve, and went in the same way substantially with flagons of wine, making merry and drinking by the way in the same riddles or sieves, to the kirk of North Berwick in Lothian, and that after they had landed, took hands on land and danced this reel or short dance, singing all with one voice: Commer ye go before, commer go ye / If ye will not go before, commer let me. At which time she confessed that this Gillis Duncan did go before them playing this reel and dance upon a small trump, called a Jew's trump, until they entered the kirk.[2]

After hearing this, James was 'in a wonderful admiration',

> and sent for the said Gillis Duncan, who upon the like trump did play the said dance before the king's majesty, who in respect of the strangeness of these matters took great delight to be present at their examination.

Tompson's evidence, with its mass of detail, allows the listeners to visualise – almost to witness – the witches' journey. However, James wants more. He summons Gillis Duncan to perform the dance for him, summons her not as a witness but as an entertainer. She is asked to *act out* her own behaviour, to turn the case against her into a theatrical event, to transform a tune which might have been freighted with occult significance into a pastime for a ruler.[3] We should pause to note that this was a woman who had perhaps been tortured, had certainly been terrified, asked to perform the 'crime' which would cost her this pain as a species of entertainment. We do not know what Gillis thought, but we do know what James said. What delights the king about Gillis's performance is 'the strangeness of these matters'. Like other societies, early modern society is compelled to define itself in terms of a constantly adjusted figure of otherness, an otherness which could represent that which society hoped to avoid or repress. Yet although stagings like this one presume strangeness as their *raison d'être*, they also work to *produce* the performer as other. By becoming a performer, Gillis Duncan established a series of relationships between herself and the king. He watches; she is what he watches. James estranges her from the court, who become the spectators who attend her performance. He also becomes her symbolic master; she now exists only to please him, to offer him wonder and strangeness. James is master of the witches who had threatened to master him. He restores the hierarchy and order threatened by the witches. The witchcraft that seemed dangerous when secret becomes visible as a performance. James's command turns the forensic and rhetorical proceedings of the court into an explicitly ideological drama, a drama in which symbolism replaces truth, and meaning is re-created – one might almost say recreated. This affirms royal power as the privileged spectator and interpreter of a spectacle offering otherness only to be dispelled by legitimate authority. In the moment of commanding Gillis Duncan's song, James becomes the author of his own masque and antimasque. Her dance is the origin of the many all-singing, all-dancing witches subsequently offered to king and commonwealth in Jacobean drama.

At the same time, James's staging is *reductive*. Complex narratives which have shape and meaning in popular culture and female household spaces are reduced to a single story of witchcraft as an all-but-incomprehensible song. This reductiveness comes about when women's stories of witchcraft are appropriated to serve male political, social and intellectual agendas, or (to put it differently) when witchcraft is staged as a theatrical spectacle of otherness which exists to subtend the maintenance of hierarchy and order. It is *not* a natural or an inevitable outcome of 'early modern witch-discourses', but a highly specific *intervention* in those discourses, one which serves particular interests. James's investment in staging witchcraft as a royal command performance functions to confirm his own role as discerning interpreter. In fact, the king 'interprets' nothing; one might even reverse the usual readings and opine that he is reduced to helpless silence by the song he orders. The song-and-dance show does not move forward the narrative of the trial. Seemingly a mere delay, a frivolity, it is as if James were deliberately trying to play the role of the effete absolutist interfering in the affairs of the law. No wonder, then, that after becoming king of England, James discovered another and more effective way to use witchcraft cases to establish his position as discerning interpreter of visual, aural and other signs. Always eager to appear abreast of intellectual fashion, James did not regard *Daemonologie* as his final or only word on the subject of witchcraft. Tacking to catch a fresh intellectual breeze, he was soon just as ready to deploy scepticism as belief in examining cases of witchcraft and possession, asserting belief in the case of the Essex divorce and scepticism in numerous cases of possession, carefully unmasked as fraudulent by the detective powers of the king.[4] Using the forensic discourses of interrogation and observation, and the nascent discourses of the medicalisation of hysteria, James tried to ground the monarch's authority in new science as well as old superstition. For instance, James intervened to get Elizabeth Jackson released after reading Edward Jorden's medicalising account of Mary Glover's 'possession' as a form of hysteria.[5] In his pamphlet on Mary Glover's 'possession', Jorden presents Glover's hysterical body and speech as an object of the knowing eye and ear of empiricism. Such stagings appealed to James; they offered an even more powerful means of defining the observer as the possessor of knowledge and interpretative skill than the discourses of Continental demonology. When in 1605 James encountered another case of possession involving a young woman named Anne Gunter, he at once enlisted the help of Edward Jorden to determine the genuineness of the case, showing his respect for Jorden's theories of hysteria.[6]

Such stagings of empiricism's triumphs over the supernatural are still figured by historians as a civilising break with the rhetorics of demonology which are valued in the case of Gillis Duncan. Placing the discovery of hysteria side by side with the revision of Gillis Duncan's dance-tune, however, suggests continuity rather than change. The fraudulent or hysteric woman offers herself as a more secure object of enquiry than the witch, since she is stripped of all power before examination. At the same time, the gaze of the empirical observer is invested with greater power than the gaze of the spectator, for the empiricist can tell the difference between acting and being, determining the truth that the body and gestures may seek to conceal. Gillis Duncan and Mary Glover are both presented as spectacles, objects of the knowing look. Both look forward to Charcot and the figuration of the female body and rambling speech of the hysteric as disorderly or carnivalesque spaces which ceaselessly transgress the bounds of decorum.[7] This presentation offers them as figures of disorder, figures against whom order can be defined. Such presentation allows the king to become the site of interpretative truth set over against a disorder which is not mysterious, but completely comprehensible in the authoritative discourses of science and medicine. At the same time, this new interpretative power allowed James to represent himself – in Habermas's useful term – as Christlike and even Godlike in his power to tell truth from fiction. Like a precious gem sensitive to poison, James could act as a touchstone of genuine virtue. No role could have been more suitable for an absolutist king.

. . . .

[Omitted here is a discussion of the staging of witchcraft in the anti-masque to Ben Jonson's *Masque of Queens*.   Ed.]

It might seem odd to treat Macbeth after *The Masque of Queens*; traditional literary histories see Shakespeare as Jonson's inspiration and not vice versa, since *Macbeth* was certainly on stage at the Globe in 1606. However, the version of *Macbeth* which survives is the product of later revision; attempts to bring the text back to the putative purity of its first staging can only be conjectural. What survives is a play reworked for the witch-fashion set by Jonson's masque; in this Borgesian sense, Jonson is Shakespeare's precursor and not vice versa. The wish to return the play to pre-Jonsonian origins is reflected in the contextualisations offered for its dramatisation of witchcraft. Since James is actually alluded to in *Macbeth* in the scene where the witches display Banquo's heirs, conventional wisdom sees the witches as a compliment to him; or, as we might put it today, as a staging of violent misogyny for the benefit of a patriarchal absolutist paranoid about women's powers. It is traditional to see the witches of *Macbeth* as addressed to the crusading paranoiac of *Newes from Scotland* rather than the sceptical debunker of the claims of the possessed.[8] Certainly, the witches in *Macbeth* are not offered as a display of ignorance and superstition as Jonson's hags are, and their appeal to the king's interpretative power is different. Jonson's hags invite the king to see *through* them as a theatrical display which minimises the figure of the witch; the witches of *Macbeth* are equivocal or unreadable texts, which the *characters* must but cannot interpret successfully.[9] Because the play lacks any interpretative figure who can make sense of events, correct interpretation of the witches in *Macbeth* lies outside the play itself, privileging the spectators in general and one (royal) spectator in particular.

However, Shakespeare's representation of witchcraft steers clear of any endorsement of the notions of Continental pact witchcraft central to *Daemonologie*. The knowledge embodied in James's writings and speeches at the Scottish trial is *not* the knowledge which the play privileges as the correct way of interpreting the witches. Jonson's hags make constant appeals to James's learning; Shakespeare addresses himself to the king's newer preoccupation with the words used, the gestures made by the lying witnesses in possession cases. As *prophets*, rather than as witches, the Weird Sisters raise the questions of meaning and truth which James had begun to understand as central to witchcraft.

Rather than presenting a single discourse as the 'answer' to witchcraft, Shakespeare refuses any such direct solution, insisting that the menace and the pleasure of witchcraft as a spectacle lies ultimately in its destabilising inscrutability. At the same time, the witches are an awkwardly compressed mass of diverse stories, inscrutable in another sense. Or existing simply to be scrutinised: the witches of *Macbeth* are a low-budget, frankly exploitative collage of randomly chosen bits of witch-lore, selected not for thematic significance but for its sensation value. Pandering shamelessly to the novelty-hungry news culture of Jacobean London, and to a court and intellectual elite increasingly eager for narratives of folklore which would demonstrate their separation from a credulous peasantry, the witch-scenes brazenly refuse any serious engagement with witchcraft in favour of a forthright rendering of witches as a stage spectacular. These all-singing, all-dancing witches bear about as much relation to the concerns of village women as *The Sound of Music* does to women's worries about childcare in the 1990s. Shakespeare buries popular culture under a thick topdressing of exploitative sensationalisation, unblushingly strip-mining both popular culture and every learned text he can lay his hands on for the sake of creating an arresting stage event. Learned interpretations of the play which eagerly make sense of the witches and relate their activities cogently to the main action are untrue to the play's unbridled sensationalism, which looks less appealing once the listener is conscious of the female voices suppressed.

The muddled signifier that is the witches does have effects. If we read the witches' confusion as an unavoidable part of a play where confusion is a preoccupation, we can see how the witches sometimes seem to figure that confusion 'intentionally'.[10] The play encourages slippage between definitions of the witch which made sense in village society, and definitions of the witch which made sense to a learned sceptic like Scot, and definitions of the witch which made sense to European demonologists and their followers, and definitions of the witch which made sense to humanist scholars. This slippage has been replicated by many of the critics who, taking up the challenge of outdoing Macbeth which the play appears to set, have tried to interpret the witches. For example, Peter Stallybrass argues that the Weird Sisters 'have features typical of the English village witch'; what he means by this becomes clouded when he elucidates it in terms of their physical appearance, sourcing this to Reginald Scot, as if Scot were a disinterested observer of village life rather than a writer with the particular interests and agendas of Protestant scepticism. For Scot the recognisability of witches was a sign that their accusers were prejudiced, but his is not the interpretation offered by the play. Stallybrass's strategy is further exposed when he speaks of Shakespeare's reluctance to '*reduce* the play's witches to village widows'.[11] This assumes that such a portrayal would automatically *be* reductive; actually, the imaginings of village women are far more complex than the Weird Sisters. Stallybrass's view uncritically reflects the Jacobean dramatists' scepticism about 'popular' superstition as nothing but a set of stories with commercial value. *Shakespeare* could only find significance in the stories of village witchcraft if they became signs of events in the public sphere; failure to churn butter or the death of a child hardly matters unless it signifies something about where Scotland stands. The *stories* of village witchcraft become metaphors for events elsewhere, and the significance they had for their original tellers becomes a layer of meaning beneath the text, a memory-trace which the play does not encourage us to uncover. The effect of the witchcraft scenes in which tropes of village witchcraft are used depends on the stories and events half narrated in them *remaining* utterly unreadable and inscrutable, so that the stories themselves function not as metaphors for *real* concerns and anxieties, but as signifiers of impenetrability and strangeness, signs of fog, filthy air, and foul is fair.

In becoming a kind of enactment of unreadability, the play draws attention to a current problem in feminist readings of early modern drama, which currently always sees scopophilia as bad, and theatrically problematised identities as good. The fact that witchcraft was a role did not always make it an interesting subversion of gender boundaries. Once convicted and hanged, the witch's opportunities for exciting unfixings of the assumptions of others were rather limited. Besides, the transformation of a witch into nothing but a theatrical event suggests that patriarchy may actually have an interest in theatricality. Such roles can become a way of mocking identities and beliefs that may feel authentic to other people. If you were (someone who believed they were) a witch, or a person who believed a witch had killed your child or taken away your livelihood, the term 'witch' might not be a spectacular curiosity, but a real part of your identity. Could it be that this authentic or 'real' witch was more awkward and unmanageable as a signifier than the theatrical display of sorcery? Shakespeare may have been shadowing James's move away from detecting 'real' witches to detecting witches as the forgeries of fraudulent actors.

At the same time, the significance of the play's reductiveness can only be understood if we are willing, speciously enough, to recover the traces of the stories of village widows in a text which seeks to deny them. I will start with the witch's colloquy in Act I, scene iii:

> 1st Witch: Where has thou been, sister?
> 2nd Witch: Killing swine.

The reference is so brief that any reading feels like over-expansion. Witches attacked pigs in village stories, but here those stories are condensed into a single gesture. Read in the context of the witches' first appearance as enigmatic weatherworkers and prognosticators, the single word 'swine' gestures less at an English village context than at the elaborate pig-fictions of Continental demonology, which systematically conflated notions of the pig's uncleanness with groups deemed beyond the pale, including Jews and witches.[12] The last thing that is conjured up here is a domestic animal, a plump porker on which a family might depend for winter protein; rather, the pig is already reduced to a metaphor of disorderliness and uncleanness. This tiny fragment of introit prepares us for the longer story of 'village' witchcraft on which one of the Sisters then embarks:

> A sailor's wife had chestnuts in her lap
> And munched and munched and munched; 'Give me,' quoth I
> Aroint thee, witch, the rump-fed roynon cries.
> Her husband's to Aleppo gone, master of the *Tiger*;
> But in a sieve I'll thither sail
> And like a rat without a tail
> I'll do, and I'll do, and I'll do.

We could react to this by seeing it as an allusive version of women's trial stories, and thus we could respond by reconstructing a 'popular' story of witchcraft from the text, filling in its lacunae so that it reads as follows. The witch asks for food, and is rudely refused. The food she asks for is a staple of the diet of the poor; bread was sometimes made with chestnut flour when wheat was scarce. Having refused the witch, the sailor's wife replies with something like an averting charm; 'Aroynt thee, witch' is not common parlance, and seems like words of power designed to dismiss the witch.[13] But the witch is not to be got rid of so lightly. Like all witches, she has supernaturally close knowledge of the family's affairs; she knows where the husband's ship sails. And she plans a revenge, a revenge which will destroy the family's livelihood; not the standard one, but there are cases which predate the play in the West Country trial records of witches wrecking ships by creating storms.[14]

The Third Witch's speech is thus inscribed in terms of popular witch-stories, and it may be that some at least of the audience would have heard it in these terms. None the less, it also transforms such conceptions. There are already signs that female anxieties are being replaced by male anxieties. The witch does not strike directly at the female domains of body, household and children, but indirectly through the husband. Her power over him is sexualised, as numerous feminist critics have pointed out; it is the power to drain the moisture from his body, exhausting his vital essence.[15] This notion of witchcraft does not figure in women's stories, but is crucial to the fantasies of demonologists. In *Macbeth*, women's stories are put to work as part of the more grandiose male narrative of the play; the Third Witch's tale foregrounds metaphors of rebellion, threats to patriarchy, disorder in nature. Because the story presents itself as a series of metaphors, what was rich, complex and coherent in the stories of village women is reduced to signs of vague disorder here. The passage also gestures, apparently randomly, at a recent news story which had nothing to do with witchcraft, the ill-fated voyage of the *Tiger*. This investment in the topical and novel, irrespective of context, points to the sensationalism which flattens out any deeper coherences in the hag's story in the interests of novelty.

This flattening effect is partly brought about by the singsong, incantatory quality of the last three lines. The witch ceases to tell a story, and begins to speak in irregularly rhyming octosyllabic lines, the metre of witch's songs, like the song of Gillis Duncan that so intrigued James. When the Third Witch resumes her narrative of revenge she speaks entirely in this idiom of incantatory verse. As the play continues, the verse comes to signify the witches' collective difference from other characters in the play, and by extension their difference from ordinary men and women. Interestingly, rhyming couplets with very short lines were one of the hallmarks of the representation of witches on the Jacobean stage; they are also used in *The Masque of Queens* and in Middleton's *The Witch*, while in *The Witches of Lancashire* the culprits speak in couplets to each other and in blank verse or prose when passing incognito as ordinary women. Like the villain's black hat in a western, the octosyllabic couplet became a simplistic convention which divides evil from good. In the world of uncertainty that is *Macbeth*, the one thing we and the other characters can be sure of is that the witches are *witches*, and not simply rather odd old women. Their speech is marked off from that of the other characters in a manner which insists on their iconic status and also on their difference from the human.[16] They are not ordinary women who have sinned, but a special class of being, like monsters or mermaids. Banquo's words on their appearance confirm the witches' ontological oddity using the language of unreadability:

> What are these
> So withered and so wild in their attire
> That look not like the inhabitants of the earth
> And yet are on't? Live you, or are you aught
> That man may question? You seem to understand me,
> By each at once her choppy finger laying
> Upon her skinny lips. You should be women
> And yet your beards forbid me to interpret
> That you are so.

Banquo is labouring to interpret the witches, and his comments on them stress their indeterminacy. The witches inhabit a borderland between clearly marked states. They are on the earth, but they do not look like its inhabitants; they should be women but they have beards. Similarly, their words are ambiguous, inviting a variety of interpretations. The witch-figure can stand for nothing concrete, but must evoke the disorder of the play's notion of order by indeterminacy. Ironically, this failure of interpretation becomes an interpretation: indeterminacy, and hence chaos, *is* the witches' meaning.

This simple interpretation is supported by the impossibility of finding a coherent pretextual context for the witches; the fact that their accoutrements, language and behaviour are borrowed from hither and yon without regard for truth or theory reinforces their metaphoric status as figures of and for confusion. They shimmer uncertainly because they are both authentic prophetesses and village witches seen from above, both Weird Sisters or Fates and beard sisters, or stereotypes from Scot.

Although Banquo says the witches understand speech, they do not respond to his questions or Macbeth's. They do not engage in conversation. They make statements, a function of their status as prophets, since they have anticipated all encounters. Their refusal – or inability – to interact with people further marks their words as different from those used by others; they make hieratic or prophetic statements, not communicative utterances. Even when the witches have disappeared, Macbeth and Banquo remain uncertain about them rather than newly certain about the future; they debate their vanishing, and argue about whether they dissolve into air or earth. Are they fairies? Fates? This is precisely the kind of sceptical, probing debate that the learned members of the audience might have been expected to engage in. Although the two thanes do not reach any conclusion (naturally, since the whole point was to urge the audience to enter the interpretative fray), Banquo's position does evolve into providentialist scepticism not unlike Reginald Scot's as the play proceeds. Since Banquo is the representative of James, this suggests that the king was being asked to authenticate his rule as lawful rather than tyrannical precisely by taking up a sceptical position, or rather that Shakespeare understood how discourses of scepticism could naturalise the king's absolutism as privileged spectator more naturally than discourses of paranoid belief.

This becomes more evident in the witches' later appearances, appearances which also reveal that James does not quite have it all his own way with his text, and also that another set of interpretations was possible for those with different knowledges and agendas. The cauldron scene is probably the scene people remember most clearly from the play. It is usually seen in relation to Continental sabbaths, in which unbaptised babies were said to be boiled to make flying-ointment. One of the unsavoury ingredients piled into the 'charmed pot' by the Weird Sisters confirms this: 'Finger of birth-strangled babe / Ditch-delivered by a drab' (IV.i.30–1). The babe in question has been strangled at birth by its prostitute mother, who as an unmarried woman has given birth to it in a ditch, perhaps because fleeing the boundaries of her own parish; it is therefore unbaptised, and unbaptised or chrism children were sought by witches for their potions, because of their extreme vulnerability to evil. The results of the spell also echo and adapt flying-ointment; here, too, the result of the mixture is supernatural power, prophetic rather than ambulatory. Time rather than distance is annihilated. So far, so coherent: however, the scene also borrows from all over the place: from Lucan's Thessalian witch in the *Pharsalia*, who prophesies for a would-be usurper by reanimating a corpse; from the lore of teeny-weeny fairies which Shakespeare helped to create; from Shakespeare's own *Henry VI, Part II*, where Margery Jourdain and others conjure up spirits to give them clairvoyant knowledge of the future. The play's Continental borrowings are not especially privileged; they do not offer a way to understand the text. Continental narratives are merely one possible source of raw materials among others.

The cauldron scene also contains a deformed trace of English women's anxieties, centring on its preoccupation with food and babies. Mocked as popular superstitions, those anxieties are also reshaped as male fears. The list of noxious substances read out by the witches, which constitutes the incantation, is a *recipe*, albeit a parodic one; this becomes more tenable when we recall that books of housewifery were often composed in rhyme in the early modern period, as an *aide-mémoire*, and when we remember that some counter-magical charms were preserved in recipe books.[17] The injunction 'Cool it with a baboon's blood / Then the charm is firm and good' alludes especially clearly to discourses of cookery; the imperative verb echoes injunctions like 'bake in slow oven'. Cauldrons, now linked with witches thanks to the memorability of this very scene, were once simply the ordinary cooking ustensil of those too poor to own an oven.[18] The witches' cauldron is a reminder of women's control over food production. Like village witches, the witches of *Macbeth* use this power to reverse it; instead of transforming the natural into the cultural, they produce the unnatural. The list of cauldron ingredients is selected to give a *frisson* of shock rather than to follow English or Continental practice; the sole point is to transgress the boundaries of the acceptable and clean. All that the ingredients have in common is their repulsiveness. This is the sensationalism of the Jacobean stage at its worst.

The trace of the family cooking-pot visible in the witches' cauldron draws attention to a sphere of feminine power separate from sexuality but equally threatening to men. Cooking at this point in the play represents other forms of misfeeding, since the purpose of the potion is to produce the prophecies which will deceptively lure Macbeth to his death. The witches' potion is 'cooked' in the sense of 'cooking the books'; constructed to deceive innocent men. The underlying metaphor here may be poison, death served up in the guise of friendship, as it is to Duncan. Poison also represents women's power to intervene decisively in public affairs by using their power over food preparation. The effect of the witches' cookery is to give them power over Macbeth, to reverse gender norms, to pluck a kingdom down, but also to remove a tyrant, right a wrong, restore lawful rule.

In all these ways, then, the cauldron as cooking-pot registers some distinctively *male* anxieties arising from the buried trace of tropes of female anxiety embedded in witch-stories. The cauldron is not just a cooking-pot. It is also a womb, a space from which metaphorical and actual children are born. The 'children' in question are the speakers and the embodiments of the tellingly ambiguous prophecies which the entire rite is designed to produce.[19] The cauldron's firstborn replicates its contents; an armed head is a severed souvenir reminiscent of the bits of murderers and heretics which have gone into the stew. But it also recalls the world of military hack-and-slay and tyranny created and inhabited by Macbeth. Hence this 'child' is most truly Macbeth's son, the more so since it is himself, foretelling his last appearance as a severed head. The second apparition is a child, and a newly born child at that, covered in the blood which signifies his unnatural separation from the mother. This violent separation from the maternal marks the unnaturalness of the witch's cauldron as a mechanism of birth, but also offers the child-prophecy as an unreadable fantasy of autotelic male identity, forever separated from the mother. In other words, the second child gestures at a fantasy of male power which the witches are specifically seen to trouble; a fantasy of man finally divided from the troubling and troubled mother/wife. This fantasy is strengthened with the appearance of the third child, who represents not just the power of the king over nature, but a genealogy produced apparently exclusively from the male figure of Banquo.

Of course, this is what the figures signify when 'read' correctly by Macbeth. But when first introduced, they *seem* to signify the opposite of what they really portend: the possibility of dismemberment or death, eternal attachment to woman, the limits of royal/male power over nature. Ironically, these fears become Macbeth's shaky safeguards in the witches' hands, but as it turns out, such fears are fantasies. In actuality, as the play understands, men *can* be born without woman, and man's power over nature extends to uprooting whole forests.[20] In the world of the play, the latter is natural, and women's role in the generation and birth of children is associated retroactively with the unnatural rule of the Macbeths. In general, then, the children of the cauldron represent male fears which para-doxically and harmfully become male fantasies, dreams-come-true which annihilate Macbeth. What has vanished from the scene is any sense of *female* fears or fantasies about the person of the witch. The witches remain 'bad' mothers, but bad mothers dealing in dead and symbolic children rather than real ones. Anxieties about a maternal power which would replace the mother's own role are displaced into anxieties about relations between a deformed maternity and a paternity that would be autotelic. What had once been women's stories and agendas are repackaged as affairs of the male heart, and as affairs of state.

Even this makes too much of a scene primarily mocking and comic in content. The cauldron contents also signify the ridiculous-ness of popular superstition; the witches' ingredients are grisly, but they are also infantile in their dirtiness, silliness, elaborateness, a list to recall Scot's bugs to frighten children. They are not a sincere list of what someone really thought witches might use, but a piece of infantile gothic. Their messiness, disorder and rather simplistic otherness, involving a body-part from every racial or religious other available, do indeed invert order, but they also act as a comic inver-sion not of the values of the absolutist court, but of the good sober carefulness and containment of the *bourgeois* household and its economics of prudence and containment. These strands of mockery give the court the opportunity to elevate itself above both peasants and godly city matrons. But for those in the know about the court, there is a pointer to its own less lovely excesses; the witches repre-sent the unnaturalness of the Macbeths' tyranny, a tyranny which blocks the circulation of power, creating some nasty spillages. Cunningly offering its ambiguity as a way to sell itself to opposing schools of thought on witchcraft, *Macbeth*'s nasty witch-brew palters with the audience in a double sense as well; it offers both king and commons a chance to feel superior to each other.

Even *this* reading may be excessively earnest for a scene staged
to end with the words 'and now about the cauldron sing / Like
elves and fairies in a ring'. Here as elsewhere, fairies signify that
part of popular superstition readable as emphatically over. In
concluding the manufacture of a spell with a trope which com-
pares the witches to fairies, the Weird Sisters are bracketed as
figments of the dramatic imagination. In doing this, Shakespeare
credits himself with inventing figures which are recensions of
other people's half-remembered stories, from Lucan to ordinary
women. The *frisson* of fear that the witches still have for some
Bardophiles is an echo of the fears of others, the others who originally wrote and believed the stories. However, *we* can credit
Shakespeare with granting witches and fairies the diachronic
significance they still have for us. The sheer banality of Hecate's
lines, especially 'like elves and fairies in a ring' points to the joint
infantilisation of octosyllabic couplets and the supernatural. Both
are now associated not with childhood, but with a naïve and pre-
electronic childhood of times past. Ironically, the witch-stories
written for today's more knowing and sceptical children contain
the most sophisticated readings of the tone of *Macbeth*: the comic
witch Meg appropriates the language of the Weird Sisters, chant-
ing 'Bubble bubble, rock and rubble, oil boil and cauldron
bubble'.[21] This points to the cultural power of Shakespeare's
witches, but also to their aesthetic impoverishment. The Weird
Sisters are nothing more and nothing less than *Macbeth*'s missing
comic sub-plot.

From *The Witch in History* (London: Routledge, 1996),
pp. 199–202, 206–214.

NOTES

[Diane Purkiss argues that *Macbeth* shamelessly exploits contemporary interest in witchcraft in order to produce a lurid stage spectacular, composed
of a bricolage of fragments from both popular culture and witch scholarship. Historical documents and canonical texts are read alongside each
other as instances of social performance – at stake here are the familiar
dyad of the power of theatre and the theatricality of power. The essay
opens by juxtaposing an élite male who has been the focus of much new
historicist attention with the non-élite women who engaged his interest as
the objects of witch-trials, a pairing that reminds us, as do Barbara
Hodgdon's references to women spectators, of the difficulty of retrieving

the cultural participation of such women. Shakespeare's play is read as a site where competing understandings of culture emerging from these two viewpoints can be seen in tension.

Omitted is a section considering the cultural agency of Queen Anne, with reference to the representation of the witches in Jonson's *Masque of Queens*; I am grateful to Professor Purkiss for allowing me to make this cut. Ed.]

1. On James's role in determining practices at this trial, see Christina Larner, 'James VI and I and Witchcraft', in *Witchcraft and Religion: The Politics of Popular Belief* (Oxford: Blackwell, 1983), pp. 7–15.

2. *Newes from Scotland, Declaring the Damnable Life and Death of Dr Fian* (1591; reprinted in *Witchcraft in England, 1558–1618*, ed. Barbara Rosen (Amherst, MA: University of Massachusetts Press, 1991), p. 195. See also Robert Pitcairn, *Criminal Trials* (Edinburgh, 1833).

3. For a similar transposition into theatre, see Stephen Greenblatt's account of Samuel Harsnett in 'Shakespeare and the Exorcists', in *Shakespearean Negotiations* (Oxford: Clarendon, 1988), pp. 94–128, esp. pp. 108–9.

4. For readings of the politics of James's rhetoric of witch-beliefs, see Stuart Clark, 'King James's *Demonologie*: Witchcraft and Kingship', in *The Damned Art: Essays in the Literature of Witchcraft*, ed. Sydney Anglo (London: Routledge & Kegan Paul, 1977), pp. 167–73; Lucia Folena, 'Figures of Violence: Philologists, Witches and Stalinistas', in *The Violence of Representation: Literature and the History of Violence*, ed. Nancy Armstrong and Leonard Tennenhouse (London and New York: Routledge, 1990), pp. 219–38; unfortunately, neither Clark nor Folena considers the politics of James's conversion(s) to scepticism.

5. On James's involvement in the case of Mary Glover, see Henry Paul, *The Royal Play of Macbeth* (New York: Macmillan, 1950), pp. 98–103, 111, and Michael Macdonald, *Witchcraft and Hysteria in Elizabethan London: Edward Jorden and the Mary Glover Case* (London: Tavistock/Routledge, 1991), pp. xlviiiff.

6. Macdonald, *Witchcraft*, p. xlviii; Paul, *Royal Play*, pp. 118–27; C. L'Estrange Ewen, *Witchcraft in the Star Chamber* (London: privately printed, 1938).

7. See Mary Russo, 'Female Grotesques: Carnival and Theory', in *Feminist Studies/Critical Studies*, ed. Teresa de Lauretis (London: Macmillan, 1986), pp. 213–29; Claire Wills, 'Upsetting the Public: Carnival, Hysteria and Women's Texts', in *Bakhtin and Cultural Theory*, ed. Ken Hirschkop and David Shepherd (Manchester: Manchester University Press, 1989), pp. 130–51.

8. For an account of James's engagement with multiple cases of possession exposed by him as fraudulent, see Paul, *Royal Play*, pp. 75–127. Dymphna Callaghan has recently argued that the play stages a conflict between scepticism and belief – see her 'Wicked Women in *Macbeth*: a Study of Power, Ideology and the Production of Motherhood', *Reconsidering the Renaissance*, ed. Mario A. Di Cesare (Binghamton, NY: Medieval and Renaissance Texts and Studies, 1992), pp. 355–69.

9. On the importance of equivocation and ambiguity in *Macbeth*, see, among others, Steven Mullaney, 'Lying like Truth: Riddle, Representation and Treason', in *The Place of the Stage: License, Play and Power in Renaissance England* (Chicago, IL: Chicago University Press, 1988), pp. 116–34. On the significance of interpretation in witchcraft and magic generally, see Greenblatt, 'Shakespeare and the Exorcists', pp. 108–9, and Karen Newman, 'Discovering Witches: Sorciographics', in *Fashioning Femininity and English Renaissance Drama* (Chicago, IL: Chicago University Press, 1991), pp. 65–6.

10. Shakespeare's conflation of classical goddesses and early modern witches has often been noted, but most commentators have tried to sort it out rather than simply point it out; see, for instance, W. C. Curry, *Shakespeare's Philosophical Patterns* (Baton Rouge, LA: Louisiana State University Press, 1937), and Anthony Harris, *Night's Black Agents: Witchcraft and Magic in Seventeenth-Century English Drama* (Manchester: Manchester University Press, 1980). Harris provides a depressing instance of criticism which assumes village witch-beliefs involve the 'trivial' (pp. 38–9). Mischievously and disingenuously, Terry Eagleton argues that the witches are really the heroines of the play – see his *William Shakespeare* (Oxford: Blackwell, 1986), ch. 1. This reading has been surprisingly influential among the historically naïve.

11. Peter Stallybrass, '*Macbeth* and Witchcraft', in *Macbeth*, ed. Alan Sinfield (London: Macmillan, 1992; first published 1983), pp. 29–30, emphasis mine. For a similar confusion, see Sarah Beckwith, 'The Power of Devils and the Heart of Men: Notes towards a Drama of Witchcraft', in *Shakespeare in the Changing Curriculum*, ed. Lesley Aers and Nigel Wheale (London: Routledge, 1991), pp. 143–61. Literary critics have often relied on Stuart Clark's piece 'Inversion, Misrule and the Meaning of Witchcraft' (*Past and Present*, 87 [1980], pp. 98–127) for their interpretive framework, largely because its rhetoric of inversion fits with the ideas of the early modern stage as carnival so popular with the post-new historicist Renaissance scholar.

12. Peter Stallybrass and Allon White, *The Politics and Poetics of Transgression* (London and New York: Methuen, 1986) ch. 1.

13. Cf. *King Lear*, III.iv.129: 'And aroint thee witch, aroint thee!', used by Edgar in a similar context of exorcism. Scholars are still unsure of the

origins of the phrase, but its obscurity (in this play above all) may be part of its power.

14. Usually identified as deriving from *Newes from Scotland*; James believed his life had been threatened by the witches' attempts to raise a storm at sea (see Barbara Rosen (ed.), *Witchcraft in England, 1558–1618* [Amherst, MA: University of Massachusetts Press, 1991] p. 197). However, there are similar cases in the English records: in 1601, a Devon woman named Anne Trevisard was accused of causing a ship to founder after a sailor's wife had insulted her (L'Estrange Ewen, *Witchcraft and Demonianism*, pp. 194–5). Weatherworking is more usual on the Continent; see Luisa Accati, 'The Spirit of Fornication: Virtue of the Soul and Virtue of the Body in Fruili, 1600–1800', trans. Margaret A. Galucci, in *Sex and Gender in Historical Perspective*, ed. Edward Muir and Guido Ruggiero (Baltimore and London: Johns Hopkins University Press, 1990), pp. 110–40. Nashe illustrates the influence of these continental ideas on English intellectuals in *The Terrors of The Night* (1594) in *The Works of Thomas Nashe*, ed. R. B. McKerrow, 5 vols (Oxford: Blackwell, 1966–74), vol. I, p. 359.

15. 'I'll drain him dry as hay / Sleep shall neither night nor day ... Weary seven nights nine times nine / Shall he dwindle, peak and pine'. See Janet Adelman, '"Born of woman": Fantasies of Maternal Power in *Macbeth*', in *Cannibals, Witches and Divorce*, ed. Marjorie Garber, *Selected Papers from the English Institute* (Baltimore, MD: Johns Hopkins University Press, 1987), and Marjorie Garber, *Shakespeare's Ghost Writers: Literature as Uncanny Causality* (London and New York: Methuen, 1987).

16. By contrast, the plays which do not seek to dismiss all witch-beliefs do not use verse in this way. Plays like Dekker, Ford and Rowley's *Witch of Edmonton*, which is an account of a contemporary witch-trial, do not use singsong verse to separate witches from the rest of the village community, but tend to emphasise their ordinariness, their indistinguishability from other villagers. Elizabeth Sawyer speaks in blank verse like everyone else, sometimes in prose. Similarly, plays like Heywood's *The Wise Woman of Hogsdon* and Lyly's *Mother Bombie*, which portray witches as tricksters keen to extract money painlessly from the gullible, do not present witches as inhabiting a different verse form from everyone else.

17. See, for example, Thomas Tusser, *Five Hundred Points of Good Husbandry*; and see Stephen Mennell, *All Manners of Food: Eating and Taste in England and France from the Middle Ages to the Present* (Oxford: Blackwell, 1985); on magic in recipe books, see Richard Kieckhefer, *Magic in the Middle Ages* (Cambridge: Cambridge University Press, 1990), p. 9.

18. See Caroline Davidson, *A Woman's Work is Never Done: A History of Housework in the British Isles, 1650–1950* (London: Chatto & Windus, 1982), ch. 1.

19. For a case involving prophetic witches, see Paul, *Royal Play*, pp. 115–17. The fatal ambiguity of the prophecies in *Macbeth* is the one clear sign of a direct appeal to James's turn towards scepticism; there is a humanist discourse of long standing which sees prophecies as a menace to order because of their verbal disorder and ambiguity; of especial interest in this respect is *A Defensative Against the Poyson of Supposed Prophecies* by Henry Howard, Earl of Northampton, 1583; the Earl of Northampton was one of James's principal supporters and later courtiers. See Diane Purkiss, 'Producing the Voice, Consuming the Body: Seventeenth-Century Women Prophets', in *Women/Writing/History*, ed. Susan Wiseman and Isobel Grundy (London: Batsford, 1992), pp. 139–58, esp. 154–6, for a more sustained account.

20. Rebecca Bushnell points out that Macbeth's femininity is linked with the traditional image of the tyrant in 'Tyranny and Effeminacy in Early Modern England', in *Reconsidering the Renaissance*, ed. Di Cesare, pp. 339–54.

21. Helen Nicoll and Jan Pienkowski, *Meg and Mog* (London: Picture Puffins, 1972), p. 10.

11

The Colour of Patriarchy: Critical Difference, Cultural Difference and Renaissance Drama

ANIA LOOMBA

Like Middleton's Beatrice-Joanna, but in conditions quite unlike hers, I 'feel a giddy turning in me'.[1] Mine is occasioned by an oscillation from Renaissance to postcolonial studies: the first being the right kind of thing an Indian student of English literature was supposed to do, and the other, a concern she ought to make a priority today. The oscillation defines me as a changeling in both areas – traditional Shakespeareans in India are upset at my suggestion that the bard be removed from the fulcrum of literary studies, other colleagues because I continue to teach Shakespeare even when I have the choice not to.[2] Out of the Indian context, I am resentful at the possibility of being ghettoised into talking solely about the intersection of race and gender, and upset when enough attention is not paid to that subject. On all counts, it is difficult to escape what Martha Minow has nicely described as 'the dilemma of difference' whereby 'both focussing on and ignoring difference risk recreating it'.[3]

Thanks to the pedagogic and cultural hangovers of colonialism, these seemingly disparate areas occasionally intersect and make the giddy turnings worthwhile. The encounters are variegated: *Hamlet*, for example, is, for many male postgraduate students in Delhi, the ultimate representation of 'the human condition'; it is also the name of a prize-winning variety of mango developed recently in Trivandrum in south India. In the small north-eastern border state of Mizoram, it approximates a folk cult show, while a road sign on a Himalayan highway cautions speeding drivers by asking them whether they want 'to be or not to be'. Together, these encounters reveal some of the strands of the postcolonial fabric.[4]

But Renaissance and postcolonial studies also meet each other via their common interest in marginalised peoples of different sorts, and in their disparate attempts to theorise and recover subaltern resistance (or agency) and locate it in relation to power. The difficulty of doing that with respect to the female subject has been an especially pressing concern within both areas and has almost become an index of critical politics. It has been alleged, for example, that those histories and theories of the colonial encounter which find it practically and theoretically impossible to recover the female subaltern voice rehearse and contribute to the continuing marginalisation of colonised people, especially women.[5] It appears that there are analogous problems in recent Renaissance studies. Some years ago, Walter Cohen's review of political criticism of Shakespeare astutely juxtaposed (but without especially interrelating) the 'strangely quietist feel of these radical critiques' (referring particularly to new historicist work) with his contention that in these readings 'women have disappeared'.[6] More recently, some feminist critics have polemically amplified aspects of this critique, contending that the effect of new historicists' and cultural materialists' inadequate focus on female presence and agency in Renaissance drama 'has been to oppress women, repress sexuality, and subordinate gender issues'.[7]

Such critiques might appear to be manifestations of the by now widespread reservations about the politically quietist implications of 'poststructuralism' and 'new history' – reservations which are framed within the larger problem of squaring critical inquiry with politics which has so bedevilled poststructuralist theory in general. Women and 'third world' critics have been especially uncomfortable with some poststructuralist assumptions and methods: it has been variously alleged that the agency of the marginalised subject is obscured when that subject is theorised as discontinuous, or as merely 'the site' for the intersection of various discourses; that a Foucauldian emphasis on the relational aspects of power and resistance implies the ultimate containment of the latter; that if power is theorised as dispersed and fragmented then it emerges as either too benign or too pervasive; and that poststructuralist scepticism about knowledge and metanarratives only results in intellectual angst and political paralysis.[8] These problems point to very real difficulties involved in theorising social difference – race, gender, class, caste, and other social differentials cannot be easily accommodated without risking an endless fragmentation of subjectivity.[9]

'The Renaissance' has been both an especially fruitful site for poststructuralist critical work and an embattled one.[10] The potential alliance between various strands of political criticism is becoming increasingly fissured, although there is widespread regret about these critical/political ruptures as well as continuing attempts to heal them. In the course of what Ann Thompson rather mildly characterises as 'an uneasy relationship' between feminism and various forms of historical and cultural materialist criticism, the sprawling debates that took place between Marxism and feminism in the 1960s and 1970s are revisited, but only implicitly, and often in a way that is not conducive to posing a viable alternative to these poststructuralist shortcomings in the theorising of gender issues, and especially female agency, within Renaissance drama.[11]

Since this essay will run the risk of exemplifying what Lynda Boose rightly criticises as 'the contestatory model of scholarship' which 'turns the literary profession into a shoot 'em out at the You're-Not-O.K. Corral', I want to underline the compulsion that a self-conscious criticism necessarily faces in having to confront the basis of its differences with others.[12] As Jean Howard puts it,

> essays which explain how and why one does and should read in a particular way are both more generous and more risky since they do not try to seal themselves off from what is polemical by aspiring to a timeless commonsense, but expose what is difficult and what is at stake in 'making knowledge' at *this* historical moment.[13]

Boose criticises the contestatory model by contrasting it with a sisterhood and a familial supportiveness that is supposed to mark the relations among American feminist Shakespeareans. My own differences with her and others are articulated in the hope that the exclusions which both 'sisterhood' and 'the family' have sometimes historically been party to need not be reinscribed in the present context.

Both Lynda Boose, in 'The Family in Shakespearean Studies', and Carol Neely, in 'Constructing the Subject', seek to redress the alleged neglect of women by cultural materialists and new historicists (who are conflated in different ways by both critics) by invoking their own experiences as critics (as I have done), and by situating these within the history and political agenda of American liberal feminism. Therefore, let me briefly discuss the question of critical self-reflexivity. Cultural materialists have been addressing this for some time, but today it has become almost fashionable: now there is a wider recognition and discussion of the ways in which Shakespearean criticism might 'negotiate power relations in our own social context'.[14] But there is a potential paradox here: even though it is increasingly acknowledged that intellectual differences about 'what happened in history' or 'textual meaning' are shaped by our own political differences, such a recognition does not end critical claims to a 'truer' historicism or a 'better' literary criticism. In other words, the desire to situate the writer–critic ostensibly stems from the need to contest universalist notions of knowledge or value but sometimes ends up replicating such notions. An analogous circularity is evident in those inquiries into cultural difference which are undertaken from, or which return to, a position of self-privileging. Orientalist discourses are of course notorious in this respect. But Gayatri Spivak argues that some influential French feminists also privilege Western culture precisely via their 'occasional interest in touching *the other* of the West'.[15] While at some level all inquiry stems from the question 'who am I?' the distinction between situating oneself critically and critical self-obsession is still worth taking trouble over.

The issue of self-reflexivity is also involved with the historical and epistemological status of 'experience', an issue which motivated feminist research to attach great importance to locating oneself in one's discourse. While 'experience' is important in recalling the reality of both oppression and agency and thus a way of countering the debilitating effects of some recent poststructuralist perspectives, it is hardly a transparent concept. First, the gaps between what is 'out there' and 'what is internalized' cannot be swept under the carpet; second, experience itself is so profoundly coloured by various social contexts and differentials that it only underlines the fact that women are a heterogeneous group.[16] The experience of one group must be placed alongside those of others: the relations between them also determine and circumscribe the validity of each. To make these connections is also one way in which we can negotiate the paradoxes of difference, and determine overlaps even as we pay attention to specific and varying contexts.

As Susie Tharu and K. Lalita point out (while setting their new anthology of women's writing in India in the context of the Western feminist academy), 'when the new validity women's experience acquired as a resource that could be drawn on for critical discussion was conflated with the empiricist idea that experience was the source of true knowledge, experience lost the critical edge it had acquired as a political tool', feminism was annexed to a bourgeois humanist scheme of things, and finally, the experiences and issues of Western feminism were offered as 'natural'.[17] Such a trajectory is evident in both Boose's and Neely's essays. Their own experience is not understood as specific and relative; rather, it swells to define what both of them are at some pains to establish, that is, what Neely calls a female 'subjectivity, interiority, identity which is continuous over time and is not the product of ideology' and 'some area of "femaleness"' which is understood as standing free of both history and context (p. 7). Both of them begin by rightly pointing out the dangers of dissolving gender into analogies. Gerda Lerner's pioneering guideline for gender critique emphasised exactly this: 'all analogies – class, group, caste – approximate the position of women but fail to define it adequately. Women are a category unto themselves; an adequate analysis of their position in society requires new conceptual tools'.[18] I have expressed my discomfort with the way in which the analogies between gender and power relations in the Renaissance have been used to explicitly undermine the specificity of the former.[19] But where Lerner cautioned against letting the uniqueness of women's position deteriorate into asserting a simplistic hierarchy of oppression, Neely ends up reiterating that gender is 'a primary category' (p. 15). It has been pointed out in so many earlier feminist debates that the primacy of gender as an analytical category can only be asserted by devaluing other social differences and thereby the 'experiences' of 'other' women.[20] That this warning needs to be repeated in the context of Renaissance studies, especially at a time when such studies are beginning to consider issues of cultural difference, is perhaps a measure of the way in which the centrality of 'The Renaissance' to Western culture constantly exerts a pressure to discuss it entirely within the values and parameters that are a legacy of that socio-cultural tradition.

'Sisterhood' has never precluded fundamental political differences among women. But in Boose's essay, and Neely's, it is invoked very easily precisely at the expense of all variegation between women even within the United States, let alone the rest of the world. It is not surprising, then, to find that while these critics reiterate Walter Cohen's point about the neglect of gender in political criticism of Shakespeare, they do not acknowledge his observation that 'Third World and other ethnic studies are regrettably relegated to the same subordinate role (as women) despite their obviously political thrust' (p. 19). A focus on woman and one on race and cultural difference are both collateral and divergent tasks. But Boose unfortunately chooses to pit them against each other: 'when gender is not being ignored in materialist critiques, it repeatedly ends up getting displaced into some other issue – usually race or class' (p. 729). Studies of race in early modern Europe (as a theoretical parameter, as a historically constituted category, and as a factor in analysing textual strategies as well as responses to them) are pitifully few and I cannot think of even one instance where race is critically *prioritised* over gender.

Such a demarcation of gender from other categories of difference predictably maps onto a whole series of other divisions – notably the ones between text and context, gender and history, family and politics. In Boose's essay, all of the former are the terrain of feminism, and the latter the interests of Marxism. The twain can never meet, it is implied, not by pointing out the very real tensions between them but simply because 'American feminists are committed to liberal rather than radical Marxist politics' and 'what has never been clear to American liberal feminism is how one can serve feminism and Marxism too' (p. 724). First, the long history of Marxist debates on the intersection between the social and the individual is reduced to a hackneyed caricature of a crudely deterministic materialist criticism which is the hallmark of right-wing attacks on cultural materialists, which Boose would like to distance herself from (p. 731, n. 22). Second, the interconnections between private and public are muted, and the binary oppositions which have historically rendered women invisible are resurrected. To argue, as Neely does (p. 12), that 'a focus on power, politics, and history, and especially, the monarch, turns attention away from marriage, sexuality, women and the masterless', is to abandon the former set of historically demarcated and contested spaces as those in which women cannot be inserted. Instead of positing the family as a privileged place for locating women, as both Boose and Neely do, feminists can demonstrate, as indeed they have done in other contexts, how these spaces are themselves gendered. I'll return to this later; here I only want to argue that surely the multiple alternative histories of the family which black and 'Third World' feminists have been making visible, and the linkages between the development of the family and those of imperialism, colonialism and capitalism, should problematise a simple invocation of that institution, and of the place of women within it.[21]

Michèle Barrett, among others, has discussed the ideological and historical contours of the ways in which the literary text, the psyche and 'woman' are linked by virtue of their compartmentalization from the social, the historical and material.[22] Boose defends her rehearsal of this process by arguing that,

> given feminism's very different *historical* relationship to 'history,' it seems thoroughly consistent with the feminist goal of liberating women *from* their history that the mainstream feminist interpretations of Shakespeare did indeed marginalize the historical and concentrate instead on the literary text. (p. 735)

One wonders where this leaves feminist historians, for whom 'liberating' women entails rewriting history itself. Surely, it is possible to *question* dominant historiography without having to *retreat* from history. The 'literary text', moreover, is at least as problematic a category for feminists as is 'history', and a legitimate form of feminist critique has been to question canonical texts as well as their dominant cultural and institutional deployment, which notoriously also marginalised the historical in the name of the literary. This should hardly need to be restated today, except that scepticism on the part of other feminists about the special status of the Shakespearean text becomes the target of Boose's wrath. She is of course perfectly right in pointing out that canon-bashing (particularly in the case of the Bard) may cut the academic branches we perch on, because so many jobs depend on our continuing to teach Shakespeare. It is also true that women readers may take pleasure in Shakespeare, as in other canonical texts. But possible pleasure and professional exigencies are strangely mutated into an insistence that we must not feel too alienated from Shakespeare's plays, or find them effecting patriarchal closures. Those who do, like Kate McLuskie, are reduced to another tired caricature – that of the 'tough', 'uncompromising', puritanical feminist, who, we are told, can 'only warn us away from Shakespeare in terms that warn us away from pleasure' (p. 725). Via this stereotype, our choices as feminists are narrowed and we are not allowed to question, beyond a certain acceptable point, the value of the Shakespearean text.

In the recent and lengthy controversy over Shakespeare in *The London Review of Books*, an analogous pleasure-in-the-text formula emerges. Boris Ford attacks cultural materialists thus:

> I found myself speculating when they last read one of Shakespeare's major plays as they might perhaps listen to one of Bach's unaccompanied cello sonatas or Mozart's string quartets: because they find them profoundly moving, or spiritually restoring, or simply strangely enjoyable.[23]

In both cases, pleasure-in-the-text quickly leads to pleasure-in-culture. It is disturbing to find how close Boose comes to Ford in reading Shakespeare as emblematic of Western culture and that culture as self-evidently worth 'enjoying' or valuing: 'And logically, Shakespeare must be only the beginning: if one is to renounce Shakespeare for his patriarchalism, then surely one must also renounce the enjoyment of most of Western drama ... and for that matter, most of Western literature' (p. 725). Now the message of colonial education was precisely that if Indians did not find Shakespeare's plays 'pleasurable', they did not possess intelligence or culture. 'Pleasure' in that context was clearly synonymous with approbation, and in continuing to conflate the two, Boose and Ford deny the pleasures of negative critique, which (I am glad to report) are considerable in the Indian academy where Shakespeare's hallowed status is still institutionally secure. At a recent conference in New Delhi (which ironically was devoted to interrogating the history and ideologies of English in India), a well-known novelist similarly accused political criticism of devaluing 'emotion': 'you have become too cold and analytical' he informed me. I could only recount to him the passions that were unleashed in my classrooms once students had the freedom to criticise the Bard, as opposed to the dull apathy that the demand for reverence usually produced. 'Pleasure' for many Indian students of Shakespeare would critically hinge on whether or not they were given the choice to agree or disagree, be moved or angry, restored or bored – and not only by Shakespeare and the Western canon, but by any text.[24] To say this is simply to recall the necessary investment of marginalised readers in insisting on the freedom to respond to complex texts in multiple ways and the important role of feminist theory in stressing (even celebrating) exactly this possibility and the diversity of positions from which readers respond.

I do not intend to suggest that a negative critique is the only kind of pleasure that canonical texts make available to traditionally marginalised students/readers. To respond from the fullness of one's specific situations is also to discover *new and different sources of textual pleasure* or issues to identify with: I certainly find that I enjoy *Antony and Cleopatra* and *Othello* a great deal more today than I did as a student when I wasn't allowed to comment on the racial difference of their central figures. (In both cases, incidentally, I ended up thinking that Shakespeare wrote a better play than I did at first.) Stephen Greenblatt also notes a 'tendency ... in those explicitly concerned with historical or ideological functions of art to ignore the analysis of pleasure or, for that matter, play', but goes on to caution that 'transhistorical stability or continuity of literary pleasure is an illusion ... the task then would be to historicize pleasure, to explore its shifts and changes, to understand its interests'.[25] This is an enormously difficult order and sensitivity to the diversity, shifts and changes among contemporary readers might be one way of equipping ourselves for reconstructing the identities and responses of past recipients of these texts.

The question of literary reception also allows us to interrogate the ongoing controversy about female agency in these plays. Those who find Shakespeare patriarchal are severely criticised by both Boose and Neely for somehow contributing to the neglect of women's power and agency. Carol Neely argues that feminist criticism needs to 'over-read, to read to excess, the possibility of human (especially female) gendered subjectivity, identity and agency, the possibility of women's resistance or even subversion' (p. 15). I think that is right, and in fact have argued, in the context of colonial history, why the recovery of subaltern agency must presuppose its existence in order to unearth it from indifferent archives and hostile historiography.[26] I also disagree with many of those critics who read Renaissance theatre as unmitigatedly patriarchal. But neither position needs to deny that women in the plays are tortured, mutilated and punished for their attempted independence and agency.

To begin with, we may sift textual meaning from the fate of the characters within the plays: it can be argued that precisely these punishments expose the workings of a hostile patriarchal order and its strategies in suppressing women so that a feminist reading of *Othello*, for example, is not dependent upon a radically resistant Desdemona.[27] Agency is often made visible precisely by the violence of the dominant response against its expression, as I shall indicate via Webster's *The White Devil* later in this essay. This play, like so many others of the period, also demonstrates the ways in which agency can often manifest itself through compliance with the structures of power, through a utilisation of dominant strategies, stereotypes and ideologies.

Moreover, and this surely is the crucial question, whose agency is finally at stake for feminist criticism? That of Shakespeare's or Middleton's or Webster's female figures? That of the female critic? Or that of the women students, readers, spectators of the drama? Not only Lynda Boose and Carol Neely, but surprisingly Ann Thompson, writing from the opposite perspective of trying to reconcile materialist and feminist criticism, imply a straightforward connection between the agency of female literary characters and that of real women reading the plays. If, as Brecht remarked in relation to his Mother Courage, the purpose of playing is to make the *spectator* see, then the readers' agency does not exist in direct relation to that of the literary figures in the plays, and in fact the relation might actually be an inverse one. Such demarcation makes possible the positive politics of the negative critique. A feminist pedagogy should not have to gloss over the victimisation of women – precisely the lack of agency in the represented lives of women can become a pedagogical and critical means for mobilising consciousness and agency in the lives of the readers. The radicalism or otherwise of Renaissance and Jacobean theatre is a contentious and difficult issue within recent political criticism; the position that a critic takes on it can hardly be a reliable or straightforward index of her own politics.[28] It is indeed a strange (and dangerous) literary-critical manoeuvre which will suggest that I am complicit with colonial ideologies if I trace the powerful workings of colonial discourse in *The Tempest*. The ideological positions contained within a text – even if we could agree on what these are – are not binding on its readers/spectators/critics. Therefore, *The Taming of the Shrew*, with its less recuperable representation of women, could as effectively function as the basis of a radical critique of literary education in India or bardolatry in general (to take just two examples) as, say, *Antony and Cleopatra*.

The confusion about women's agency in this debate also has much to do with the privileging of text over history, which I earlier remarked upon. Benita Parry suggests that the agency of the colonised is either misunderstood or neglected by recent colonial discourse theorists partly because they do not pay sufficient

attention to the various contexts of that voice, privileging discourses and texts over, say, institutions and political movements.[29]
The distinction between the two sets is not unproblematic, but
here I'm concerned that the very opposite suggestion is being made
– that the *text* (as explicitly contrasted to history) is offered as a
sufficient ground for recovering the agency of the marginalised.
That this should happen within non-traditional Shakespearean
studies only indicates that the legacy of English literary studies of
the last century is difficult to challenge on one of its central sites –
the Shakespearean play.

In this essay, I have sporadically referred to the colonialist history
of Shakespeare's plays and the current teaching situation in India
not simply to insert my own critical stake into debates about
Shakespeare and feminism, but also to point out that even discussions of race, imperialism, colonialism, cultural difference and otherness can be insular. Boose's suggestion that 'if race, ethnicity and
religion have mapped a differential investment for blacks onto
Othello and Jews onto *The Merchant of Venice*, gender construction
has always already dictated a disproportionate feminist investment
in a number of issues which span the canon' (p. 721) reduces critical
investment to only one of its many starting points. 'Blacks' may also
be invested in more than a rereading of *Othello*. The notion of 'race'
must transcend the black presence in the plays and inform understandings of gender, the state, political life and private existences,
otherwise the 'others' within Shakespeare as well as in the
Shakespearean academy or classroom will be granted only a token
legitimacy which will disguise, among other things, the dynamic and
intricate intersections of these categories in the creation of
Renaissance culture as well as our own contemporary cultures.
These connections would include the following: the relationship
between the Western family and emergent colonial discourses; the
overlap and tensions between various types of patriarchal ideologies
in the early modern period; the construction of newer forms of patriarchal discourses via the deployment of canonical texts (such as
Shakespeare) in a variety of contexts (for example, Indian and South
African classrooms); the ways in which relations of gender and race
inform and shape teaching situations in various parts of the world
and the relationships between them. As I hope the rest of this essay
will indicate, these difficult, even occasionally fuzzy, connections are
conducive rather than detrimental to a critical focus on gender and
the recovery of female agency.

[An extended passage exploring John Webster's *The White Devil* in the light of these concerns has been omitted here.   Ed.]

. . . .

I have been suggesting the necessity of weaving between and even within different categories of difference: not just the category of 'women' but also the category of 'race' needs to be acknowledged as heterogeneous. The outsider in the literature of the period is not always literally of a different colour; after all, the slave population of Europe consisted of Tartar, Greek, Armenian, Russian, Bulgarian, Turkish, Circassian, Slavonic, Cretan, Arab, African (Mori), and occasionally Chinese (Cathay) slaves. Peter Stallybrass rightly questions the assumption that the interests of different marginalised groups automatically, or simply, converge, and shows that in the case of Renaissance representations of 'the world turned upside down' the unity of oppressed groups 'emerged as a precarious alliance, often honoured as much in the breach as in the observance'.[30] These tensions between various 'others' serve as a crucial check against confusing intersections with parallels; against simply mapping various forms of oppression upon each other, cataloguing endless 'overlaps' to the point where the specificity of each is blurred. As Brittain and Maynard point out, 'because there are cultural explanations for both racism and sexism does not mean that they deal with the same phenomenon ... the oppression of black women undercuts the usefulness of the "parallels" exercise'. They also astutely note that 'the distinction we make between sex and gender seems to have no counterpart in the discourse on race'.[31] Dominant discourses of course strategically collapse as well as emphasise distinctions in those they seek to control. British colonial strategy in India, for example, worked toward stratifying the local population into several races. The repeated distinctions drawn between Aryan and Dravidian rested upon an equation of the latter with Africans and worked towards persuading the Indian élite that they were not racially discriminated against. (As it happens, the precarious pan-Aryanism thereby suggested played some role in smoothing the course of Western literature in the Indian classroom, by offering connections between the 'great' authors of both cultures.) At the same time, colonialist discourse constantly had to draw linkages between its various others; both strategies can be detected in the following pronouncements of Sir Harry Johnson, the first commissioner of British Central Africa, in 1894:

> On the whole, I think the admixture of yellow that the negro requires should come from India, and that Eastern Africa and British central Africa should become the America of the Hindu. The mixture of the two races would give the Indian the physical development which he lacks, and he in turn would transmit to his half-negro offspring the industry, ambition, and aspiration towards civilized life which the negro so markedly lacks.[32]

An analogous reminder of the ways differences are simultaneously marshalled and flattened by dominant discourses and institutions is offered by several studies that point out how the Irish provided a model for slavery and colonialist discourses in both Africa and India.[33] My point is that to recognise both differences between various categories of 'difference' as well as the importance of alliances is necessarily to undertake a somewhat tortuous and dizzy critical path, one which is sensitive not just to 'the text' but also to its placement. For example, the endless critical debates about Othello's precise skin colour, one may recall, often strain to deny its political importance, so that, paradoxically, to insist on the crucial significance of blackness may involve moving away from the question of Othello's exact shade.[34] That play also demonstrates both the divergences and alliances between different sorts of patriarchy: black and white, familial and public, virulent and more 'human', and the same variegation can be observed in other plays, both where there is a black presence and where there isn't.

The diversity of those who were regarded as 'outsiders' and the overlaps between race, region, class and gender do not minimise the importance of colour consciousness, which already had a history which newer interactions drew upon and remoulded. As Norman Daniel puts

> xenophobia and hysteria were compounded at the inception of the Crusades and it is a mistake to view them as isolatable phenomena ... Fighting and robbing, killing, trading, making profits, taking rents or tributes, all these were closely linked to philosophical and theological analysis, to the composition of history and propaganda, and even to love of one's neighbour. The Crusades renewed the idea that we need not do as we would be done by. They were also an expression of a much older history of suspicion. . . . The expectation of dif-

ference goes back to the cultural intolerance of 'barbarians' which is one of the less useful legacies of Greece.[35]

To insert gender into this history is to note how similar dichotomies between woman and man, inner and outer, private and public, shape the development of family, nation, home, race and culture. In *The White Devil* or *The Duchess of Malfi* domestic and State power are represented as occupying literally the same sites, and, as discussed above, the language of control uses (and fluctuates between) both gender and colour. The way in which they are meshed together is evident from some of the material made available by Jean-Louis Flandrin, whose studies of the early modern family do not address either gender or race explicitly but who points out the ways in which the terms 'kins-folk', *'lignage'*, 'race', 'home', and family appear in seventeenth- and eighteenth-century French dictionaries as more or less synonymous.[36] The concept of the house, writes Flandrin, is intermediate between those of *race* and of 'household'; it 'linked the continuity of the family with the perenniality of settlement in a particular place'. This fluctuation between 'race' and 'house' is also evident in Montaigne's essay 'Of Names':

> It is a wretched custom, and with most injurious consequences in our land of France, to call each person by the name of the estate, and it is the usage that most leads to confusion between different races. The younger son of a good house, having had as his appanage a piece of land under the name of which he has been known and honoured, cannot honourably abandon it; ten years after his death the land passes into the hands of stranger who follows the same usage; you may well guess how confused we become when we try to ascertain the origin of these men.[37]

Flandrin points out that such ambiguity meant that descent could be traced through women whenever it suited the preservation of the household.

The dwindling of this concept of the household by the sixteenth century can be related to changes in class, gender and race relations, each of which called for a stricter definition of the family in order to preserve property and cultural identity. While the lower classes (especially people like travelling salesmen) were perceived as black, actual contact with non-white peoples intensified parochialism into racism. The fear of female mobility and the fear of 'outsiders' fuel each other – in early modern Europe, as in countless other patriarchal cultures. For example, we learn, from Flandrin again, that the exogamous policy of the Church was contrary to the everyday practice of the French peasantry:

> In many villages, if not in all, the 'big boys' grouped together as an institution, made efforts to establish their monopoly over the marriageable girls of the parish. Every girl married to an outsider represented, in fact, for the less fortunate among them, an increased probability of remaining a bachelor and a servant in the house of another. Thus it was that with cudgel blows, if one is to believe Retif and some other observers, they dissuaded outsiders from associating with the village girls. Furthermore, they proclaimed the dishonour of such girls as became interested in others than themselves.[38]

In various cultures and historical contexts, female sexuality has been seen as 'responsible' for a necessary tightening of the family structure and for the need for hierarchy, differentiation and privacy. Renaissance and Jacobean plays, as well as other writings of the time, are literally littered with instances which demonstrate the linkage between deviant femininity and outsiders, even in the most casual or 'insignificant' moments.[39] In *The Two Gentlemen of Verona*, for example, Proteus remarks that

> ... the old saying is:
> Black men are pearls in beauteous ladies' eyes.

Julia's disavowal

> 'Tis true, such pearls as put out ladies' eyes;
> For I had rather wink than look upon them
> (V.i.11–14)

confirms her 'lack' of sexuality and therefore her status as a desirable and moral woman. Black women are rare in the plays, but even when they are briefly invoked, their 'place' is clear:

> DESDEMONA How if she be black and witty?
> IAGO If she be black and thereto have a wit,
> She'll find a white that shall her blackness hit.
> (II.i.131–3)

The unruly female body is both a symptom and the result of a threatened national culture: in Middleton and Dekker's *The Roaring Girl*, Moll's unfeminine attire consists of 'the great Dutch slop', or breeches which her tailor promises her will be 'open enough' to accommodate her desire for free movement; Sir Alexander Wengrave fears he has 'brought up my son to marry a Dutch slop and a French doublet; a codpiece daughter' (II.i.88, 95, 97–8).[40] In the 1620 pamphlet *Hic Mulier*, which virulently attacks female crossdressing, women who display the desire to fashion themselves and 'mould their bodies' are described much in the same way as Vittoria is: they are 'all Odious, all Devil', 'Mer-Monsters' and if their activities 'be not barbarous, make the rude Scythian, the untamed Moor, the naked Indian, or the wild Irish, Lords and Rulers of well-governed cities'.[41]

This essay has only been able to gesture towards the various textual and contextual linkages between patriarchal control, state power, parochialism, colonialism and racial prejudice that need to be made. Of course it is possible to use such connections to read gender relations, sexual anxiety or threats from and to women as merely signs for something else – cultural anxieties, a crisis of governance, and so on. I have tried to argue that such reductionism cannot be corrected by matching it; instead we can use a fuller, if more heterogeneous and problematic, understanding of women to relocate them as central to all cultural and historical processes. Colonialism is manifestly the history of the intersection of various and colour-coded patriarchies. The common operations of these patriarchies might lead us to posit a globally oppressed, transcultural womanhood, but even as we point to a widespread history of gender oppression, we must be alert to the difference that the colour of patriarchy (and the colour of feminism?) makes to an analysis of female subordination and agency. In so far as the Renaissance has provided a crucial 'originary' moment for the supporting structures of Western culture such as the state and the family, the study of these structures can often become a culturally inward-looking exercise which takes these structures as universal, or worse, as normative. Even as students of the Renaissance today focus upon those constituencies and groups (women, blacks) who function as the enabling 'others' of Renaissance culture, it becomes clear that no study that assumes as normative the structures of the state or the family (then or now) can develop a vocabulary sensitive enough to recover adequately the histories of oppression, let alone to reconstruct acts of disobedience. Further, our attempts to recover the agency of 'woman' will constantly have to reckon with critical and pedagogic investments in the idea of 'family'; the need is to dispense with the family romance, both in relation to the community of Shakespeareans today, and in the analysis of the Renaissance family. The widespread and sometimes strange existence of Shakespeare in postcolonial worlds is only one useful reminder of this diversity (of the black sheep, perhaps!) in the Shakespearean 'family'.

From *Women, 'Race' and Writing in the Early Modern Period*, ed. Margo Hendricks and Patricia Parker (London: Routledge, 1994), pp. 17–34.

NOTES

[Returning Shakespeare to his place in a rich matrix of early modern cultural texts, this wide-ranging essay meditates on the implications, in a variety of global contexts, of recent developments in politically committed approaches to Renaissance studies. Ania Loomba traces differences within feminist Shakespeare criticism, insisting that scholars must go forward with the difficult but necessary task of understanding as fully as possible the intersections of patriarchal, colonial and other structures of power, in relation both to Renaissance culture and the contemporary situations in which Shakespeare continues to be studied, written about and performed.

In order to maintain the present volume's close focus on Shakespeare, a discussion of the intricate interrelations of gender, race and class in *The White Devil* is omitted, at the point indicated. I am grateful to Professor Loomba for allowing me to make this cut. Ed.]

I would like to thank Suvir Kaul, Sumit Guha, Lars Engle, Margo Hendricks and Patricia Parker.

1. Thomas Middleton, *The Changeling*, in *Thomas Middleton, Three Plays*, ed. Kenneth Muir (London and Melbourne: Dent, 1975), I.i.52.

2. See my 'Teaching the Bard in India', *JEFL* (Special Issue on 'Teaching Literature'), nos 7 and 8, June and December 1991 (Hyderabad Central Institute of English and Foreign Languages), pp. 147–62.

3. Quoted by Joan W. Scott, 'Deconstructing Equality-versus-Difference: or, the Uses of Post-structuralist Theory for Feminism', *Feminist Studies*, 14: 1 (Spring 1988), 29. On the tensions between difference and equality see also Michèle Barrett, 'The Concept of "Difference"', *Feminist Review*, 26 (Summer 1987), 28–41.

4. See A. Loomba, '*Hamlet* in Mizoram', in Marianne Novy (ed.), *Cross-Cultural Performances: Differences in Women's Re-Visions of Shakespeare* (Urbana–Champaign and Chicago: Illinois University

Press, 1993) for discussions of this meeting ground, and an analysis of the political unconscious of the *Hamlet* performances.

5. Benita Parry, 'Problems in Current Theories of Colonial Discourse', *Oxford Literary Review*, 9: 1–2 (1987), 27–58.

6. Walter Cohen, 'Political Criticism of Shakespeare', in Jean E. Howard and Marion F. O'Connor (eds), *Shakespeare Reproduced: The Text in History and Ideology* (New York and London: Methuen, 1987), pp. 37–8.

7. Carol Thomas Neely, 'Constructing the Subject: Feminist Practice and the New Renaissance Discourse', *English Literary Renaissance*, 18: 1 (Winter 1988), 7; see also Lynda E. Boose, 'The Family in Shakespearean Studies; or – Studies in the Family of Shakespeareans; or – The Politics of Politics', *Renaissance Quarterly*, 40: 4 (Winter 1987), 707–42. All subsequent references to these essays have been incorporated in the text. See also Ann Thompson, 'Are there any Women in *King Lear*?' in Valerie Wayne (ed.), *The Matter of Difference: Materialist Feminist Criticism of Shakespeare* (Ithaca, NY: Cornell University Press, 1991), pp. 117–28.

8. Doubts about the political uses of poststructuralism are expressed by Perry Anderson, *In the Tracks of Historical Materialism* (London: Verso, 1980); Nancy Hartsock, 'Rethinking Modernism: Minority versus Majority Theories', and Kumkum Sangari, 'The Politics of the Possible', both in *Cultural Critique*, 7 (Fall 1987), 187–206 and 157–86 respectively; 'Patrolling the Borders: Feminist Historiography and the New Historicism', *Radical History Review*, 43 (1989), 23–43. Postmodernism is usefully summarised by Jane Flax, 'Postmodernism and Gender Relations in Feminist Theory', *Signs*, 12: 4 (Summer 1987), 621–43. Joan W. Scott, 'Deconstructing Equality-versus-Difference', argues for the political potential of poststructuralism, as does Michael Ryan, *Marxism and Deconstruction: A Critical Introduction* (Baltimore, MD: Johns Hopkins University Press, 1982). A sensitive account of both the overlaps and the differences between feminist historiography and new historicism is provided by Judith Newton, 'History as Usual? Feminism and the New Historicism', *Cultural Critique*, 9 (Spring 1988), 87–121. See also Leslie Wahl Rabine, 'A Feminist Politics of Non-Identity', and Mary Poovey, 'Feminism and Deconstruction', both in *Feminist Studies*, 14: 1 (Spring 1988), 11–31 and 51–65, respectively, and 'Critical Theory and the History of Women: What's at Stake in Deconstructing Women's History', dialogue section in *Journal of Women's History*, 2: 3 (Winter 1991), 58–108.

9. Walter Cohen remarks, 'the addition of race, sexuality, subjectivity, the body, or all of these issues to the list would only highlight the dilemma – the need for an account that overcomes both monistic

reduction and pluralistic vacuity' ('Pre-revolutionary Drama', in Gordon McMullan and Jonathan Hope [eds], *The Politics of Tragi-Comedy: Shakespeare and After* (London: Routledge, 1992), p. 146).

10. The centrality of Renaissance studies to new historicism and cultural materialism is evident from various recent discussions of these perspectives, especially Judith Newton, 'Family Fortunes: "New History" and "New Historicism"', *Radical History Review*, 43 (1989), 5–22. See also various essays in H. Aram Veeser (ed.), *The New Historicism* (New York: Routledge, 1989). Comparisons between the two analytical methods and their relationship to Renaissance studies have been widely commented on, including by Jonathan Dollimore, 'Introduction: Shakespeare, Cultural Materialism and New Historicism', in Jonathan Dollimore and Alan Sinfield (eds), *Political Shakespeare: New Essays in Cultural Materialism* (Manchester: Manchester University Press, 1985), pp. 2–17, and 'Shakespeare, Cultural Materialism, Feminism and Marxist Humanism', *New Literary History*, 21: 3 (Spring 1990), 471–93; Walter Cohen, 'Political Criticism of Shakespeare', pp. 18–46; Don Wayne, 'Power, Politics, and the Shakespearean Text: Recent Criticism of Shakespeare', in *Shakespeare Reproduced*, pp. 47–67; Louis A. Montrose, 'Renaissance Literary Studies and the Subject of History', and Jean E. Howard, 'The New Historicism in Renaissance Studies', both in *English Literary Renaissance*, 16: 1 (Winter 1986), 5–12 and 13–43 respectively. For the backlash against these perspectives see Edward Pechter, 'New Historicism and its Discontent', *PMLA*, 102: 3 (1987), 292–303; Richard Levin, 'Unthinkable Thoughts in the New Historicizing of English Renaissance Drama', *New Literary History*, 21: 3 (Spring 1990), 434–47 and various letters in the recent Bardbiz controversy in the *London Review of Books* – especially those by James Wood, 22 March, 24 May and 10 August, 1990.

11. Thompson, 'Are there any Women in *King Lear*?' is one recent attempt to reconcile feminist and materialist criticism of Shakespeare. Both Boose ('The Family') and Dollimore ('Shakespeare, Cultural Materialism') lament the fissured alliance, although Boose clearly does not regard it as having been a real possibility.

12. Boose, 'The Family', p. 718.

13. Howard, 'New Historicism', p. 31.

14. Don Wayne, 'Power, Politics', p. 61. See also Valerie Traub, 'Desire and the Difference It Makes', in Valerie Wayne, *The Matter of Difference*, p. 81.

15. Gayatri Chakravorty Spivak, 'French Feminism in an International Frame', in *In Other Worlds: Essays in Cultural Politics* (New York: Methuen, 1987), p. 137.

16. Sandra Harding, 'Introduction: is there a Feminist Method?', in Harding (ed.), *Feminism and Methodology* (Bloomington, IN: Indiana University Press, 1987), p. 7. See also Gisela Bock, 'Women's History and Gender History: Aspects of an International Debate', *Gender and History*, 1: 1 (Spring 1989), 11.

17. Susie Tharu and K. Lalita (eds), *Women's Writing in India*, vol. 1 (New York: The Feminist Press, 1990), pp. 30–1.

18. Gerda Lerner is quoted by Joan Kelly, *Women, History, Theory* (Chicago, IL: University of Chicago Press, 1984), p. 6. In a recent article, 'Reconceptualising Differences among Women', *Journal of Women's History* (Winter 1990), 106–21, Lerner emphasises that women cannot be treated as a unified category.

19. See Ania Loomba, *Gender, Race, Renaissance Drama* (Manchester: Manchester University Press, 1989), p. 56.

20. See, for example, Hazel V. Carby, 'White Woman Listen! Black Feminism and the Boundaries of Sisterhood', in *The Empire Strikes Back: Race and Racism in Britain in the Seventies*, Centre for Contemporary Cultural Studies (London: Hutchinson, 1972), pp. 212–35, and Gloria Joseph, 'The Incompatible *Ménage à Trois*: Marxism, Feminism, and Racism', in Lydia Sargent (ed.), *Women and Revolution: A Discussion of the Unhappy Marriage of Marxism and Feminism* (Boston, MA: South End Press, 1981), pp. 91–107.

21. See, for example, Angela Davis, *Women, Race and Class* (London: The Women's Press, 1982), and Patricia Hill Collins, *Black Feminist Thought: Knowledge, Consciousness, and the Politics of Empowerment* (London: Unwin Hyman, 1990).

22. Michèle Barrett, 'Ideology and the Cultural Production of Gender', in Judith Newton and Deborah Rosenfelt (eds), *Feminist Literary Criticism and Social Change* (London: Methuen, 1986), pp. 70–102.

23. Dated 12 July 1990.

24. See my letter in *The London Review of Books*, 15 August 1991.

25. Stephen Greenblatt, *Learning to Curse: Essays in Early Modern Culture* (New York and London: Routledge, 1990), pp. 9–10.

26. See my 'Overworlding the "The Third World"', *Oxford Literary Review*, 13 (1991), 184–5.

27. See Loomba, *Gender, Race, Renaissance Drama*, Ch. 2.

28. See Dollimore, 'Shakespeare, Cultural Materialism', pp. 475–6.

29. Parry, 'Problems in Current Theories', p. 43.

30. Peter Stallybrass, 'The World Turned Upside Down: Inversion, Gender and the State', in Wayne, *The Matter of Difference*, pp. 201–2.

31. Arthur Brittain and Mary Maynard, *Sexism, Racism and Oppression* (Oxford: Basil Blackwell, 1984), pp. 5–6.

32. Cedric Robinson, *Black Marxism: The Making of the Black Radical Tradition* (London: Zed Books, 1983).

33. In a 1952 article, 'The Origins of Columbian Cosmography', Arthur Davies pointed to connections between Irish and blacks in colonial discourses. He is quoted by Robinson, who also notes that the Irish provided the prototype for the white servant (ibid., p. 104).

34. See Loomba, *Gender, Race, Renaissance Drama*, pp. 106–8.

35. See Robinson, *Black Marxism*, p. 121.

36. Jean-Louis Flandrin, *Families in Former Times: Kinship, Household and Sexuality*, trans. Richard Southern (Cambridge: Cambridge University Press, 1974), p. 4.

37. Quoted in ibid., p. 11.

38. Ibid., p. 47.

39. The interlocking of a variety of discourses that construct 'woman' or otherness are, of course, starkly evident in plays such as *The White Devil*, and others where there is a central black presence and a deviant woman, such as *Othello, Titus Andronicus* and *Antony and Cleopatra*. But it can also be detected elsewhere in interchanges or moments that are apparently more marginal to the vocabulary of blackness. In *Love's Labour's Lost*, extreme sexual adoration which is also a surrender of the self is expressed in the image of a 'rude and savage man of Inde' who

> At the first op'ning of the gorgeous east,
> Bows not his vassal head and, strucken blind,
> Kisses the base ground with obedient breast.
> (IV.iii.217–21)

In the same play, since 'Black is the badge of hell, / The hue of dungeons, and school of night', the ultimate test of love is its ability to remain unchanged even if the lover were black (IV.iii.250–75). By the same token, a repentant Claudio in *Much Ado About Nothing* expresses his new steadfastness by saying that he'll marry Hero, 'were she an Ethiope' (V.iv.38). Citations from both plays are from *The Riverside Shakespeare* (Boston, MA: Houghton Mifflin, 1974).

40. Thomas Dekker and Thomas Middleton, *The Roaring Girl*, in Russell A. Fraser and Norman Rabkin (eds), *Drama of the English Renaissance* (New York and London: Macmillan 1976), pp. 334–68.

41. *Hic Mulier*, reprinted in Katherine Usher Henderson and Barbara F. McManus, *Half Humankind, Contexts and Texts of the Controversy about Women in England, 1540–1640* (Urbana and Chicago, IL: University of Illinois Press, 1985), pp. 268–9.

Further Reading

In order to keep the scale of this bibliography manageable, I have not singled out individual essays in journals or edited collections of books for special mention, and I have focused on material published during the period covered by the book, that is 1985 to 1999.

Feminist or gender-focused criticism of Shakespeare appears quite frequently in journals such as *English Literary Renaissance*, *Renaissance Drama*, *Shakespeare Quarterly*, *Shakespeare Survey*, and *Studies in English Literature, 1500–1900*. All of these also have important bibliographic or review sections which are useful for finding additional material. Other journals, including *ELH* and *Textual Practice*, publish relevant articles and reviews occasionally.

Good electronic journals in this field are *Early Modern Literary Studies*, http://www.purl.oclc.org/emls/emlshome.html, and *Renaissance Forum*, http://www.hull.ac.uk/renforum/, though to date they have both paid more attention to feminist scholarship in their review sections than in essays. For Shakespeare-related websites and electronic discussion groups, see http://www.ardenshakespeare.com/main/ardennet/; 'Mr William Shakespeare and the Internet' at http://daphne.palomar.edu/shakespeare/; and the SHAKSPER discussion group (subscription by application to editor@ws.bowiestate.edu). The unmoderated newsgroup humanities.lit.authors.Shakespear is a primarily non-academic site for discussion.

COLLECTIONS OF ESSAYS ON GENDER IN RENAISSANCE LITERATURE AND CULTURE

Though not all the essays in each of these volumes are specifically about Shakespeare, these collections helpfully serve to site his plays in the context of the larger feminist project to understand the role of gender and sexuality in early modern culture. Many of the collections are co-edited, and many of the same names recur in the contributors' lists, testifying to the importance of collaboration among feminist scholars in delineating this field of inquiry.

Jean R. Brink (ed.), *Privileging Gender in Early Modern England* (Tempe: Sixteenth-Century Studies Conference, 1992).

Viviana Comensoli and Anne Russell (eds), *Enacting Gender on the English Renaissance Stage* (Urbana: University of Illinois Press, 1998).

Margaret Ferguson, Maureen Quilligan and Nancy J. Vickers (eds), *Rewriting the Renaissance: The Discourses of Sexual Difference in Early Modern Europe* (Chicago: Chicago University Press, 1986).

Susan Frye and Karen Robertson (eds), *Maids and Mistresses, Cousins and Queens: Women's Alliances in Early Modern England* (Oxford: Oxford University Press, 1999).

Patricia Fumerton and Simon Hunt (eds), *Renaissance Culture and the Everyday* (Philadelphia: University of Pennsylvania Press, 1999).

Margo Hendricks and Patricia Parker (eds), *Women, 'Race', and Writing in the Early Modern Period* (London: Routledge, 1993).

David Hillman and Carla Mazzio (eds), *The Body in Parts: Fantasies of Corporeality in Early Modern Europe* (New York: Routledge, 1997).

Dorothea Kehler and Susan Baker (eds), *In Another Country: Feminist Perspectives on Renaissance Drama* (Metuchen, NJ: Scarecrow, 1991).

Carole Levin and Karen Robertson (eds), *Sexuality and Politics in Renaissance Drama* (Lewiston: Edwin Mellen Press, 1991).

Mary Beth Rose (ed.), *Women in the Middle Ages and the Renaissance: Literary and Historical Perspectives* (Syracuse, NY: Syracuse University Press, 1986).

Valerie Traub, M. Lindsay Kaplan and Dympna Callaghan (eds), *Feminist Readings of Early Modern Culture: Emerging Subjects* (Cambridge: Cambridge University Press, 1996).

James Grantham Turner (ed.), *Sexuality and Gender in Early Modern Europe: Institutions, Texts, Images* (Cambridge: Cambridge University Press, 1993).

Helen Wilcox (ed.), *Women and Literature in Britain, 1500–1700* (Cambridge: Cambridge University Press, 1996).

Susan Zimmerman (ed.), *Erotic Politics: Desire on the Renaissance Stage* (New York: Routledge, 1992).

COLLECTIONS OF ESSAYS ON SHAKESPEARE

Though all the books in this section are about Shakespeare, they are not all equally attentive to gender issues. However, they do all contain important essays that have shaped the development of feminist Shakespeare criticism.

Deborah E. Barker and Ivo Kamps (eds), *Shakespeare and Gender: A History* (London: Verso, 1995).

Dympna Callaghan (ed.), *A Feminist Companion to Shakespeare* (Oxford: Blackwell, 2000).

Dympna Callaghan, Lorraine Helms and Jyotsna Singh, *The Weyward Sisters: Shakespeare and Feminist Politics* (Oxford: Blackwell, 1994).

John Drakakis (ed.), *Alternative Shakespeares* (London: Methuen, 1985).

Shirley Nelson Garner and Madelon Sprengnether (eds), *Shakespearean Tragedy and Gender* (Bloomington: Indiana University Press, 1996).

Terence Hawkes (ed.), *Alternative Shakespeares*, vol. 2 (London: Routledge, 1996).

Jean E. Howard and Marion O'Connor (eds), *Shakespeare Reproduced: The Text in History and Ideology* (London: Routledge, 1987).

Ania Loomba and Martin Orkin (eds), *Postcolonial Shakespeares* (London: Routledge, 1998).

Jean Marsden (ed.), *The Appropriation of Shakespeare: Post-Restoration Reconstructions of the Works and the Myth* (Hemel Hempstead: Harvester, 1991).

Valerie Wayne (ed.), *The Matter of Difference: Materialist Feminist Criticism of Shakespeare* (Hemel Hempstead: Harvester, 1991).

CRITICAL STUDIES OF SHAKESPEAREAN DRAMA

Diverse in approach, theoretical framework, and choice of texts, the books listed here represent, but do not exhaust, the many ways in which feminist scholarship has enriched Shakespeare criticism.

Janet Adelman, *Suffocating Mothers: Fantasies of Maternal Origin in Shakespeare's Plays, 'Hamlet' to 'The Tempest'* (New York: Routledge, 1992).

Catherine Belsey, *The Subject of Tragedy: Identity and Difference in Renaissance Drama* (London: Methuen, 1985).

——, *Shakespeare and the Loss of Eden* (Basingstoke: Macmillan, 1999).

Philippa Berry, *Shakespeare's Feminine Endings: Disfiguring Death in the Tragedies* (London: Routledge, 1999).

Dympna Callaghan, *Woman and Gender in Renaissance Tragedy* (London: Harvester Wheatsheaf, 1989).

——, *Shakespeare without Women* (New York: Routledge, 1999).

Peter Erickson, *Patriarchal Structures in Shakespeare's Drama* (Berkeley: University of California Press, 1985).

Alison Findlay, *A Feminist Perspective on Renaissance Drama* (Oxford: Blackwell, 1999).

Barbara Freedman, *Staging the Gaze: Postmodernism, Psychoanalysis, and Shakespearean Comedy* (Ithaca, NY: Cornell University Press, 1991).

Kim F. Hall, *Things of Darkness: Economies of Race and Gender in Early Modern England* (Ithaca, NY: Cornell University Press, 1995).

Lorraine Helms, *Seneca by Candlelight and Other Stories of Renaissance Drama* (Philadelphia: University of Pennsylvania Press, 1997).

Lisa Hopkins, *The Shakespearean Marriage: Merry Wives and Heavy Husbands* (Basingstoke: Macmillan, 1998).

Jean E. Howard, *The Stage and Social Struggle in Early Modern England* (New York: Routledge, 1994).

Lorna Hutson, *The Usurer's Daughter: Male Friendship and Fictions of Women in Sixteenth-Century England* (London: Routledge, 1994).

Theodora Jankowski, *Women in Power in the Early Modern Drama* (Urbana: University of Illinois Press, 1992).

Lisa Jardine, *Reading Shakespeare Historically* (London: Routledge, 1996).

Coppélia Kahn, *Roman Shakespeare: Warriors, Wounds, and Women* (London: Routledge, 1997).

Ania Loomba, *Gender, Race, Renaissance Drama* (Manchester: Manchester University Press, 1988).

Katherine Eisaman Maus, *Inwardness and Theatre in the English Renaissance* (Chicago: University of Chicago Press, 1995).

Jodi Mikalachki, *The Legacy of Boadicea: Gender and Nation in Early Modern England* (London: Routledge, 1998).

Louis Montrose, *The Purpose of Playing: Shakespeare and the Cultural Politics of the Elizabethan Theatre* (Chicago: University of Chicago Press, 1996).

Karen Newman, *Fashioning Femininity and English Renaissance Drama* (Chicago: Chicago University Press, 1991).

Stephen Orgel, *Impersonations: The Performance of Gender in Shakespeare's England* (Cambridge: Cambridge University Press, 1996).

Patricia Parker, *Literary Fat Ladies: Rhetoric, Gender, Property* (London: Methuen, 1987).

——, *Shakespeare from the Margins: Language, Culture, Context* (Chicago: University of Chicago Press, 1996).

Gail Kern Paster, *The Body Embarrassed: Drama and the Disciplines of Shame in Early Modern English Culture* (Ithaca, NY: Cornell University Press, 1995).

Phyllis Rackin, *Stages of History: Shakespeare's English Chronicles* (Ithaca, NY: Cornell University Press, 1990).

Mary Beth Rose, *The Expense of Spirit: Love and Sexuality in English Renaissance Drama* (Ithaca, NY: Cornell University Press, 1988).

Juliana Schiesari, *The Gendering of Melancholia: Feminism, Psychoanalysis, and the Symbolics of Loss in Renaissance Literature* (Ithaca, NY: Cornell University Press, 1992).

Michael Shapiro, *Gender in Play on the Shakespearean Stage: Boy Heroines and Female Pages* (Ann Arbor: Michigan University Press, 1996).

Marilyn L. Williamson, *The Patriarchy of Shakespeare's Comedies* (Detroit, IL: Wayne State University Press 1986).

Deborah Willis, *Malevolent Nurture: Witch-Hunting and Maternal Power in Early Modern England* (Ithaca, NY: Cornell University Press, 1995).

PERFORMANCE

Penny Gay, *As She Likes It: Shakespeare's Unruly Women* (London: Routledge, 1994).

Barbara Hodgdon, *The Shakespeare Trade: Performances and Appropriations* (Philadelphia: University of Pennsylvania Press, 1998).

Carol Rutter, *Clamorous Voices: Shakespeare's Women Today*, ed. Faith Evans (London: Women's Press, 1988).

Elizabeth Schafer, *Ms-Directing Shakespeare: Women Direct Shakespeare* (London: Women's Press, 1998).

APPROPRIATIONS

Kate Chedgzoy, *Shakespeare's Queer Children: Sexual Politics and Contemporary Culture* (Manchester: Manchester University Press, 1996).

Christy Desmet and Robert Sawyer (eds), *Shakespeare and Appropriation* (London: Routledge, 1999).

Peter Erickson, *Rewriting Shakespeare, Rewriting Ourselves* (Berkeley: University of California Press, 1991).

Marianne Novy, *Engaging with Shakespeare: Responses of George Eliot and Other Women Novelists* (Athens, GA: University of Georgia Press, 1994).

—— (ed.), *Women's Re-Visions of Shakespeare* (Urbana: University of Illinois Press, 1990).

—— (ed.), *Cross-Cultural Performances: Differences in Women's Re-Visions of Shakespeare* (Urbana: University of Illinois Press, 1993).

—— (ed.), *Transforming Shakespeare: Contemporary Women's Re-Visions in Literature and Performance* (New York: St Martin's Press, 1999).

Ann Thompson and Sasha Roberts (eds), *Women Reading Shakespeare, 1660–1900* (Manchester: Manchester University Press, 1997).

Notes on Contributors

Frances Dolan is Professor of English, and an Affiliate of the History Department and the Women's Studies Program, at Miami University in Ohio. She is the author of *Dangerous Familiars: Representations of Domestic Crime in England, 1550–1700* (1994), and *Whores of Babylon: Catholicism, Gender, and Seventeenth-Century Print Culture* (2000). She is the editor of *The Taming of the Shrew: Texts and Contexts* (1996) and of five plays for the new Pelican Shakespeare. She is currently working on a study of marriage, inequality, and violence in England and America.

Lizbeth Goodman is Director of the Institute for New Media Performance Research and Senior Lecturer in Theatre and Performance Studies at the University of Surrey. She was formerly Chair of the Shakespeare Multimedia Research Project and the Gender in Writing and Performance Research Group at the Open University/BBC. She is the author of *Contemporary Feminist Stages* (1993) and of *Sexuality in Performance: Replaying Gender in Theatre and Culture* (1998). She is editor of *The Routledge Reader in Gender and Performance* (1998), *Mythic Women/Real Women* (1999), and co-editor of the forthcoming *Routledge Reader in Politics and Performance* (1999). She is also the editor of *Literature and Gender* (1996), *Feminist Stages* (1996), and co-editor of *Shakespeare, Aphra Behn and the Canon* (1996).

Barbara Hodgdon is Ellis and Nelle Levitt Professor of English at Drake University. She is the author of *The End Crowns All: Closure and Contradiction in Shakespeare's History* (1991), *Henry IV, Part 2* in the Shakespeare in Performance series (1996), *The First Part of King Henry the Fourth: Texts and Contexts* (1997), and *The Shakespeare Trade: Performances and Appropriations* (1998). She is currently preparing the new Arden 3 edition of *The Taming of the Shrew*.

Jean E. Howard is Professor of English at Columbia University and Director of the Institute for Research on Women and Gender. She writes on Renaissance literature and on problems in contemporary literary theory. Her books include *Shakespeare's Art of Orchestration: Stage Technique and Audience Response* (1984), *The Stage and Social Struggle in Early Modern England* (1994), and, with Phyllis Rackin, *Engendering* *a Nation: A Feminist Account of Shakespeare's English Histories* (1997). In 1987 she co-edited, with Marion O'Connor, *Shakespeare Reproduced: The Text in History and Ideology* (Methuen) and she is one of the four editors of *The Norton Shakespeare* (1997).

Ania Loomba is Professor of English at the University of Illinois at Urbana Champaign. She is the author of *Gender, Race, Renaissance Drama* (1989), and *Colonialism/Postcolonialism* (1998), and editor of *Postcolonial Shakespeares* (1998). Currently she is working on a volume called *Shakespeare and Race* for Oxford University Press.

Kathleen McLuskie is Professor of English at Southampton University. She has worked on feminist approaches to early modern culture and her publications include *Renaissance Dramatists* (1989) and *Dekker and Heywood: Professional Dramatists* (1994). She is currently working on the commercialisation of drama in early modern England and editing *Macbeth* for Arden 3.

Steven Mullaney teaches at the University of Michigan in Ann Arbor. He is the author of *The Place of the Stage: License, Play, and Power in Renaissance England* (1988) as well as numerous essays on early modern culture. Currently he is completing a book on emotions in the sixteenth century, titled *Earning Ideology: Theater and Other Technologies of Affect in the Age of Shakespeare*.

Diane Purkiss is Professor of English at the University of Exeter. She is the author of *The Witch in History* (1996) and has edited *Three Tragedies by Renaissance Women* for the Penguin Renaissance Dramatists Series. Her research interests focus on Shakespeare, witchcraft and the supernatural, fairies, feminist theory, and theories of history.

Phyllis Rackin teaches literature and women's studies at Pennsylvania University. A past president of the Shakespeare Association of America, she has published numerous articles on Shakespeare and related subjects and three books on Shakespeare: *Shakespeare's Tragedies* (1978), *Stages of History: Shakespeare's English Chronicles* (1990), and *Engendering a Nation: A Feminist Account of Shakespeare's English Histories*, written in collaboration with Jean E. Howard.

Alan Sinfield is Professor of English in the School of English and American Studies at Sussex University, where he teaches on the MA programme 'Sexual Dissidence and Cultural Change'. His recent publications include *Faultlines: Cultural Materialism and the Politics of Dissident Reading* (1992), *Cultural Politics – Queer Reading* (1994), *The Wilde Century* (1994), and *Gay and After* (1998). He is editor of the journal *Textual Practice*.

Ann Thompson is Professor of English at King's College, London. She edited *The Taming of the Shrew* for the New Cambridge Shakespeare series (1984) and is currently one of the General Editors of the Arden Shakespeare (third series), for which she is also co-editing *Hamlet* with Neil Taylor. She is General Editor of a series of books on feminist criticism of Shakespeare published by Routledge, and co-editor with Sasha Roberts of *Women Reading Shakespeare, 1660–1900* (1997).

Valerie Traub teaches English literature and women's studies at the University of Michigan. She is the author of *Desire and Anxiety: Circulations of Sexuality in Shakespeare Drama* (1992), and co-editor of *Feminist Readings of Early Modern Culture* (1997). Her latest book, *The Renaissance of Lesbianism in Early Modern England*, will be published shortly.

Index